D0948965

The Forgiving Life

The Forgiving Life

A Pathway to Overcoming Resentment and Creating a Legacy of Love

Robert D. Enright, PhD

American Psychological Association • *Washington, DC*

Second Printing, April 2014

Published by
American Psychological Association
750 First Street, NE
Washington, DC 20002
www.apa.org

To order
APA Order Department
P.O. Box 92984
Washington, DC 20090-2984
Tel: (800) 374-2721;
Direct: (202) 336-5510
Fax: (202) 336-5502;
TDD/TTY: (202) 336-6123
Online: www.apa.org/pubs/books
E-mail: order@apa.org

In the U.K., Europe, Africa, and the Middle East, copies may be ordered from
American Psychological Association
3 Henrietta Street
Covent Garden, London
WC2E 8LU England

Typeset in Sabon by Circle Graphics, Inc., Columbia, MD

Printer: Maple-Vail Books, York, PA
Cover Designer: Naylor Design, Washington, DC

The opinions and statements published are the responsibility of the authors, and such opinions and statements do not necessarily represent the policies of the American Psychological Association.

Library of Congress Cataloging-in-Publication Data

Enright, Robert D.
  The forgiving life: a pathway to overcoming resentment and creating a legacy of love / Robert D. Enright. —1st ed.
     p. cm.
  Includes bibliographical references and index
  ISBN-13: 978-1-4338-1091-6
  ISBN-10: 1-4338-1091-3
  1. Forgiveness. 2. Love. I. Title.
  BF637.F67E573 2012
  155.9'2—dc23

2011035040

British Library Cataloguing-in-Publication Data
A CIP record is available from the British Library.

Printed in the United States of America
First Edition

To my brother, William Enright Jr., who battled cancer to the end as a hero does.

CONTENTS

PREFACE

Are you aware of the wounds in the world? If you pay attention to the evening news, you surely know of the wounds caused to the flesh, but I am talking about another kind of wound, the emotional wound that is not so easily seen. Have you been aware of these lately in others? These unseen wounds are visible if you pay attention—in people's facial expressions, in the language they choose to use, within the tensions they carry on them like heavy chains around their necks. The world is full of wounds.

In 2001, I dedicated my book *Forgiveness Is a Choice* to "Nancy, with whom I have discovered the secret to a long and happy marriage."[1] I dedicated that book to her while she lay in a hospital bed in our home. She was dying of a particularly hard-to-treat form of cancer. The "secret" that I refer to was our willingness to love each other in such a special way that we practiced forgiving each other for our all-too-human imperfections. Our love for each other and then the loss of her helped me to see deeper and farther than ever before. I saw more clearly the wounds that so many people carry inside of them every day. Some of those deep wounds come from life's circumstances, as did Nancy's, mine, and our two sons' wounds when she was diagnosed with a fatal disease. Other internal wounds come from injustices inflicted on us by other people, from their own place of pain. We can do something about the incessant wounds of the world, caused by injustice, I thought.

Yet, we cannot be conquerors of so many wounds inflicted on us, and we cannot help others be conquerors, if we consider only one injustice and forgive only one person. Over the years, I have mused about so many injustices caused by so many wounds, and I have realized that to go after all of this woundedness, we must go beyond practicing forgiveness to actually living The Forgiving Life. This entails forgiving, then forgiving some more, then learning to love this moral virtue until it becomes a part of us.

The intent of this book is to bring you on this path, to the door of The Forgiving Life, and through that door so that you arrive home, comfortable with forgiveness, trusting it, and thankful that it is in the world and a part of your life. It starts with understanding and then goes deeply into you as wisdom. It becomes not just a thing that is in you, but a part of the very fabric of the real you, the important you, the core you, and then you may want to give it away to others. This is where we are heading in this book.

Am I exaggerating when I say that forgiveness is vital in this world? Desmond Tutu, the South African activist, said that there is no future without forgiveness, stating that in the title to one of his bestselling books.[2] What did he mean? For one thing, he was reflecting on the history and the hope for South Africa, as the country struggles with the wounds of apartheid and seeks a better way. Another of his points was that there are so many wounded people in his country that they need the medicine of forgiveness. Otherwise, they could head in an undesirable direction filled with resentment.

Are you ready to begin the journey? We start in Chapter 1 with a brief description of what I call our Theory of Forgiveness. A theory is like a story in that it connects forgiveness to other important aspects of life, such as resentment, love, emotional well-being, and good relationships. A theory of forgiveness tells the story of how all of these issues interrelate and why forgiveness is important for you and the world. We discuss this theory in Chapter 2 with those of you who are reading this book because you have experienced a trauma. I want to speak with you in particular because your wounds are deep and need special attention.

Chapters 3 through 6 introduce you to our pathway to forgiving, a pathway that I created and with my colleagues have studied and implemented since 1985. In Chapter 7, we take a little breather from the process to explore in-depth what we mean when we say, "I forgive you." Chapter 8 presents you with an overall plan for approaching the complex process of forgiving all or most people who have ever been deeply unfair to you. In Chapter 9, you are given the opportunity to take a forgiveness test to see the degree to which you currently forgive these people. It will help you to decide whom to forgive first. Chapters 10 through 16 guide you through this forgiveness process, first with a member of your family of origin, in which you grew up, and then with other important relationships. As you will see, we expand your world of forgiveness by including more and more people. In Chapter 16, you have a chance to step back, climb up on the summit, and view your accomplishments to this point in the book.

Chapters 17 and 18 center on your helping children to forgive, and then I challenge you to consider giving forgiveness away to others, in families, schools, workplaces, places of worship, and other groups. We end in Chapter 19 by my challenging you to consider your own legacy—what will you be leaving behind in this world? As you will see in the chapters to follow, too many people leave their wounds, which end up wounding others, who then leave their own wounds to the next generation, and on it goes. If this is true, that people can leave a legacy of woundedness, is it not possible to imagine leaving goodness for generations to come? Consider the supernova, long since gone from the universe as it exploded, but continuing to provide light for those who take the time to look. What will you leave behind? This book is intended to help you decide that.

Now, for your sake and for those whom you will meet after reading and following the exercises in this book, let us begin to lead The Forgiving Life as we, together, confront and overcome your wounds resulting from others' injustices. My hope is for an exhilarating journey with emotional and relational healing for you and others as its end point.

ACKNOWLEDGMENTS

I am indebted to the hundreds of people who have entered into dialogue with me in the great conversation that is forgiveness. Without all of these spirited exchanges of ideas, this book would not be possible. Thank you Maureen Adams, Susan Herman, and Harriet Kaplan, editors within APA Books, for your expert help as we moved forward. Thank you, Mary Lynn Skutley, editor extraordinaire of APA Books, for your masterful help and for having the vision to see, so many years ago now, that the psychology of forgiveness would spread across the planet. And it did. Thank you to my family for your unwavering support and love that accompany the family as a forgiving community.

Part I

THE BASICS

CHAPTER 1

A THEORY OF FORGIVENESS IN BRIEF

What is The Forgiving Life and why is it important? In this book, we approach The Forgiving Life like a pathway, but because its importance may take some time to emerge, let's start slowly, with an analogy that illustrates a pathway you might have explored quite a bit in your life: a career. In our analogy, we'll follow a young woman named Inez, whose career path took a definite form early in her life but whose pathway to forgiveness, as we'll see in later chapters, was not so clear at first.

Suppose that a young Inez, just out of secondary school, reads a story about a person who has spent 30 years as a service worker in a nursing home. The story is so inspiring that Inez decides to explore this possibility for herself of being in service to the elderly in a nursing home. Does the reading of the story and the inspiration that followed make her a service worker to the elderly? I know that your answer is, "No, of course not," but a more important question is, "Why?" What does she need to be a service worker to the elderly in the true sense?

Suppose further that Inez takes a course on nursing homes at her local community college and receives a grade of A for the course. Is she now a service worker to the elderly? Suppose she likes the course a great deal and makes plans for an advanced course in the area. Is she a service worker? Again, if you answer no, then what is missing?

Now suppose that she goes back to college and gets a degree in social work, specializing in this area of care to the elderly by taking five courses on this and related topics. When others ask what her major is, Inez the college student says, "Oh, I'm in service work to the elderly. I have a practicum in which I will be an assistant at a nursing home for 3 weeks." Now is Inez-the-scholar a service worker to the elderly?

Suppose she gets a doctoral degree in the area of social work, specializing in nursing home care and administration. Suppose that she has a 1-year internship in nursing home care. Now would you grant her the status of service worker to the elderly?

What if Inez is hired at a well-known nursing home, where she administrates, teaches the staff, and implements new ideas? Is she now more of a service worker to the elderly than when she majored in this area of specialization and received the doctorate? Why?

Now suppose we have two people who followed the same academic path to the same nursing home. Both are in the similar areas of administration, teaching, and innovation. The first person has a detached lack of interest in it all, despite years of schooling. She would rather be hot-air ballooning over Minneapolis. The other, Inez, remains engaged in the topic, thinking creatively about it and engaging staff and residents in new ideas. Are they both service workers to the elderly in the same way? If not, why not? What are the major distinguishing features between them?

I have asked you the questions in the previous paragraphs to bring home the following six important points about living The Forgiving Life:

- Reading this book, if it is helpful to you, is a positive step. Yet, this alone does not mean that you are living The Forgiving Life, especially if you read it once and then sell it on an Internet auction site. There is much more to it than that. You might read this book, for example, more out of curiosity than anything else. In other words, you may be peeking into the window of forgiveness without knocking on the door, entering, and spending valuable quality time with it at home.

- Even if you have spent time in another book working on forgiving one person for one act of injustice, this does not necessarily mean that you are living The Forgiving Life. It would be easy to let all of the learning just drift away as the cares of the world or other distractions smother your interest in and pursuit of a forgiving life.
- Even if you have forgiven five people, each for a serious unfairness, you may or may not be living The Forgiving Life. It is more than a series of forgiveness acts. You can do this kind of forgiving and never reflect on what you did. You can do this kind of forgiving and never let the actions sink so deeply into you that you begin to say, "Forgiveness is a part of my life; it is a part of who I am."
- If you do begin to reflect on forgiveness and conclude that you like it—if you understand it and if it is beginning to be a part of you—then I ask you to address this challenge: To what extent have you forgiven people from your past? To what extent have you forgiven people across family, workplace, and neighborhood? To what extent has forgiveness pervaded your life?
- Do you see that it is possible for you to make a commitment to putting forgiveness on the front burner of life, making it a high priority in your relationships from the past and in your current relationships across the various settings in which you live? In other words, can you see that it is possible for you to make forgiveness such a part of your identity that you may be able to say in the future, "I am a forgiving person"?

- Finally, do you see that it is possible to derive joy from making forgiveness a central part of who you are? When you do, your next question is likely to be this: "How can I let others know of the deeper meaning and applications of forgiving so that we can have a better world?"

After contemplating these points, do you see that forgiveness is so much more than a one-time action toward one person who hurt you? Do you see that it is more than a series of actions? Are you seeing that forgiveness takes root when it goes down deep inside you and you willingly say yes to it? Are you seeing that forgiveness, starting from that position deep inside you, can be a lifestyle, a way of living peacefully with others in this imperfect world? Are you seeing that forgiveness can actually be a part of your very identity, a part of your core self? Are you seeing that the love of forgiveness can lead you to helping others acquire this virtue? All of this is what I mean by The Forgiving Life.[1]

A THEORY OF FORGIVENESS

If we are to live The Forgiving Life, it might help to know why. Why bother? Why is it difficult to live such a life? If I refuse to live such a life, will there be unfavorable consequences for me? If so, why would that be? If I live The Forgiving Life, what is likely to be the outcome for me and others? Why are these outcomes likely? Social scientists tend to explain the "whys" of whatever interests them by formulating theories. A theory basically tells you a story—not a fable, but a story that links a variety of issues together—that can be tested to see if it is true.

Our theory starts with the premise that all people need to both give and receive love to be healthy and to have psychologically healthy families and communities. I am not alone in this view when we study the ancient literature, going back to the formation of the Hebrew nation thousands of years ago with the command to love one's neighbor as oneself. I am not alone when we turn to modern-day heroes such as Martin Luther King Jr., Gandhi, or Mother Teresa. Unconditionally loving others, despite the blemishes and faults that each of these heroic people had, was at the heart of their message.

I am not alone in this view when we consult modern philosophy, in which Gene Outka has shown the centrality of love for morally good human interaction. I am not alone in this view of the primacy of love when we examine the earliest roots of psychology, going back over a century to the pioneering work of the psychoanalyst, Sigmund Freud, who made the famous statement that each person's purpose is to work and to love if genuine mental health will result, a theme that continues to resonate with psychoanalysts in the 21st century. Contemporary social scientists such as Thomas Lewis, Fari Amini, and Richard Lannon make the compelling biological case that love is at the central core of who we are as humans.[2] I continue not to be alone in this view when I ask people of good common sense about what is of the utmost importance to them. All people require love, both the giving and the receiving of love; this is not an option.

On this issue, some people who use the method of religious faith to understand the world, some who use the method of deductive logic and philosophical analysis, some who use the method of psychoanalysis, and some who use the method of modern biological and social science are in agreement: The essence of our humanity is to love and be loved.

Of course, we can think of the essence of humanity in other ways. For example, it would be accurate to characterize humans as "rational beings," as Aristotle did. His idea is intriguing because only humans can understand logical deductions; work crossword puzzles; or discern what a basketball, golf ball, and Frisbee all have in common. We are rational, a unique characteristic of us as humans, but I claim—along with Lewis, Amini, and Lannon—that our rationality is not at the core of who we are. This is true simply because we can use our rationality for some very inappropriate ends. Tyrants have been known to use their rational brilliance for the development of sinister war strategies. Bank robbers are usually quite rational in their approach to hauling away the goods, that is, if they wish to avoid capture. Rationality is vital for us, don't get me wrong on that; it separates us from species lower in the hierarchy because we alone as humans deliberately and consciously pursue truth. Rationality can aid our understanding of who we should be to one another, thus aiding us in pursuing what is morally good, but it does not seem to be the primary theme when we ask what is at our core.

Rather than focus on rationality, it is probably more accurate to say that the essence of our humanity is tied to our ability to make free choices. We are not bound by instinct. Free will makes us human.[3] Yet, as in the case of rationality, our free will does not seem to be the bottom-line essence of who we are as persons because some take liberty with that free will for ill-gotten gain. For example, a person may choose to skip work when the surf is up at Malibu or choose to leave his or her partner of 15 years simply because "I choose to do so." As with rationality, free will can be very unloving, even exploitive of others.

Many philosophers, starting with Immanuel Kant, a preeminent Western thinker, have emphasized a good will as good in itself and therefore the foundation of who we are as moral beings. If we desire the moral good for each other, then our interactions for the most part will come out fine. We will have a good society. Yet, although a good will is essential, even it seems too small a candidate for what is absolutely and centrally at the core of our being. Inez might have a very good will because she intends to eventually work in a nursing home (for the sake of helping others) by first taking courses, then getting a degree and later an advanced degree. Yet, without a strong will, one that motivates her to strive toward this goal, her good will may not lead to the good career if she lacks perseverance to actually secure it.[4] And, if a person has a good will coupled with a strong will without the wisdom to create goodness in the world with that good and strong will, it amounts to little. Perhaps something that is produced by a good will, which benefits humankind in a consistent and meaningful way, is the key to our search for the bottom-line essence of our humanity. What might that be? It would have to be something that is rational (it makes sense), is not forced on us (it comes from a free will), is inherently good (it comes from a good will), and can realistically be done for good in the world (comes from a strong will).

Love, properly understood, reaches higher and goes farther in explaining who we are compared with rationality, free will, and even good will. According to Aristotle, there are four different kinds of love: the natural love that exists, for example, between a mother and her child (*storge* in Greek); the love that develops strongly among friends (*philia*); the love that is forged between romantic partners (*eros*); and a fourth love (*agape*) that is based on service to others (developed more fully in medieval times by Thomas Aquinas). The first three kinds of love (*storge, philia,* and *eros*) depend for their proper expression on agape or *service love* (loving even when you do not feel like it, loving when you are tired, loving when the other seems unlovable). C.S. Lewis, who wrote *The Chronicles of Narnia,* made this point of the philosophical centrality of agape. Agape, according to Lewis, is the highest form of love precisely because it nobly and courageously perseveres when the other kinds of love say, "Ouch! I'm outta here! Run!" With agape love, a person chooses to love, even when it hurts. In other words, it comes from a free will (we choose it) and from both a good will (we choose it to help others even if we are uncomfortable) and a strong will (we do not run away from and carry on despite the difficulty), and it makes sense (coming from a position of rationality).[5] Agape love has an inherent goodness within it that is missing from rationality and free will.

Further, without a sense of love that is deliberately in service to others, all of the other loves can be distorted and not be inherently good in themselves. Take eros as an example. Is it the best kind of romantic relationship when the partner degenerates into a "What's in it for me?" pattern? Agape balances the tendency in eros to seek one's own pleasure primarily and says, instead, "How may I serve you?" Agape is a kind of love that has dignity, quiet, and strength as it seeks to build up and even restore others. Agape helps us to see others as possessing inherent worth, a quality that is not earned. The paradox of agape in the context of forgiveness is that as a person reaches out to others who have been unjust, that person experiences considerable emotional healing (as we see in the next chapter).

I use the word *balance* in the previous paragraph. Balance was an important idea for Aristotle, who called it *temperance*. Each expression of love, whether it is storge, agape, or another variety, itself needs balance unless it becomes distorted by overdoing or underdoing it. For example, if people distort agape by begrudgingly overdoing it, they could perform supposed acts of love with deep resentment, deplete their own reserves, or burn out without being able to love well at all.[6] If people underdo agape, their efforts may be halfhearted, even indifferent, as they perform this lazy distortion of agape. The point is to strive for a good, solid expression of service love without overdoing or underdoing it. Wisdom helps us to know how much is enough.

Love then, in the form of agape, may be the most fundamental and the most important aspect of our being for this one reason: It is inherently good in that, by its definition, we seek meaningful and healthy relationships with others, and therefore it is good for others and for us. All other virtues, by themselves, do not necessarily fulfill any lasting connection between and among people. Justice, by itself, can be a rather cold virtue as, say, a magistrate almost indifferently sentences a person as a rightful punishment for a crime. Courage, by itself, can be a grim duty as, say, a soldier goes to battle because he is ordered to do so. If the need for meaningful connections is part of our religious, ethical, psychological, and biological essence, then agape love is central to that essence. If the fulfillment of meaningful connections is part of our end point as human beings, then the mature understanding and expression of agape love is a major part of that end point, or what philosophers call our *summum bonum*, or greatest good to which we strive.

Lewis, Amini, and Lannon made the scientific case that we must have love from others and must give love to others if we are to thrive in our humanity. Otherwise, the combination of our rationality, free will, good will, and strong will can and may be misdirected away from what is good. When others either fail to love us or withdraw that love, because it is so vital to us all, we tend to feel pain. The greater the removal of love, the greater the pain a person might experience. The longer and more intensively that love is removed, the longer the road to recovery might be. This scientifically testable idea leads us to the following seven subplots to our story about love and its importance to people through the practice of forgiveness.

First, when other people withdraw love from us, we might development resentment. After all, we do not deserve unfair treatment, and we do require love, not from all but at least from some. Resentment occurs when anger not only comes to visit but sits down in our hearts, takes off its stinky shoes, and makes itself too much at home. After a while, we do not know how to ask it to leave. Although some anger might be good, persistent and intensive anger that is resentment is not healthy. It can distort in the short run how we think (as we dwell on the negative), what we think (as we have specific condemning thoughts), and how we act (reducing our will to act in a morally good way).

Second, as we continually live with love withdrawn from us and a resulting resentment (with the short-term consequences of thinking with a negative pattern, thinking specific condemning thoughts, and acting poorly), we can settle into a kind of long-term distortion of who the love-withdrawing person is, who we ourselves are, and who people are in general. The basic issue here is that once love is withdrawn from us, we can begin to withdraw a sense of worth toward the one who hurt us. The conclusion is that he or she is worthless. Over time, we can drift into the dangerous conclusion that "I, too, am worthless" and "after all, others have withdrawn love from me and have concluded that I lack worth, therefore I do lack worth." Even later, we can drift into the unhealthy conclusion that there is no love in the world and so no one really has any worth, thus everyone is worthless.

As a third subplot, if the theory is correct that the essence of our humanity is agape love in our minds, hearts, and actions, then we need to take seriously this caution: If love remains outside of us for a very long time, this can do damage to our emotions and to our relationships with many different people in our lives. In a sense, the connections that we formerly had with good people can become broken, and we become disconnected from a variety of other people. We see this over and over in the published literature. The book *Helping Clients Forgive* presents scientific and clinical evidence of damaged emotions and relationships when love is withdrawn from people.[7]

A fourth subplot within our theory is that resentment can be displaced onto others not involved in the original offense. For example, when a mother withdraws love from her daughter (let's call her Caterina), then in her resentment Caterina might withdraw love from her brother. The brother, in turn, might then take out his resentment on other boys in school. When these young people grow up, they might pass the resentment to their partners and to their children, who then pass it along to their children. Do you see the potential for a domino effect of disconnection? This is the point Gandhi was making when he stated that if we keep taking an eye for an eye, then eventually the whole world will be without sight. In our theory of forgiveness, this happens because love has been withdrawn from people who do not take the time to restore that love within their own hearts. They, in turn, withdraw love from others, which leads to relational disconnection, and on it goes. Are you beginning to see why I have entitled this book, *The Forgiving Life*? It is a life that can restore connections—within the self, within the family, and within and among communities.

A fifth subplot to our story about love is that it can be restored through forgiveness. When others take their love away from us, we typically respond by withdrawing our love from them. By forgiving, we can restore our love for them. This may be a dim glimmer at first, but love understood as agape can grow even for strangers who are unjust to us as we become concerned for their welfare, for their very humanity. Our forgiving them can restore our love for ourselves and for others in general as well. Sometimes we guard our hearts so carefully that we do not allow ourselves to love even those who have been fair and loving toward us. Forgiveness can fix this. It can even reestablish meaningful connections, if we are mutually willing to reconnect.

Still regarding this fifth point, we should not think of love as a commodity, for example, like wildflowers growing along a pond, in that every time a person picks some of the flowers, we have fewer to give away in the future. Love given well to others does not mean that our hearts will have less of it now than before. Love is more like the stream that continually renews the pond. If we take water out of the pond, it is replenished, as long as the stream continues its flow into and out of the pond. Think of forgiveness as a part of that stream of agape love into and out of the heart. If you have been treated unjustly, you need to find that stream of loving forgiveness to replenish the heart.

Sixth, even if the one who caused your pain refuses to give love back to you, this does not mean that you are now stuck with a heart that is less loving because you were treated in an unloving way. No, we must remember the stream and the pond. Your forgiving another can put love back into your heart even if the other refuses that gift of love for whatever reason. The one who forgives is open to that stream, is open to the offering and receiving of love—both a vital part, perhaps the core, of our humanity.

Our seventh idea is that forgiveness stops that cycle of resentment and even revenge and can restore much that is good. Forgiveness can restore a sense of worth toward the ones who withdrew love, toward oneself, and toward other people in general. Forgiveness can restore emotional health as you find love again and start to give it away to others. Forgiveness can restore relationships, restore connections, at least to the degree that those from whom you are estranged accept your love and forgiveness and are willing to make necessary changes. Forgiveness can stop the incessant passing on of resentment to future generations. If Caterina displaces her resentment onto her brother, who displaces it onto a friend at school, who displaces it onto his mother when he gets home that evening, then an antidote is needed to all of this displaced resentment. Forgiveness is powerful medicine that can stop the ravages of resentment.

Forgiveness, when understood and practiced properly, can reverse the destructive consequences of excessive anger that can result when love is withdrawn from us. Do you see that forgiveness is a protection of your and others' very humanity? This is so because when you have love withdrawn from you by others' unjust acts, forgiveness is one way of restoring a sense of love within you, which will make you more open in the future to others' love toward you. As you love others in a better way, then they, too, have a chance to understand and practice forgiveness and find a way to stop the ravages of resentment in their own relationships and communities.

YOUR OWN LOVE STORY

Think of your life as an unfolding story, with plots and subplots, with consequences for you and others because of the good and the bad that have occurred and will occur in your life. If common sense; ancient wisdom; philosophical analysis; our modern-day heroes; psychoanalytic thinking; and Lewis, Amini, and Lannon's theory in the social sciences are all correct, then we should take seriously your history and future of love, the self-giving kind or agape. We need to take seriously your triumphs, challenges, frustrations, and failures in this area. Each time you have an interaction in which love is present or fails to be present, you add to your life's story.

The beauty of forgiveness is that it allows you to add goodness to your story even when others are intent on polluting your very being with injustices, whether by words, actions, or failures to say or act when they should. Love empowers, and because forgiveness is a variant of love, it too empowers those who are treated unfairly.

The beauty of forgiveness is evident when your story is seemingly being written with lots of sadness and bitterness. Forgiveness cannot reverse what has happened to you, but it can reverse your reactions now to what has happened. If you take forgiveness seriously, and if you practice it faithfully, you can actually add love to your story as you give it to others, even to those whom you could not now imagine as being the recipients of your love.

This is now up to you—whether your story will be written with more or less love in it—because to love and to forgive are your choice, now and in the future. To love and to forgive are part of your free will, your good will, and your strong will.[8] Although forgiveness is not some kind of magical antidote to the poison of unfairness and others' failure to love you, you should know that forgiveness is strong enough to help you go back in time, in a psychological sense, and to mend wounds from your past. You need not continue to write your story with many subplots of bitterness and resentment. If these negative emotions are weighing you down today, take heart because your story is about to change for the better, with more love in it.

The Importance of Love for You

Theory, whether of love or some other issue, might be best understood by direct experience, and so we turn to an activity to show you love's importance. Take a moment to focus on your heart as you reflect on one of your most loving relationships and a specific time in which you and that person were clearly showing agape love to each other, whether with a family member or with a friend, whether in the distant past as a child or in the present. Quiet yourself and concentrate on your heart as you remember one of the warmest interactions of your life. Try to see the other person as he or she was on that day. Where were you? Try to recreate the physical space in your mind. Was it a sunny day? A rainy evening? What was this specific interaction like for the both of you? How did the person look at you? Did his or her eyes sparkle? Did you delight in that person? What was said? Remember to be concentrating on the region of your heart as you recall. How did the person's loving response to you affect your heart that day? How are you feeling right now with respect to your heart as you recall? On a 0-to-10 scale, how happy is your heart at the present moment? How is the happiness in your heart affecting the rest of your body and mind? Can you sense the emotional and physical health accompanying this kind of love and the resulting happiness? Try to linger awhile with the image of the interaction that day. Let it soak into you so that you remember what love is like. The two of you were making a decision that day to choose to love. The fact that it was mutual is part of the happiness.

I would like you to have a written record of this experience to which we can refer back (and to which you can add) as you proceed in this book. Please take some time out from this introduction to write the description of your heart. As a working title for your essay, consider using "My Unfolding Love Story" (as a reminder, I am referring to agape and not necessarily some other form of love). The task is to describe what your heart is like right now, what the loving heart is like, as you focus on one loving interaction in your life. Try to give some detail. Those who love can give such detail.

I have requested this written record from you because at times as we proceed, the love that you experience will not be a two-way street, but will only be coming from you. Although this is not ideal, it surely is much better than a situation in which you and the other person are slowly burning with anger. The written record will help reacquaint you with genuine love and perhaps help you strive toward the goal of loving the one who was unjust to you. This is work that requires patience and sometimes "baby steps" to let love grow in you when you are feeling unlovable and feeling no love for a person who was unjust to you.

Your Agape Love Experience

If you are like most people, when you take the time to carefully reflect on one loving interaction, you are aware of a sense of deep happiness. This is not surprising because, as I discussed in the previous section, A Theory of Forgiveness, love is at the core of who we are as persons. When we move toward interactions that genuinely and positively touch our very core, we experience happiness. Aristotle reasoned that the major end point in life is happiness, which for him was to be more and more perfected in goodness.[9]

To exercise goodness is to be connected with others. The virtue of love requires connection with others for its completion. If you think about it, the goal of loving is to be loved by the other in return. Surely we can love when others do not, but the fulfillment of this virtue is to be connected in a healthy way with others.

In your essay, you may have described a sense of fulfillment. *Fulfillment* means just that—to be filled. When we are experiencing love, even for a short time, it seems as if the experience can fill our entire self across time, long after the particular interaction is over. We can bring the sense of that interaction with us as we develop.

If you are like most people, you probably described a certain sense of completion. I do not mean that your relationship was complete at that point. What I mean is that you probably felt completed (or nearly completed) as a person. One other person accepted you exactly as you were that day and loved you. You gave that love back. The love is what completed the interaction and completed you (at least in the short-run meaning of the word *complete*). You may not have achieved anything of worldly note that day, but you did achieve an experience of love that you can now take with you for the rest of your life.

If you are like most people, you probably felt a sensation of timelessness, a bit suspended from time because love is actually outside of space and time. Love transcends the physical world, it goes beyond what we experience here and now and makes the grit and grime of that world more tolerable, perhaps even more meaningful.

If you are like most people, you probably experienced a sense of giving yourself away. Love is like that; it is a willingness to give yourself, even if for a moment, to another for his or her good. If you think about it, this is what the other person did that day when loving you. He or she gave the self away to you, even if temporarily. When you gave yourself away, even in a fleeting moment, did you lose the real you, or did you experience more deeply the real you? This is one of the paradoxes of love—as you give yourself away to the other, you experience your real self, your core self. When you forgive in this way, you experience your forgiving self as you lead The Forgiving Life.

If you are like most people, you probably experienced a deeper sense of knowing who the other person is. To love is to begin to know more deeply. You have known the deepest core of the other person, his or her sense of love. At the same time, the other has had a peek into the deepest part of your core self. This is what we mean by *knowing*.

If you are like most people, you probably experienced a sense of inner contentment. This is a sense of not having wants or desires, at least for a while. As you are suspended in time with love surrounding you and being strongly in you, wants and needs cease for the moment. Of course, contentment is always fleeting in this difficult world, but giving and receiving love is one place where that contentment can be realized. As a footnote to this paragraph, our goal when we love and when we forgive is not contentment. If it were, then our focus would be on ourselves and what we want or need. To love and to forgive is to focus on the other. Contentment is a consequence of loving and forgiving; it is not our goal. By way of summary, we reflected on eight characteristics of agape love: happiness, connection, fulfillment, completion, timelessness, giving oneself away, knowing, and contentment.

These characteristics have been yours, even if fleetingly and with only one person in your life. I want this way of loving others for you, and that is what forgiveness can achieve, at least to a degree. We must remember that forgiveness is an imperfect enterprise. As with any of the moral virtues such as justice, patience, or courage, forgiveness takes time; you may not always reach your goal, and yet even an imperfect learning and expression of forgiveness-as-virtue can have great consequences for you, for the one who hurt you, and for your family and other central groups in your life.

At this point, I have an important question for you: Does this discussion resonate with your common sense? Am I making sense or talking high-minded nonsense? I ask you not to answer this question with your mind but with your heart. Please concentrate again on the area of your heart and then answer my question: Does your heart tell you that happiness, fulfillment, completion, timelessness, and all of the other characteristics of genuine love are possible for you? If the answer is "yes," then I urge you not to let others' woundedness or even your own wounds push you away from this conclusion. It will take some serious heart work to keep this focus.

I desire for you to let the seeds of the one loving encounter with the one person you described above to grow in you. "I know what love is" was the emphatic statement of the simple man, Forrest Gump. "I know what love is" is now your goal. And the paradox is that you may begin to find love out of the ashes of all your resentments and disappointments from hundreds of injustices inflicted on you by others. Yes, forgiveness is a paradox—as you practice a sense of love toward people whom you might currently consider to be unlovable, you develop a certain wisdom about both love and forgiveness. It is in the struggle to forgive that you find wholeness. As you practice forgiveness, you discover love in such a way that it is more natural, more readily available, more deeply expressed, and more consistently expressed by you across the board.

WHAT'S NEXT?

In the chapters to come, you will witness conversations between Sophia, who has journeyed long and far on the pathway to The Forgiving Life, and her friend Inez, whose career we reflected on at the beginning of this chapter. Inez is a very courageous woman intent on restoring love in her life through forgiveness. You will have the unique opportunity of observing Inez in all of her humanity—her doubt and skepticism, her triumphs and failures, and her struggle— the enduring struggle—to love through forgiveness even when it hurts. You will see that for Inez, forgiveness is not some neat, clean, straight line from resentment to a quick forgiveness and then off she goes. No, instead you will see the humanity of forgiveness in all of its imperfections and in its triumph of love over resentment. I hope that you enter into the dialogue, learning from the two people and adding your own insights while you grow as a forgiving person.

As you enter the dialogue, you will be adding to your life's story. This will be a central theme throughout the book—your own personal story, your love story. I want you to see the past, to encounter it in a positive and courageous way, and to heal from all of those incidents in which you deserved love but did not receive it from others. I want you to see your present, make adjustments now, and put more love in your life and in others' lives. I want you to see your future with all of your potential to add love to the world. Doesn't that idea—your adding more love to the world—get your blood pumping and your enthusiasm for life going more strongly?

That dialogue between Sophia and Inez begins in Chapter 3. In the next chapter, I want to talk specifically to those of you who have been profoundly hurt by others. I want to strengthen you for this journey of love.

CHAPTER 2

IF YOU ARE TRAUMATIZED

Before you begin forgiving anyone, I would like to pause briefly to give those of you who have experienced or are experiencing a trauma time to ask these questions: Do I really want to forgive? How can I be kept safe while I forgive? Is there scientific evidence to give me confidence that this will be worthwhile? Should I forgive? I ask these questions in particular because they are the ones I typically get from those who are deeply wounded and are not sure if forgiveness is for them.

WHAT DO I MEAN BY TRAUMA?

Beth-Anne, a 27-year-old bank clerk, was sexually molested by her brother when she was 10 years old. Shortly after that time, she began to wet the bed and to experience disturbing nightmares at least three times a week. She did not tell her parents about the assault. She kept her personal torment private until she attended a college course on positive social relationships. She began to cry in class and, after a number of counseling sessions, was able to confront what happened to her more than a decade before. She was afraid to consider forgiveness because her trust was so damaged. She thought that to forgive her brother would make her vulnerable to him.

David's father ran off when David was only 8 years old. He never called or wrote to David. Silence was all David ever received from his father. He grew up and began to achieve in his chosen career as an engineer. One day his father showed up without warning and asked him to go to dinner. Anger welled up in David to such a degree that he refused to talk with his father, thinking "Why should I now give him any of my time after all of the time he stole from my childhood?" The thought of forgiveness seemed absurd to David. He reasoned that he was better off without his father.

Miguel was happily married until his spouse announced that she had been having an affair with her boss. It turned out that she had been secretly seeing the boss on business trips and that their intimacy had been going on for a year. She asked Miguel to take her back. He thought that forgiveness was a cheap way out for her: Forgive, forget, and all will be well. He fumed at his wife and her boss for the bitter betrayal of him and their family.

Brownyn lost her first-born child to murder when he was only 7 years old. A single mother raising three other children, 8 years later she was still burdened by depression and recurring thoughts of the murder. She began a course of study at a local community college but found it hard to concentrate. She did not sleep well, had low energy, and had no confidence that she would be able to get the degree that would allow her to enter a university and pursue a teaching credential. She was afraid to forgive because she thought it would dishonor her child. The murderer had never been caught, and her quest was for justice. She thought that forgiveness might weaken her resolve to find the killer.

In each case here, the injustice was profound, and therefore the wounds that these brave people experienced were equally profound. Severe wounds sometimes make us want to stop time so that we do not have to confront the everyday details of life. We need time to heal, and the fast-moving world does not always allow for that. Forgiveness is challenging enough to make the head spin as the world spins on. Forgiveness under such circumstances is sometimes seen as irrelevant, or absurd, or dangerous, or highly morally inappropriate.

DO I REALLY WANT TO FORGIVE?

Why would anyone want to forgive under these circumstances? I suggest a different perspective on trauma and forgiveness. It is not forgiveness itself that is creating the sense of fear or disgust or danger or moral evil. Instead, it is the grave emotional wounds that are leading to these thoughts and feelings about forgiveness. When people are wounded, they naturally tend to duck for cover. When someone comes along with an outstretched hand and says, "Please come out, into the sunshine, and experience the warmth of healing," it can be too much. The person then blames the one with the outstretched hand or the warmth of the sun or anything else "out there" for his or her discomfort, when all the while the discomfort is residing inside the person. And this reaction is perfectly understandable, given the trauma.

If you blow out a knee while working out and it is gravely painful, is it not difficult to go to the physician? At the doctor's office, you face the sharp white lights of the examining room; the nurses scurrying about; and the unpleasant discussions with your doctor about surgery, recovery, and rehabilitation. It all seems to be too much. Yet, it is not the physician or the nurses or the thought of the scalpel or the rehab that is the ultimate cause of all the discomfort. That ultimate cause is the blown-out knee. Isn't it the same with forgiveness? You have within you a deep wound caused by others' injustice, and now the challenge is to heal.

Forgiveness is one way to heal from the trauma that you did not deserve. Like the blown-out knee, the trauma needs healing. So, I urge you to separate in your mind the wound from forgiveness itself. My first challenge to you, then, is to answer this question: Is it forgiveness itself that is the basic problem, or is it the wound and then all the thoughts of what you must do to participate in its healing? Forgiveness heals. Forgiveness does not further traumatize. To forgive is to know that you have been treated unjustly and, despite the injustice, make the decision to reduce your resentment toward the offending person and eventually work toward mercy. That mercy can take the form of kindness, respect, generosity, and even love. Do you want these in your life? Forgiveness can help strengthen them in your heart or even help them grow again for you.

HOW CAN I BE KEPT SAFE WHEN I FORGIVE?

Forgiveness, properly understood and practiced, is safe. It is only when we misunderstand forgiveness that this false notion of forgiveness can be dangerous for us. When you genuinely forgive, you do not say, "I now forgive. Therefore, what the person did to me was OK and will always be OK." No. To forgive is to acknowledge that another person has (or persons have) been unfair to you, and now you are emotionally wounded. We do not condone what another did to us.

When you genuinely forgive, you do not say, "I forgive you. Now I will enter into a relationship with you even if you are dangerous." No. Forgiveness is an act of mercy, and that mercy can be given from a distance if the other refuses to change and is a danger to you. Forgiveness and reconciliation differ. Forgiveness comes from within you as a freely chosen response of mercy to a person who is unjust. Reconciliation involves two people coming together again in mutual trust. You can forgive and not reconcile. At the same time, you do not want to take this previous statement to extreme lengths and refuse to reconcile with a repentant, honest, and now trustworthy person simply because forgiveness as a concept and reconciliation as a concept differ.

When you forgive, you do not say, "Because I forgive you, I now trust you." You can forgive and still not trust. If the person is showing you that he or she is a danger to you, then mistrust of his or her behavior is warranted. At the same time, and I state this specifically for those who have experienced trauma, be careful not to confuse a general mistrust and specific mistrust toward a particular person. In other words, many traumatized people have a pervasive mistrust that needs work. Sometimes the traumatized person meets a truly good person who is reliable and safe to be with, yet the mistrust from past relationships is so great that the traumatized person just cannot give of himself or herself in the new relationship. Knowing this and working deliberately on the previous issues of mistrust will help. Forgiveness will help. Time will help. Trust is such a delicate thing and needs work if it is to improve.

IS THERE SCIENTIFIC EVIDENCE TO GIVE ME CONFIDENCE THAT FORGIVENESS WILL BE WORTHWHILE?

The short answer is "yes." Since the publication in which J. H. Hebl and I guided elderly women through our forgiveness process,[1] our research team has conducted 10 published studies with our forgiveness approach with a variety of people. Please see the descriptions of these journal articles in Table 2.1. In each case, we randomly assigned people to either forgiveness therapy, using our model that we introduce in the coming chapters, or a control group, in which there was no forgiveness therapy.

As you can see in the table, we have worked with such traumatized people as incest survivors, people in residential drug rehabilitation, emotionally abused women who in some cases had to seek a protective shelter, terminally ill cancer patients, and middle-school youth who were so distracted by anger that they were about to fail in school. In every study, those who had forgiveness therapy with us

---

TABLE 2.1. Research on Forgiveness Therapy and Education

Research	Reference
Elderly women with a variety of injustices against them. The forgiveness group improved more in emotional health than did the control group, whose members discussed their emotional wounds without working on forgiveness in particular.	"Forgiveness as a Psychotherapeutic Goal With Elderly Females," by J. H. Hebl and R. D. Enright, 1993, *Psychotherapy: Theory, Research, Practice, Training, 30,* pp. 658–667.
College students who, while growing up, had a parent who was emotionally distant. The forgiveness group showed significant improvement in emotional health compared with the control group.	"Forgiveness Education With Parentally Love-Deprived College Students," by R. Al-Mabuk, R. D. Enright, and P. Cardis, 1995, *Journal of Moral Education, 24,* pp. 427–444.
Incest survivors. The forgiveness group became emotionally healthier than did the control group after 14 months. Differences between the groups were observed for depression, anxiety, hope, and self-esteem. The results were maintained in a 14-month follow-up.	"Forgiveness as an Intervention Goal With Incest Survivors," by S. R. Freedman and R. D. Enright, 1996, *Journal of Consulting and Clinical Psychology, 64,* pp. 983–992.
Men hurt by the abortion decision of a partner. The participants in the forgiveness group became emotionally healthier than did those in the control group after a 12-week program of individual intervention. Differences between the groups were observed for anger, anxiety,	"Forgiveness Intervention With Post-Abortion Men," by C. T. Coyle and R. D. Enright, 1997, *Journal of Consulting and Clinical Psychology, 65,* pp. 1042–1046.

TABLE 2.1. Research on Forgiveness Therapy and Education (Continued)

and grief. The results were maintained at a 3-month follow-up. When the control group went through the forgiveness process, its members also showed significant improvement in emotional health.

Participants in drug rehabilitation. The forgiveness group became emotionally healthier than did the control group, similar to the previous study. The experimental participants' need for drugs declined substantially, relative to the control group. Results were maintained at a 4-month follow-up.

"Effects of Forgiveness Therapy on Anger, Mood, and Vulnerability to Substance Use Among Inpatient Substance-Dependent Clients," by W. F. Lin, D. Mack, R. D. Enright, D. Krahn, and T. Baskin, 2004, *Journal of Consulting and Clinical Psychology, 72,* pp. 1114–1121.

Cardiac patients. Again, the experimental (forgiveness) group became emotionally healthier than did the control group. At a 4-month follow-up, the experimental group had more efficiently functioning hearts than did the control group.

"The Effects of a Forgiveness Intervention on Patients With Coronary Artery Disease," by M. A. Waltman, D. C. Russell, C. T. Coyle, R. D. Enright, A. C. Holter, and C. Swoboda, 2009, *Psychology & Health, 24,* pp. 11–27.

Emotionally abused women. Results are similar to the above studies in terms of emotional health (decreased anxiety, depression, and posttraumatic stress disorder symptoms and increased self-esteem).

"The Effects of Forgiveness Therapy on Depression, Anxiety, and Post-Traumatic Stress for Women After Spousal Emotional Abuse," by G. Reed and R. D. Enright, 2006, *Journal of Consulting and Clinical Psychology, 74,* pp. 920–929.

(continued)

TABLE 2.1. Research on Forgiveness Therapy and Education (*Continued*)

Terminally ill, elderly cancer patients. After a 4-week intervention, the forgiveness group showed greater improvement in psychological health (less anger, more hopefulness toward the future) than did the control group. Physical indicators of both groups showed declines.

"A Palliative Care Intervention in Forgiveness Therapy for Elderly Terminally-Ill Cancer Patients," by M. J. Hansen, R. D. Enright, R. W. Baskin, and J. Klatt, 2009, *Journal of Palliative Care, 25,* pp. 51–60.

Adult children of alcoholics. Two group interventions were compared: forgiveness and conflict resolution centered on one member of the participant's family of origin who abused alcohol. After a 12-week intervention, both groups improved in depression, anxiety, anger, self-esteem, and relations with others. When the control group then went through the forgiveness intervention for another 12-weeks, its members continued to improve in emotional health.

"Treating Adult Children of Alcoholics Through Forgiveness Therapy," by C. L. Osterndorf, R. D. Enright, A. C. Holter, and J. Klatt, 2011, *Alcoholism Treatment Quarterly, 29,* pp. 274–292.

At-risk middle-school students in Wisconsin. Those in the experimental (forgiveness) group improved more in emotional health and in academic achievement than did the control counterparts.

"Can School-Based Forgiveness Counseling Improve Conduct and Academic Achievement in Academically At-Risk Adolescents?" by M. E. Gambaro, R. D. Enright, T. A. Baskin, T. A., and J. Klatt, 2008, *Journal of Research in Education, 18,* pp. 16–27.

improved significantly in their emotional health. A finding worth noting is that those who benefited from forgiveness therapy did not become perfect forgivers. In many cases, the people went from being low on forgiveness to being average (relative to the different samples we have studied). Yet, this was sufficient for them to improve substantially in their emotional health, with (for example) decreased anxiety and depression and an increase in self-esteem and hope for the future.

Because we have worked with such a wide variety of people in a wide variety of settings and with different facilitators, we find these results very encouraging. They certainly do not present an iron-clad guarantee that anyone who starts down the forgiveness path will experience deep emotional healing, but they do suggest that you should go into this forgiveness effort with confidence. Our approach to forgiveness therapy works.

This next section is for those of you who wish more detail regarding the scientific methods we used in our research. If you are not interested in that, then I urge you to skip to the final section of this chapter, Should I Forgive?

Overview of Our Scientific Method When Studying Forgiveness Therapy

I describe in this section some of the details in two published studies: One concerned men and women in a drug rehabilitation program, and the other focused on men with cardiovascular disease. In each case, the participants had deep emotional wounds and needed to forgive. Each forgave using the very same process model of forgiveness that you will be learning about in this book. In both of these studies, as well as in every published therapy study with the process model of forgiveness, the scientists used true scientific experiments. By this I mean the following:

1. People were randomized to either the forgiveness group or a control group (which did not receive forgiveness therapy but instead either waited to receive it or had an alternative treatment).

2. Each person was given a series of psychological tests before the therapy began (the *pretest*), very soon after the therapy ended (the *posttest*), and after a period of time elapsed following treatment (the *follow-up test,* which was 4 months in both studies, although follow-up testing has been between 1 month and 14 months in different forgiveness programs). In each case, the measures chosen are some of the best in the field. Others have used them widely, and they are popular.

3. All therapists/educators were trained in the use of forgiveness therapy and whatever therapy was used (if any) in the control group. For most of the studies, the researchers audiotaped each therapist and had a person uninvolved in the research listen to the tape to be sure that the therapist was following the written manual for that day and was not being overly enthusiastic with one group over the other. They did this to minimize therapist bias or even error in delivering the programs.

4. The researchers applied standard statistical tests to see whether the people in the forgiveness group improved more in their psychological health than did the people in the control group. When this happens, the experimental designs allow the researchers to talk about cause and effect. By this I mean that we can say, "The forgiveness therapy caused a change in the people's psychological well-being."

People in Drug Rehabilitation

For the study with patients in drug rehabilitation, 14 men and women who suffered with drug dependence were admitted to a residential facility for treatment.[2] About 90% of all drug rehabilitation is done on an outpatient basis. Typically, inpatient care is reserved for those who are suffering the most. All 14 people came to the program with substantial psychological depression. To begin, the researchers randomized each person to one of two groups. The first group focused both on the patient forgiving someone in his or her life for a very deep injustice and on the patient going through the typical program at the facility. The control group focused exclusively on the patient going through the typical program at the facility, which included information on the effects of drug use on the body, strategies for avoiding stress, and social support. Each patient met individually with the counselor for about 1 hour twice a week for 6 weeks.

The statistical analyses showed that those in the group that emphasized forgiveness reduced more in depression, anxiety, anger, and vulnerability to drug use and increased more in forgiveness and self-esteem than did those in the control group. These positive findings held at the 4-month follow-up testing. What caught the researchers' attention the most seems to be this: Those in the forgiveness group, just as was found in the study with incest survivors, went from considerable psychological depression to nondepressed, and this held at the 4-month follow-up. Those in the control group went down in depression, but they remained clinically depressed at posttest and at follow-up testing.

One of the patients, Carol, worked on forgiving a man who had sexually assaulted her years before. Following that incident, her drug dependence increased markedly until she ended up in the rehabilitation facility. During forgiveness therapy, Carol learned that the man who had assaulted her was himself the victim of sexual assault as a child. He was now doing to others what had happened to him. Carol realized during therapy that this man continued to have a great deal of power over her because she lived daily with a burning resentment toward him. Her forgiving him for this attack did not mean that she would be invulnerable to him or other attackers because to forgive does not mean to reconcile or to unquestioningly trust others. As a result of the forgiveness therapy, Carol went to nondepressed status and remained there at the 4-month follow-up. One year after leaving the treatment facility, she was working for the state department of vocational rehabilitation and was doing fine.

Men With Coronary Artery Disease

In this study, 17 men with coronary artery disease were randomized into either a forgiveness therapy group or a control group that focused on heart health (proper diet, exercise, dealing with stress). Each man met for approximately 1 hour per week for 10 weeks with a counselor.[3]

The researchers focused in this study on what the field refers to as "myocardial blood flow" through the heart, which is assessed by a computer imaging technique. They focused on this issue for two reasons: (a) Those with coronary artery disease have less of this blood flow through the heart than people without this disease, and (b) research has shown that anger tends to reduce this kind of blood flow. Thus, when people with coronary artery disease have been treated very unjustly by others and remain angry (unforgiving), there is a tendency for even more blood flow restriction to occur in the heart. This makes the person vulnerable to angina, sudden death, and other coronary complications.

The researchers first screened each patient to be sure that he had a significant interpersonal hurt and that he remained unforgiving. They then assessed the myocardial blood flow through his heart when he was at rest and then while he retold his story of deep hurt. Those who showed myocardial defects became part of the study.

Following treatment, the researchers found that patients in the forgiveness group not only improved in forgiveness but also had less blood flow restriction in their hearts at the 4-month follow-up testing than they did at pretest compared with patients in the control group. In other words, when they recalled their story of deep injustice, their hearts functioned better than did the hearts of those in the control group, and they functioned better than they did at the pretesting.

Forgiveness can have an effect on the body. The researchers were cautious in this conclusion. They were not making the claim that forgiveness therapy actually restored the hearts to normal. The forgiveness therapy reduced anger and therefore helped the heart to function a little better than before forgiveness therapy.

Third-Grade (Primary 5) Children in Belfast, Northern Ireland

Forgiveness education basically is more about education than it is about psychology. The curriculum guides (explained in more detail in Chapter 18) are written for teachers and parents as well as for counselors who have the goal of addressing students through an instructional approach. The point of the guides is to introduce children to the concepts—the basic foundations—that they will need to be strong forgivers in adulthood. They need to know about inherent worth and about kindness, respect, generosity, and love. They need to know what forgiveness is and is not. They need some time to practice the virtues.

In the study with third graders (Primary 5 in Belfast), as well as in the four other studies done with classroom teachers, the scientists randomized each classroom either to the experimental condition (in which the teachers instructed the students in forgiveness) or to the control condition (in which the teachers did not provide forgiveness education for the children).

Because we have five studies of forgiveness education in classrooms, we have replicated the results. By this I mean that we have done the same kind of study five times with different teachers and different children in two different cultures (Belfast and Milwaukee's central city), and we continue to find the same results.

As in the studies on forgiveness therapy with adults, in this study each student was given a series of psychological tests before the educational program began (the pretest) and 1 month after the teacher finished the program. As in the studies on adults, in each case the measures chosen are some of the best in the field and included anger and depression inventories for children developed by Aaron Beck, a well-respected psychiatrist, and the Enright Forgiveness Inventory for Children, a variant on the adult version.

In this and all other published studies to date, the educators and the school counselor (for the middle-school study) were trained in the use of forgiveness education. The researchers then either had the teachers provide detailed accounts of their teaching or be observed by a person not involved in the research who recorded whether the teacher had followed the written manual for that day. Across all five studies, the researchers applied standard statistical tests to each child or adolescent (not to each classroom) to see whether the students in the forgiveness group improved more in their psychological health than did the students in the control group.

In the study of 8- and 9-year-old children in Belfast, there were 35 students across three classrooms in the forgiveness program and 49 students across three different classrooms in the control group.[4] For both the experimental and control groups at pretesting time, on the average, the children were more angry and depressed than the children who did not come from such a challenging environment.

The experimental students were taught forgiveness through the medium of stories such as *The Velveteen Rabbit* by Margery Williams and my book, *Rising Above the Storm Clouds*.[5] The teachers spent about 1 hour each week for 15 weeks working with the students on such topics as the meaning of forgiveness, the theme of inherent worth in each person, and the importance of the moral virtue of love in forgiveness.

The statistical analyses showed that those students who had forgiveness instruction once a week for 15 weeks decreased more in anger and depression and increased more in forgiveness than did the students in the control group, who did not have forgiveness education (they did have it a year later). Those in the experimental group actually went to average levels of both anger and depression after the intervention. Prior to the forgiveness program, the children were higher than they should have been in both anger and depression.

The researchers compared the strength of these results with other, published results of group interventions with adults conducted by trained psychologists. The results were as strong as forgiveness therapy conducted with adults by the trained psychologists. The teachers did an excellent job from both a teaching standpoint and a scientific standpoint.

SHOULD I FORGIVE?

Even when people get a glimmer of hope and now want to forgive, questions remain. Even when people know that they can be kept safe when they forgive, they can be hesitant. Even with the scientific evidence, there is an important question looming: Should I forgive? This question does not address motivation (the person's wants), or the consequences of forgiveness (e.g., safety issues), or even the evidence itself that forgiveness works (the scientific evidence). This question instead centers on the moral issue of forgiveness: Is it a morally good thing to do and, if so, why? Is a forgiveness act good in itself?

Not everyone agrees that forgiveness is morally good. For example, in 1887, the German philosopher Nietzsche said that only the weak forgive. In other words, if you have to keep a job, then you forgive the boss to keep a paycheck coming. If you find another job, so

Nietzsche's story goes, then you can boldly share what is really on your mind as you strut out the door. Yet, was Nietzsche talking about genuine forgiveness? I don't think so. To forgive is to deliberately offer goodness in the face of your own pain to the one who was unfair to you. This is an act of great courage, not weakness. As we see in subsequent chapters, forgiveness—like justice or patience or kindness or love—is a virtue, and all virtues are concerned with the exercise of goodness. It is always appropriate to be good to others, if you so choose and are ready to do so. As a caution, if you have only one dollar to feed your hungry child and you get a phone call requesting that you give to the local animal shelter, you should not exercise goodness toward the shelter if it means depriving your child of basic needs. Yet, if the circumstances are right and if you have an honest motive to give mercy to someone who hurt you, then going ahead with forgiveness is morally good. Why? Because you are freely offering kindness or respect or generosity or even love (or all four together), and this might change you and the other person and others in the world. Even if no one is changed by what you do, it is always good (given the right motivation and circumstance) to offer mercy in a world that too often seems to turn its collective back on such an act.

Are you ready to explore forgiveness in greater depth? I am not asking you to forgive just yet. Instead, I am asking if you are willing to continue exploring the concept, which we will do for the next five chapters.

Part II

OVERVIEW OF THE FORGIVENESS PROCESS

CHAPTER 3

HOW TELLING AND LISTENING TO STORIES CAN HELP

We are all in the process of writing our stories. Everyone will have a legacy, whether it is primarily good or bad, whether it is a story of helping people with their wounds or adding more wounds to the world. We are about to meet one such person, Inez, who is sensing that something is wrong and that there is something much deeper in life that she does not have. She has lived for much of her life without a strong sense of love. Surely, she has experienced love, giving and receiving it. Yet so many important people in her life, from childhood to the present (she is 35), have been so wounded by others that they have wounded her in an emotional sense. Despite this, she is a strong, courageous woman intent on making a difference—within herself and then for others in this world.

She has begun to change her life through dialogue with her friend, Sophia, 20 years older and with lots of "forgiveness miles" accumulated over decades; Sophia has studied, practiced, and taught about forgiveness as a life's calling.

THE DIALOGUE

The vast majority of my professional work with others has centered on dialogue. Whether it involves education or helping people work through their conflicts, much of the work on forgiveness takes place in the special forum of dialogue, the give-and-take of ideas and strategies between interested people. I like dialogue because it assumes the following:

- We are all learners when it comes to forgiveness, even those of us with more than a quarter of a century of experience in the area. We never outgrow our capacity to know.
- Each member of the dialogue brings some important insights and experiences to the table. I have found that most people have some degree of wisdom about what forgiveness is and is not.
- Dialogue opens each person to change and deeper insight from the other's experience. We learn from each other.
- Working out forgiveness with others can act as a strong motivator to continue on the forgiveness path. In a certain sense, those with whom we dialogue help us focus on the task of becoming forgivingly fit.
- Dialogue can expand our vision and help us see new areas in which we need to forgive.
- Dialogue can expand our vision further and help us see new areas in which we can bring our knowledge to others for their benefit.
- Dialogue, as a way of knowing and changing, has been used for thousands of years, as we know from Socrates' dialogues—preserved for all time in Plato's writings in ancient Greece. Dialogue as a teaching technique has withstood the test of time.

THE FORGIVER AND YOU

Inez's story is intended to spark your thinking about your own story. It is a typical, not exact, reconstruction of what goes on when someone willingly explores forgiveness through dialogue.

I challenge you to become involved in the dialogue. Don't just sit back and watch as Inez attempts to understand forgiveness and then to apply it in a variety of her life's circumstances. Become a participant in the dialogue, in this great conversation about forgiveness. It is my hope for you that your engagement with the exchanges between Inez and Sophia will help lead you onto the path of living The Forgiving Life.

THE INITIAL CONVERSATION

> *Inez:* I'm discouraged. Sterling [her husband] seems so distant with me, angry even. I try so hard. My stepchildren and I get along very well, but lately they have been pulling back too. I think they see their father's unhappiness with me. [*Inez puts her head down, seemingly ashamed and embarrassed at saying this.*]
>
> *Sophia:* Are you unhappy with yourself?
>
> *Inez:* [*looking up surprised*] No . . . no . . . I don't think so. I have always tried to live my life so that I have self-respect. [*It is obvious that she had not considered this question before.*]
>
> *Sophia:* This is a good first step. Respecting yourself is a good sign. It seems that others in your life, however, are not respecting you.
>
> *Inez:* [*again looking up surprised*] Yes, a lack of respect. Yes.
>
> *Sophia:* I think I can help you with this.

The Details

Inez was raised in a two-parent family in Texas. The father owned his own machine-repair business and spent long hours away from the family. Her mother ran the household. She did so with an authoritarian style, sometimes impatient with the children because she was angry at the frequent absence of her husband from the family. Inez is the youngest of three children; the oldest is her brother, McCade, and the middle child is her sister, Katina.

Both parents had good intentions toward the children, but because of their chronic busyness they rarely had time to just be with them. It is the kind of situation that I have described in one of my journal articles as "parental love deprivation."[1] The parents, to put it directly, just were not there for Inez. They were especially not emotionally present to Inez in particular because she was the youngest of the children, and the parents were more distracted and tired when she was young. As a result, she did not learn to trust at an early age and has carried this burden with her through her adult life.

Would you call what Inez faced with her parents a trauma, similar to what we discussed in the previous chapter? Even though she did not experience an actual abandonment, as I described for David, she may have experienced something more subtle but nonetheless similar. In both cases, the parents withdrew love. In both cases, children were forced to find their own way without the support of parents, which every child deserves. In Inez's case, the withdrawal of love was so subtle that she might not have realized what was happening, and so her trauma could be just as serious as David's. After all, Inez's parents were physically present, making the detection of the love withdrawal more difficult. The legacy for both David and Inez is a lifelong struggle to trust.

To continue her story: Inez attended local schools and received a 2-year college degree from the local community college while living at home with her parents. She was married at age 21 to Enrico, and they were divorced 3 years later with no children. Since that time, she has worked as a service representative for an insurance firm and then for a telecommunications company. She had a 1-year period of unemployment after being laid off from her first job because of a downturn in the economy. At the age of 30, she met Sterling, who was 3 years older than her, through mutual friends. One year later they were married. Sterling brought a daughter and a son into the marriage—Kailey, now age 12, and Cade, now age 7. At present, Inez continues to work part time at a local nursing home while taking courses part time toward an undergraduate college degree in social work, which she hopes will help her as she advances in service to the elderly in nursing homes.

Four years into their marriage, Inez and Sterling have hit a rough spot in the road. Sterling is a seventh-grade teacher at the local middle school. They struggle a bit financially but are not overly concerned about finances. The children will be going to college in the future, so the family is feeling some financial pressure over those costs.

The Dialogue Continued

> *Sophia:* What do you think is going on?
>
> *Inez:* Sterling keeps telling me that I am not giving enough to the marriage and family and I resent it. I have to work, he knows that. I have only a year and a half left to my college degree. It will help me get the better job I've always wanted. I'm going nowhere in my present position.
>
> *Sophia:* It can be hard balancing it all.
>
> *Inez:* Yes, and he has trouble balancing it all, too. He is no saint, but don't say that I said that. He gets so distracted with his sports on TV. It's the same old thing over and over. Dinner, he in front of the television, me lonely, and then he complains that I don't do enough for him. I can't stand it.
>
> *Sophia:* It sounds like the tension has built and the resentments are beginning to run deep.

Inez: The resentments are running deep, in both directions.

Sophia: What do you mean?

Inez: Well, he is resenting me and I am resenting him. The resentments are running back and forth between us.

For the rest of this conversation, Inez and Sophia continue to outline sources of conflict on which Inez would like to work. It is only a beginning. It will take several conversations for both to see where the central conflicts lie and what work needs to be done.

Fast Forward in Time

It is best to ease into the issue of forgiveness. If one were to suggest it in a first conversation, unless the one who has been treated unjustly has that goal in mind from the beginning, then he or she may become resistant to the idea or even angry with the suggestion. Inez has carefully explored the tensions between Sterling and her.

Sophia: Have you thought of forgiving Sterling?

Inez: [*wide-eyed*] Forgive him? He says, "You never do enough around here!" How absurd. He is wrong! No, I won't forgive him.

Sophia: What is holding you back?

Inez: Him, that's who is holding me back. I can't just forgive him and admit defeat. If I forgive him, I just cave in and go back to this stagnation-as-usual thing. He wins. I lose. Where is my self-respect then? No, I can't do that.

Sophia: I'm curious about something. You referred to forgiveness as "caving in." Is that what it means to you?

Inez: Sort of. He demands, I get resentful, then I forgive. He gets his demand and I get my resentment and off we go again, round and round. It never ends.

Sophia: I'm curious about something else. You said, "Then I forgive." Do you see forgiveness as a one-time, quick fix?

Inez: [pausing] Well, yes, sure. Isn't that what you have in mind?

Sophia: I'm bringing up forgiveness because you used the word *resentment* more than once, and forgiveness is a major way of reducing resentment and making you feel a whole lot better inside. Resentment can do some serious damage to our emotional health if we let it have free rein inside of us.

Inez: You seemed unhappy with my idea that forgiveness is something you do as a one-time attempt. "I forgive you." Isn't that it?

Sophia: That may be part of what forgiveness is, but that is not the whole story. When we forgive, we have been treated unfairly by another person. You have picked out Sterling as someone who has been unfair.

Inez: You've got that right.

Sophia: When we forgive, we struggle to get rid of resentment caused by the other's unfairness.

Inez: I'm not too keen on that little word *struggle*.

Sophia: Did I use the word *struggle*? If I did, I really did mean to say that. To forgive is not an easy task. It is a process that can take days, weeks, months, or even years. [*Inez looks a little worried by the word* years.] Yet, as a person works to rid herself of resentment, that resentment gradually lessens.

Inez: I like that little word *lessens*.

Sophia: Yes, and besides reducing resentment, when you forgive, you strive to offer goodness to the one who hurt you. Forgiveness is part of the moral virtue of mercy. When you forgive, you have mercy on the one who hurt you.

Inez: Goodness? To the one who hurt me? Mercy? On the one who acted like a ninny?

Sophia: [*smiling*] Yes, even to ninnies.

Inez: It's my choice, right? I'll have to think about it.

Sophia: When you think about it, you might want to remember a few things: that forgiveness is an act of mercy toward someone who treated you unfairly; that it is your choice whether to forgive a particular person for a particular injustice; that when you forgive, you will struggle, yes, struggle, to get rid of resentment toward the person who hurt you; that you will be challenged to offer goodness, again to the person who hurt you; that forgiveness is a moral response, not a response to get your own way or to manipulate the other person—a response of goodness; and that when you forgive, you do not excuse or condone because these are not necessarily moral responses. When you forgive, you do not forget, but you remember in new ways. Forgiveness is not the same as reconciliation.[2]

Another thing to keep in mind is that this process can take some time.

BACK TO THE BASICS—YOU

Having been a part of this dialogue between Sophia and Inez, how will you now add to this dialogue? Has someone in your life treated you unjustly? Are you sure that you are not misunderstanding something? In other words, might the person have an extenuating circumstance, a good excuse, so that what you think is an injustice really isn't? I ask just to be sure. If you conclude that you have been treated unfairly, I now have another question for you. What do you think of the definition of forgiveness so far? It is a process, freely chosen by you, in which you willingly reduce resentment through some hard work and offer goodness of some kind toward the one who hurt you. Where do you agree and disagree with this? What would you say to me, for example, about the idea of offering goodness toward someone who acts in an offensive way toward you? If you say, "I just won't put up with all of the unfairness anymore, and forgiveness will not aid me in that," then I want you to know that you are not alone in this assessment.

Many people are hesitant, even afraid, to forgive because they fear that the other will take advantage of them. "Forgiveness is for wimps," I have heard many times. Yet, is that true? Is the offer of goodness, true goodness, extended from a position of your own pain, ever done in weakness? How can one offer goodness through a position of pain and see it as weak? And see the giver of this goodness as weak? My point is this: We all may need to delve more deeply into what forgiveness is so that we can make the best decisions possible for ourselves, for our loved ones, and for the ones who hurt us.

DO YOU WANT TO BECOME A FORGIVING PERSON?

At this point in your life, how do you see yourself relative to forgiveness? You may be someone who has thought some about the topic and perhaps has practiced forgiveness from time to time. I ask you now to write about the different errors concerning what forgiveness is and is not, which you have brought to this book. For instance, did you

- think that forgiveness is a somewhat superficial act ("I'm sorry"; "Oh, that's OK, I forgive you"),
- confuse forgiveness with excusing,
- confuse forgiveness with reconciliation,

- think that you should now throw justice out the window because you have forgiven, or
- see yourself as vulnerable to another's nonsense because you have forgiven?

What has surprised you about forgiveness and what do you see as its strengths and weaknesses? When you are ready, let us continue the dialogue with Inez and Sophia in the next chapter.

CHAPTER 4

FORGIVENESS IS A PROCESS

In this chapter, you will be listening to the exchange between Sophia and Inez regarding the unfolding process of forgiveness. As you will see, we use a particular model for bringing about forgiveness. This model is summarized in Appendix A at the back of the book. The model has what we call four phases: Uncovering, Decision, Work, and Discovery. When a person decides to forgive, he or she usually begins with Uncovering and moves through the phases one at a time, with Discovery coming near the end of the forgiveness path.

Please keep in mind that this is not some kind of neat-and-tidy process through which you will be progressing in a steplike fashion. Forgiveness is not that predictable. You may find yourself going back to parts of the process you thought you had conquered long ago. For example, you may be near the end of the process and discover that you still harbor considerable anger toward the person (anger comes near the beginning of the entire forgiveness process). You then may cycle back to the beginning, do some work on your anger, and jump back to the end of the process. Be ready to go backward and forward in the forgiveness process, depending on your particular needs with a particular person whom you are currently forgiving. With this in mind, let's enter the conversation.

Inez: At the end of our most recent talk, I was not so sure that I wanted to continue.

Sophia: Did something upset you?

Inez: Yes, you.

Sophia: How was I upsetting for you?

Inez: You don't know? You used that little word *forgiveness.* You scared me.

Sophia: What scared you about it?

Inez: I don't want to forgive because I don't want to be vulnerable. I can't forgive because Sterling and I have been fighting for too long.

Sophia: You have been fighting? I don't think you mentioned actual fighting until now.

Inez: Well, you know. He stays in front of the TV and sulks, and I stay in the kitchen and sulk.

Sophia: It is a kind of passive fighting rather than something active, then.

Inez: Yes, that's a good way of putting it. We are passive.

Sophia: You are passive and angry.

Inez: And resentful, and bored, and lonely.

Sophia: We can approach this issue from a different angle than forgiveness. For instance . . .

Inez: [*interrupting*] No, please. I said I was scared, but I did not say that I don't want to think about forgiveness. I'd like to learn more.

Sophia: OK, but I want to be sure that this is what you choose and that you want to continue in this vein.

Inez: Yes, I am sure.

Sophia: Then I would like to share with you what I call the *roadmap of forgiveness*—the basic path that you likely will take as you forgive someone who has hurt you. [*See Appendix A.*]

Inez: That would be Sterling.

Sophia: One thing to consider at first is this: Sterling might not be the very first person whom you forgive.

Inez: [*looking surprised*] Why is that?

Sophia: Sometimes, when we begin a forgiveness journey, we take a look at the big picture: Who hurt you and when? You now have a long history with many people. Think about it for a minute. You were born into a family with your mom and dad and a brother and a sister. You went to school all the way through a 2-year college and now you are in college again. Along the way, you made friends and lost friends. Perhaps you even made a few of what some would call enemies. You were married to Enrico and have had more than one boss in your employment history. You have two stepchildren. That is well over 20 people with whom you have interacted in a meaningful way, if you include teachers and bosses, and I did not even count the friends and enemies.

Inez: I see what you mean.

Sophia: I am not saying that you will not start the forgiveness journey with Sterling in mind. You might or might not, but if you want to continue forgiving— what I call "leading the forgiving life"—you won't stop with just one person. You may decide to extend forgiveness to many others in the months and years to come.

Inez: There you go again, Sophia, with that not-so-little word *years*. What am I getting myself into?

Sophia: You may be getting yourself into a new way of looking at the world. You may be getting into living a forgiving life if you so choose.

Inez: A forgiving life. That sounds like a lot more than just saying, "I forgive you," and then the birds start singing and the sun starts shining.

Sophia: Yes, The Forgiving Life is far more than that. Here is a different way to look at it, perhaps. Have you ever heard owners of exercise gyms talk of New Year's resolutions?

Inez: No, I can't say that I have.

Sophia: I know a few owners, and they might not be representative of all, but each one has told me that they make a significant amount of money from people who sign up for a gym membership early in each calendar year. Many who sign up then have a New Year's resolution to get into good physical shape.

Inez: Seems like a good idea to me.

Sophia: Yes, it is what philosophers call a *good will*. They have the very best of intentions. Yet, many of those who sign up last about a month and fade away. They do not have what we will call a *strong will*. They never come back, but they've paid their annual membership.

Inez: What's the point with me and forgiveness?

Sophia: This—you are not going to live The Forgiving Life by making a quick decision about it, getting all excited about a new way, trying it for a month, and then dropping it altogether. You have to work at it, stay at it, and persevere through struggles if you will lead The Forgiving Life.

Inez: I wouldn't be one of those who signs up and then leaves after a month.

Sophia: The people who sign up for the gym memberships don't mean to drop them either, but they do.

Inez: So, how can I avoid that?

Sophia: First, keep in mind that it is easier to drop the whole thing than you think. And knowing that, don't let it happen. Have a strong will.

Inez: That I have.

Sophia: I know that. Second, please keep in mind that The Forgiving Life is a steady marathon, not a quick sprint to a finish line. You will need to stay at it.

Inez: Inez, the marathoner! I like that.

Sophia: Third, you will be practicing the moral virtue of forgiveness. The practice of any virtue engages your mind, your emotions, and your actions. Our bodies get tired with this kind of effort, so allow yourself time to rest and recover.

Inez: Could you explain that a little more, please?

Sophia: You do not want to strive after forgiveness with mighty effort for too many hours on too many days in a row. Take breaks. Focus on other priorities. Allow yourself time to refresh. It is kind of similar to physical workouts in that if you overdo it, you exhaust and injure your muscles. It is then that too many people walk away from the gym.

Inez: OK, I'm listening.

Sophia: Please keep in mind that a person who lives The Forgiving Life persists in the practice of forgiveness, and so you should build in times of work and times of refreshment, just as you do relative to schooling, employment, and an exercise program.

Inez: Balance. Yes, The Forgiving Life interests me.

Sophia: Then I am willing to work on that with you, but we are getting ahead of ourselves. I want to explain the roadmap of forgiveness I mentioned. There are four phases you will go through as you forgive a particular person for a particular injustice against you. [*See Appendix A.*] First, you will work on uncovering your anger. When I use the word *anger*, I mean to reflect your particular emotion toward the person whom you are forgiving. For some, *anger* does not quite capture the way they feel. Instead of feeling angry, they may feel sad, or frustrated, or even hate filled, so you should choose the feeling that best describes your internal world.

Inez: OK. I'll keep that in mind.

Sophia: When you enter the Uncovering Phase of forgiveness, you already have chosen the particular person you will forgive. In your case, it might be Sterling, but it also might be Enrico.

Inez: Don't go reminding me of Enrico. I don't want to even think about him.

Sophia: That is up to you, but, if you are to live The Forgiving Life, you may want to do so. Perhaps you are not ready now, but you might be later. Besides Enrico, you might wish to start forgiving your mom or dad, or the employer who asked you to resign from your career with the insurance company.

Inez: I see that my first choice for forgiveness is not as straightforward as I had hoped.

Sophia: And that is OK. Take your time in choosing that one person. In the Uncovering Phase, you will begin to see how angry (or sad or disappointed) you are with the unfair treatment that you received from the person. You will see how the person's unfair treatment has possibly complicated your life. You will see how the person's unfairness has emotionally wounded you.

Inez: I'm zeroed in on Sterling.

Sophia: At the very beginning of the Uncovering Phase there is a question about avoiding one's anger. This deals with the psychological defenses, the shields we put up by denying, or suppressing, or repressing, or even displacing our emotional wounds. These defenses or shields are good up to a point because they help protect us from being flooded with pain, but in the long run, if we begin to hide behind those shields, we may never give ourselves a chance to see the wounds, take steps to treat the wounds, and be healed.

Inez: Do I have this kind of shield?

Sophia: You'll want to explore that.

Inez: And if I do have shields up, then I've got to come out from behind them?

Sophia: Yes, if you wish to be healed. Suppose you were afraid to go to the doctor when an infection was developing in your ankle. If you ignored it too long it could make you very sick. It could kill you. Is it any different with persistent and deep emotional wounds, those we receive from others' unfairness?

Inez: Are you saying that my mom, to use that example again, may have hurt me more than I think?

Sophia: I'm not saying that she definitely hurt you more than you think. At this point, I am only saying that if she was unjust to you, then this can sometimes complicate your life. We can explore this for each person you wish to forgive. And remember, we are not doing this to attack anyone, to put the blame on anyone. We are doing this to be merciful with each person who was very unjust to you and who hurt you.

Inez: What do you mean by "complicate my life"? You've used that expression twice now.

Sophia: For example, let's take the boss who asked you to resign.

Inez: No, you take her. I don't want her.

Sophia: [*smiling*] Let's take her as an example, OK? When she asked you to resign, this was seen as an injustice to you.

Inez: Yes, absolutely.

Sophia: A possible complication is that you were embarrassed.

Inez: Terribly. I had to walk past all of those cubicles with all of those people who kept their jobs. It was embarrassing and angering.

Sophia: And that is my very point. As you were treated unjustly, an unintended consequence is that you were embarrassed, which is another wound for you besides the termination itself.

Inez: I was not just embarrassed. Over the next couple of weeks, I was exhausted from the stress.

Sophia: That is another one of the wounds to examine in the Uncovering Phase: As you are treated unfairly, you can become tired.

Inez: I see. An injustice can make me angry and embarrassed and tired.

Sophia: Some other complications could be that as you begin to feel embarrassed, and not everyone does by every injustice, there can be a tendency to think over and over about what happened.

Inez: When I was fired, I mean asked to resign, I remember dreaming about my boss. When watching TV, I would sometimes miss the plot of a movie because my mind would wander to the day I was fired. I relived it over and over.

Sophia: Yes, and that is yet another wound, as is a comparison people tend to make between themselves and the one who acted unfairly. People tend to think, "Here I am, out of a job, embarrassed, tired, and distracted, and there is my boss with a good job and a good salary not caring about me."

Inez: I see. I also had to make a major adjustment to my work. I had to find another job and it took a while to do it.

Sophia: You see, that is yet another wound from the original injustice. So far, we have identified seven of these as a result of what happened to you, and here they are: You are possibly denying the severity of the offense, thus hampering your will to confront the injustice and bottling you up inside; you may be struggling with anger, disappointment, sadness, or some other unpleasant emotion; you were embarrassed, a situation you did not deserve, as people whispered and wondered and you may have guilt if you pushed back, in an emotional sense, with insensitivity or in some way hurt the person by your actions; you became tired; you thought over and over about what happened; you compared yourself, unfavorably, with your boss; and you had to make a permanent change in your life.

These are all part of the Uncovering Phase of forgiveness.

Inez: I'm tired just thinking about it all. I hope that's it for the Uncovering Phase.

Sophia: There is another wound, an eighth one. Sometimes as people are treated unfairly, they change their worldview, their philosophy of life, their sense of how things work in this world. For example, if a person breaks up with a partner, there might be a tendency to become pessimistic in general about such relationships, saying to oneself, "No man (or no woman) can be trusted."

Inez: I definitely had it in for bosses of all kinds after that. I mistrusted people in authority.

Sophia: This is what I mean by this eighth wound when I say that you altered your worldview. In your case, you became more negative in general toward bosses.

Inez: And I did not even know I was doing it until a colleague pointed it out to me.

Sophia: Yes, this can happen. We slip quietly into negativism and are not even aware of it. This is a wound that you did not deserve, and it is part of the Uncovering Phase.

Inez: [*silent for a while*] Is this why I am so very resentful toward Sterling? Has he wounded me eight times every time he is really, really unfair to me?

Sophia: The short answer is, yes, if he is very unjust to you, it is possible that you have received eight wounds each time severe injustice occurs.

[*Inez welled up with tears. She began to experience too many wounds all at once.*]

Sophia: Even though you cannot get rid of the injustices themselves, forgiveness can reduce or even get rid of the effects of all these wounds. For example, you cannot build yourself a time machine and go back to the place and time when your boss dismissed you so you can reverse the decision. It is part of your life's history. But this does not mean that you have to live with the effects of the injustice. The negative effects can be reversed through forgiveness.

Inez: [*again, with tears*] What do you mean?

Sophia: I mean this. If you are feeling anger or even hatred, these emotions can be reduced and even eliminated. If you are feeling resentful from being embarrassed, this can be reduced or even eliminated. If you are tired and distracted from what happened, these feelings can change as you forgive. Your worldview can change toward the more positive and the more realistic, and I can be here as coach or cheerleader if you want help with that.

Inez: I'd like the help. Thank you.

Sophia: Should we proceed with the next phase, the Decision Phase of forgiveness?

Inez: [*growing a little stronger*] Yes.

Sophia: The Decision Phase is just as it seems. You make a decision to either forgive or not to forgive. Of course, we continue forgiveness only if you say "yes" to this phase, which includes examining first how effective your current strategies are for solving your problems. It seems, for example, that your sulking in the kitchen while Sterling sulks in front of the television is not working.

Inez: [*with a slight smile*] Tell me something I don't already know.

Sophia: Forgiveness can offer one approach for dealing with this issue.

Inez: I don't get it. How will forgiveness make Sterling get off his duff and start talking with me?

Sophia: If you can forgive him and be less angry and if he can forgive you and be less huffy, then the two of you might begin to talk more civilly with each other. You might be able to rekindle the spark.

Inez: I'm listening.

Sophia: In the Decision Phase, you decide if you are ready to begin the forgiveness process.

Inez: Well . . .

Sophia: I see that you are hesitating.

Inez: Right. I'm still not entirely sure what forgiveness is. Am I caving into Sterling's huffiness? Do I give up my rights and agree with him? Will I put the past behind me? My painful past? I think that forgiveness may be a cop-out . . . but I'm not sure.

Sophia: Great points. You are seeing that it is vital to examine what forgiveness is and is not so you can decide if you are willing to consider forgiveness as an option. When we first started our conversation, it seemed you thought that forgiveness would lead to a cycle of ignoring between you and Sterling and that it could be potentially harmful and weak. You will need to examine forgiveness closely and train your mind to be a philosopher of forgiveness if you wish to lead The Forgiving Life.

Inez: I am taking two philosophy courses at college, and I like thinking that way.

Sophia: Good.

Inez: I'm ready when you are.

Sophia: At the end of the Decision Phase, you make a commitment to following the path of forgiveness. This starts with this simple but maybe profound challenge: Are you ready to do no harm to the one who hurt you? By this I mean: Are you ready not to talk trash to or about the person? Are you willing not to return injustice with injustice of your own? I don't mean if you would do something morally good for the person, such as being compassionate or loving, but only if you can commit to refraining from the negative, from any harm.

Inez: As I understand it, yes, I can commit to that for the boss who hurt me.

Sophia: What about Sterling?

Inez: I'm thinking, I'm thinking.

Sophia: When you explore the Decision Phase of forgiveness you examine old patterns of coping to evaluate whether they have been effective; examine whether you will consider forgiveness as a way of dealing with your problems, which will include a detailed examination of what forgiveness is and is not; and commit to forgiving by committing to doing no harm. You will not be forgiving at this point, but making a commitment to doing the work of forgiveness.

Inez: It looks like I have my work cut out for me.

Sophia: Good segue to the next phase, the Work Phase of forgiveness.

Inez: "Work" phase. I'm afraid to ask.

Sophia: Remember that little word *struggle*. Here is where the struggle really begins, but it sounds like I've given you enough to think about for now. Let's talk about the work phase next time we get together, OK?

BACK TO THE BASICS—YOU

What have you heard in this chapter that is confusing or unclear to you? For example, do you have someone clearly in mind to forgive? As you observe Inez, I hope you realize that you may have a number of people to forgive, from your past and your present. We will discuss later whom the best person is for you to forgive initially.

Are you clear on what an "emotional wound" is? Philosophers refer to our inner world, the world that no one else can see or truly measure in a completely accurate way, as *qualia*. Think of qualia as those inner experiences that no one else shares with you. An example is physical pain. Has a medical professional ever asked you your level of pain in a knee or elbow? When you give a number from 0 to 10, that medical professional still cannot share the exact pain that you and only you feel. It is a part of your own inner world, of your qualia. The medical professional can only share the effect of your qualia by, for example, seeing your facial expression or listening to your description of your inner world.

Emotional pains, what we are calling *emotional wounds,* also are part of your qualia. No other human being can completely share the experience of those pains with you, but you can help others know of your pains by putting a number on them, as medical professionals do with physical pain. On a 0-to-10 scale, how angry (sad, disappointed, frustrated, etc.) do you feel toward certain people who have been unfair to you (suppose that a 0 = *no anger* and a 10 = *extreme anger*)? On that 0-to-10 scale, how embarrassed are you (suppose a 10 = *extreme embarrassment*)? How tired are you on that same scale (10 = *exceptionally fatigued*)? On the 0-to-10 scale, how dramatically has your life been altered by the injustices that you have faced in life (10 = *drastic life changes*)? How pessimistic are you? Please be honest here. Have any of the injustices that you have faced led to a pessimistic view of the world? If 0 means that you are very optimistic, if 5 means that you are neither pessimistic nor optimistic, and if 10 means that you are extremely pessimistic, where do you fall on the scale? Answers to the questions that put you in the 7, 8, or higher categories should be seen as emotional wounds in need of healing. Of course, because we are talking about qualia here, it is truly your call, your judgment, about whether or not you are wounded enough to try the forgiveness exercises in this book. I do not mean to suggest that if you have only a mild annoyance that you should not forgive. Instead, I am suggesting that you may not need the detailed help I offer here for you to successfully forgive. The pathways and strategies outlined here are for the big injustices with significant emotional wounds.

Has anything you have read in this chapter distressed you? Most people are surprised to hear that when they are treated unjustly, they may suffer eight psychological wounds each time, if the injustice is severe enough. This can be overwhelming. Yet, please keep in mind that there is a way out—forgiveness. This is not a quick fix, as you might be seeing already and surely will see as you keep reading. If you persevere in the work with a strong will, you should experience some or even considerable emotional healing. Of course, I cannot guarantee this. I can only say from experience and from the scientific studies that we have run (discussed in Chapter 2) that many people experience considerable emotional relief when they forgive.

What have you done to reduce the emotional wounds? Have you talked with a friend? Tried therapy? Started an exercise program? All of these are good things, and some of them may prove helpful to you. On the 0-to-10 scale, how effective have each of these, as well as any other innovations toward healing that you've tried, been for you? If your good efforts still have you feeling wounded, perhaps it is time to consider forgiveness as one of your options for emotional healing and for the healing of a relationship.

DO YOU WANT TO BECOME A FORGIVING PERSON?

Are you beginning to get a sense of what forgiveness is and what you may have to do to forgive? Does the effort to forgive scare you? If so, what do you see as the dangers? Does the effort to forgive seem like a good challenge, one you are ready to take on? If so, what are the positives you see in this journey? Please recall that we are just beginning to explore forgiveness—we are just warming up. You will deepen your understanding of it and of the process you go through as we continue watching Inez progress toward and through this process.

CHAPTER 5

THE WORK PHASE OF FORGIVENESS

As stated in the previous chapter, there are four phases to the forgiveness process. We will examine the Work Phase here and the Discovery Phase in the next chapter. Once we have done that, we will take a little breather before you actually take your first steps along this path. In Chapter 7, we will carefully examine just what *forgiveness* is. It would be remiss of me not to do this. As Socrates and Aristotle reminded us more than 2,300 years ago, it is of paramount importance to understand whatever it is that we are examining. Their counsel was: Examine your term. If we want to forgive, we first must understand what forgiveness is. Let us listen in, as Sophia and Inez struggle to understand.

> *Sophia:* How is the forgiveness process coming for you?
>
> *Inez:* Let's see. I have emotional wounds from my mom and dad, from Enrico, from Sterling, from the woman who thought she was my boss, and so forth. Let's see . . . if I have eight emotional wounds for each time any one of them hurt me very deeply . . . I'm quickly doing the math here . . . I've got 7,121 wounds to work on!

Sophia: [*laughing*] OK, it can be overwhelming.

Inez: I am angry not only at all of these people, but also at forgiveness itself.

Sophia: Why forgiveness?

Inez: It is asking too much of me.

Sophia: How is that?

Inez: I was doing pretty well before you and I started talking about all this forgiveness stuff. Now I am feeling very wounded.

Sophia: Why is this the fault of forgiveness itself? Is forgiveness itself responsible for even one of your emotional wounds?

Inez: No, but it sure is making me acutely aware of all of these wounds, and it hurts.

Sophia: As you recall, at the beginning of the Uncovering Phase, there is a stage of dealing with the psychological defenses, or the shields, people put up to keep themselves from the pain of all the wounds they receive. I think that you are moving well beyond the put-up-the-shield part of forgiveness, and you are feeling the effects of the injustices against you.

Inez: Yes, that I am.

Sophia: Do you see that it is not forgiveness itself that is wounding you? Do you see that it is the injustices that are causing the wounds?

Inez: I guess you are trying to convince me that forgiveness is not the enemy. Forgiveness shows me the pain and the extent of it within me.

Sophia: Right. And it provides a way out of that pain. To acknowledge all of the pain you have received is courageous. It shows that you have a strong sense of justice, of what is right and wrong. You want to face head-on the injustices of your life. This is good.

Inez: It may be good, but it sure is painful.

Sophia: And forgiveness is not the origin of the pain. Yes, working through the process of forgiveness can be painful, but is that not the case with any typical medical treatment? Surgery to repair a torn rotator cuff can be challenging but necessary to restore full use of the arm.

Inez: OK, I hear you. Forgiveness is my friend. If this is the way forgiveness treats its friends, no wonder it has so few of them.

Sophia: [*smiling*] I admire your courage and your willingness to do surgery of the heart. You are wounded.

Inez: And I say "yes" to forgiveness surgery.

Sophia: Shall we then progress to the next phase of the pathway to forgiving: the Work Phase?

Inez: I'm ready.

Sophia: There are four parts to the Work Phase of forgiveness. The first of these is what I call *work toward understanding*. If we begin with Sterling, and that has yet to be determined, I wonder if you could try to see him from these angles: What was life like for him as he was growing up? Was it all sunshine and roses? Was he emotionally wounded? Can you see him as clearly as you can when he is at his worst at home, not to condone his actions or to excuse his behavior, but to better understand him? To deliberately try to know someone more deeply is actually part of loving more deeply. See his vulnerabilities as well as his injustices. See his weaknesses, not to belittle or condemn him, but because separating his actions from him as a person may help you begin to soften your heart toward him. See him in light of this question: What is the meaning of the word *person*, and is Sterling a person? If so, what are your obligations toward him as a person? See him relative to your own belief system. Who is Sterling in light of your beliefs? Although this may sound like a tall order, it can help you soften your heart even more toward him.

Inez: Isn't it the other way around? Shouldn't he be softening his heart toward me?

Sophia: Yes, that would be nice, but if your task is forgiveness, it doesn't matter whether he softens his heart toward you. You can go ahead and forgive him anyway.

Inez: I can? Shouldn't he at least apologize, or maybe grovel at my feet for an hour or so?

Sophia: We'll have to explore the precise meaning of forgiveness to be sure you want to proceed with this strategy of healing your emotional wounds and maybe your relationships.

Inez: I can't wait because I have some big questions for you about forgiveness.

Sophia: Good. Let's work together to more fully understand what it means to forgive. The next step in the Work Phase is working toward compassion. That . . .

Inez: Excuse me, compassion? Again, he needs that more than I do.

Sophia: Perhaps that is true, but can you truly, deeply forgive without compassion? What does your sense of the term *forgiveness* tell you at this point?

Inez: If forgiveness is not a caving in, if it is not letting someone walk all over my back, then maybe it does have gentleness associated with it.

Sophia: Yes, gentleness. A good word here. As you forgive, you practice gentleness toward the person, not because of what he did, but in spite of it. Compassion is that softened heart we are talking about.

Inez: From a wounded heart to a softened heart. Is that it?

Sophia: You're definitely getting it. The next step is accepting the pain, bearing the pain of what happened to you.

Inez: Gulp. . . . Did you hear me? I said, "Gulp." I thought we were going to get rid of wounds, not add to them.

Sophia: Great point. When you bear the pain of what happened to you, you do not add more pain but instead realize that you already have pain and are now going to be careful not to toss that pain to others. You will bear it. For example, when you are fuming at Sterling, is it easy or hard to transfer that pain to others, say to your stepchildren?

Inez: What do you mean?

Sophia: When you are angry, do you keep it in or does it sometimes go flying out at others, sometimes to people who are innocent bystanders, such as your stepchildren? Sometimes when people have had a hard day at the office, they come home and yell at the pet dog, when all along the yelling is really meant for the boss.

Inez: I see what you mean. Let me think. Yes, although I hate to admit it, I can be kind of rough with my stepchildren when Sterling has been huffy with me.

Sophia: Do you see that your anger is meant for him and then you take it out on the children?

Inez: Yes.

Sophia: And they do not deserve it.

Inez: Ouch!

Sophia: Right. You are showing the psychological defense of displacement when you do that—when you take out your anger on others who were not part of the injustice—and everyone does this to a greater or lesser extent from time to time. When we do this, we are not bearing the pain. We are transferring the pain to the innocent.

Inez: No wonder the world is so full of emotional wounds.

Sophia: And our forgiving by bearing the pain helps us not to transfer more wounds to others and into the world.

Inez: I'm listening.

Sophia: Here is one of the paradoxes of forgiveness: As you bear the pain of injustices, and you surely do not deserve the injustices, then you are the one who is healed in an emotional way.

Inez: I take on the wounds, bear the pain, and then I am eventually healed emotionally?

Sophia: It definitely can happen that way. I have seen it. People become stronger as they bear up under the weight of the pain that life has brought their way. This standing up and consciously deciding not to transfer the pain to others has a positive effect on us. We realize we are strong and that we can play a part in preventing even more wounds from being transferred to our loved ones.

Inez: How can you "transfer" a wound?

Sophia: What I mean by *transfer* is similar to our discussion of displacement. If you are wounded and you are insensitive to someone else because of your pain, you may pass that pain to him or her, thus creating an emotional wound inside of the person.

Inez: Yes, I see what you mean. It is the issue of a wounded person wounding others if he or she is not careful.

Sophia: Bearing the pain is at the heart of forgiveness. It is a key to healing, both oneself and one's relationships. So many people do not understand it.

Inez: I can see why. You are asking me to bear more pain.

Sophia: Again, it will not be me who is doing the asking. The forgiveness process itself will ask this of anyone who forgives. Forgiveness is not for wimps. And one more thing: Forgiveness does not ask you to bear more pain but to bear the pain you already have.

Inez: It sounds kind of round-shouldered and discouraging.

Sophia: It would be if this were the end of the story. Forgiveness does not leave you with a great big sack of woes on your back. As you bear the pain, stand up to it, face it, and have mercy on the person who placed that heavy sack onto you, then the burden begins to lift.

Inez: Not soon enough as far as I am concerned.

Sophia: The timeline for the release of your emotional pain is not absolutely predictable. It will differ for each person, and it will differ depending on whom you are forgiving. It will even differ across different injustices from the same person. Yet, the point I want to make is this: The pain does lessen and your emotions become healthier the more you stay at the task of forgiving someone for deep injustices and wounds resulting from those injustices.

[Inez sits in silence, contemplating these points.]

Sophia: The final guidepost of the Work Phase is giving a gift of mercy to the one who hurt you. You can give a gift in many different ways: a smile, a returned phone call, acknowledging a person's presence at a meeting or any get-together. This is part of what is called *agape love,* the kind of love that serves others and has their best interest at heart. So you see how forgiveness is part of mercy? You give a gift unconditionally to someone who has not necessarily done something to deserve this form of love.

Inez: Yes, I am beginning to see that. But I can't give a gift to everyone I have in mind to forgive. What if I want to forgive my grandmother? She died 4 years ago.

Sophia: You can do this even for the deceased. There is a published study of incest survivors forgiving their perpetrators.[1] One woman brought her own children to the cemetery to visit their grandfather's grave. The mom had a tasteful ceremony of respect for her deceased father, the one who took advantage of her. She was giving to her father a legacy of respect with regard to his grandchildren. It was a gift.

Inez: Wasn't that kind of dishonest? He abused her!

Sophia: Was that the extent of his life? I am in no way condoning incest. It was wrong, it is wrong, and it will always be wrong. At the same time, he was a steady worker, bringing home a paycheck on a regular basis; he had his good points as a father despite his tragic behavior; he did offer some goodness, which became all mixed together with the badness. Even more important than all of this, he was a person. Was he more than the perpetrator of incest?

Inez: Yes.

Sophia: And that is one of two points that I wish to make. Staying for a moment on this first point about the personhood of the one who offended, when we forgive, we see more details, some of which will be positive and others of which will be negative. Remember the reason for these exercises: so that you can see a vulnerable human being—a real person—not evil incarnate. This should help soften your heart toward anyone who has treated you unjustly. Second, we do not forgive because of the person's actions alone because actions alone are not complete enough when it comes to understanding any person as a person. After all, are you the sum total of what you do?

Inez: I hope not. I'm not exactly a star at all I do.

Sophia: Then no one can define you on your abilities, on your functions such as your various roles of student, or daughter, or spouse, or stepmother, or employee?

Inez: Well, in a certain way, yes, people can "define me" in those ways because, yes, I am in those roles.

Sophia: And is that all you are—a role-player?

Inez: What do you mean by that?

Sophia: I am asking if you are only the roles you have in our society.

Inez: Of course not.

Sophia: Why not? What are you or who are you beyond the roles that you play?

Inez: What are you getting at?

Sophia: It is more "what am I pointing toward?" when I say you are a person. If you are more than specific roles such as employee, student, daughter, and so forth, then there has to be more to you than that. What is it?

Inez: I am a person?

Sophia: Yes, and what does that mean?

Inez: OK, I am catching on here. I am special, unique, and irreplaceable regardless of the roles I have or how skillfully I take on those roles.

Sophia: Now for my question: Can we give the same privilege to the man who was so terribly unjust to his daughter that he committed incest against her?

Inez: It would take great effort to see him that way.

Sophia: Yes, and again I have a question: Does the great effort in any way take away from the realization that he is a person, just as you are?

Inez: I would have to train my mind very strongly to say "yes."

Sophia: Now you are beginning to see what the forgiveness process is about on a deep level. You train yourself to see the personhood, the humanity, in the other and then respond accordingly.

Inez: OK once again. Do I have it right? We forgive because we acknowledge that the offender is a person and all persons are worthy of respect because they are persons, not because of actions, either positive or negative?

Sophia: No person should be shunned, disrespected, or thrown away. An expression for this is that all people have inherent worth. The worth is inherent—built in, not earned but there unconditionally.

Inez: I can see it, but I have no idea why this would be the case.

Sophia: I think you know better than you realize. What is your definition of a person? Let us be Aristotle again and define our terms.

Inez: You might not like my definition. It is based on my particular history, on who I am.

Sophia: I hope you don't apologize for that.

Inez: I'm just afraid that you will criticize me for my particular view.

Sophia: I promise that I will not criticize you . . . although I may have a few things to say about your view.

Inez: A person is someone who is made in the image and likeness of God. I learned that in Sunday school, Genesis 1.

Sophia: And if someone in your view is made in the image and likeness of God, then what?

Inez: Then if he is good enough for God, then he is good enough for me, at least in the sense that I do not shun, disrespect, or throw away that person.

Sophia: OK. Let's press the point further. Suppose you never went to Sunday school. Let us suppose you are an agnostic or an atheist. What is a person? Give me a humanistic view on the matter.

Inez: Still, a person is someone who is unique, special, and irreplaceable.

Sophia: What is your humanistic basis for this idea? Why hold such a view?

Inez: Great challenge. For one thing, Immanuel Kant, a secular philosopher, said that we are all ends in and of ourselves and should be treated as such. Each person is an end and should not be manipulated, oppressed, or used for other people's ends. Personally, my belief system tells me that people are not "ends in and of themselves" because they are made for each other and for God, but Kant's view and mine come together in that each person must never be manipulated and used as a means to others' ends.

Sophia: So, if you are a monotheistic believer or a humanist, you can see that a person is special, unique, and irreplaceable, worthy of respect. He or she can be given the gift of mercy, then?

Inez: It appears to be so.

Sophia: Even Sterling, or Enrico, or your boss?

Inez: I knew you'd ask that. Yes, the inevitable conclusion is the same. Darn it all.

Sophia: Why the "darn it all"?

Inez: Because now I am feeling compelled to forgive each of them, and I don't want to do that.

Sophia: Compelled? By whom?

Inez: By the logic of it all. If I follow the logic of who a person is, I am hard-pressed to walk away from forgiving them, from giving what you call a "gift of mercy."

Sophia: Is it still your choice to do so, or not?

Inez: Yes, but I've just made it more difficult for myself to refuse.

Sophia: You have not made it more difficult. The "logic of it all," as you say, might be the challenge now for you. To sum up the Work Phase of forgiveness, it includes working toward understanding the person who has been unfair to you, working toward compassion for him or her, and accepting the pain of the injustice so that you do not pass that pain to others; you should also consider giving a gift to the one who hurt you because he or she is a person and all persons are worthy of receiving gifts from you.

Inez: I am a little apprehensive, but I want to move ahead.

Sophia: This discussion demanded a lot from you. Let us discuss the final phase, the Discovery Phase, of forgiveness another time.

BACK TO THE BASICS—YOU

It is time to extend your dialogue now with Inez and Sophia. What have you heard here that is surprising? What did you not expect? Why is it surprising—because it seems wrong to you or because you have not quite thought about forgiveness this way? Do you understand the issue of bearing the pain—that forgiveness does not add pain to you but instead asks you to confront the pain you have received from others in such a way that you do not throw it back to them or to other people? Do you have any fears of bearing the pain? If so, what is the source of the fears—suffering itself, not fully understanding yet what I mean by "bearing the pain"? Try to identify the source of any apprehension you currently have. Are you beginning to understand what I mean by the term *person*? We will have much more to say about this, and in greater detail, in Chapter 10 and others to follow.

DO YOU WANT TO BECOME A FORGIVING PERSON?

Just as you are learning about what a person is by thinking about someone who has been unfair to you, part of this book, as you can tell by the title, is to develop a more forgiving person within you. I hope that you are beginning to see that forgiveness is not only something you do, nor is it just a feeling or a thought inside you. It pervades your very being. Forgiveness, in other words, might become a part of your identity, a part of who you are as a person. Try this thought on for size to see if it fits: I am a forgiving person. Did that hurt or feel strange? Try it again. Of course, to say something like this and then to live your life this way will take plenty of practice. Part of that practice is to get to know the entire process of forgiveness. When you are ready to learn about the final phase of our forgiveness process, the Discovery Phase, then please turn to the next chapter.

CHAPTER 6

THE DISCOVERY PHASE
OF FORGIVENESS

The Discovery Phase of the forgiveness process is not as intense as the phase before because much of the struggle to forgive occurs in the Work Phase. Discovery in the sense meant here is the opening of oneself as a forgiver to new insights—about oneself, the one who acted unjustly, and even one's philosophy about how the world works. The final guidepost of this phase, discovering the freedom of forgiveness, concerns another paradox of forgiveness: As you reach out to the one who was unjust, with compassion and with respect for his or her personhood, you the forgiver are the one who is emotionally healed. Your forgiving may play a part in the other person's change of behavior as well, although there surely is no guarantee of that.

Let us look in now on the conversation between Sophia and Inez.

Sophia: How is the world of forgiveness treating you?
Inez: Pretty well. I can't say that Sterling and I are living happily ever after at this point. Not yet, anyway, but I was not expecting that.
Sophia: Yes, after all, you are just exploring the forgiveness process for now. You will be practicing it shortly.
Inez: I can't wait.

Sophia: Shall we explore the Discovery Phase of forgiveness?

Inez: Let's "shall."

Sophia: The first task is discovering the meaning of suffering. In this step . . .

Inez: I know I have a tendency to interrupt you when you drop word bombs.

Sophia: Word bombs?

Inez: You used the "s" word.

Sophia: Suffering? Yes, I did. Have you not suffered from the injustices from the big three: Enrico, Sterling, and your boss?

Inez: Well, on further review, as they say on football broadcasts, yes, I have suffered a great deal.

Sophia: And is not forgiveness about confronting that suffering, dealing with it, and allowing it to dissipate?

Inez: I had not quite thought of it that way.

Sophia: That is part of what forgiveness is—to deal forthrightly with your suffering by offering mercy to the one who has caused the suffering.

Inez: Why can't we just stay with the moral virtue of justice and forget about mercy?

Sophia: Because that is what you have been doing for many years now, seeking fairness, which is a good thing, but rarely does the exclusive seeking and even getting of justice heal our emotional wounds the way that the practice of mercy can.

Inez: Once again, I'm listening.

Sophia: To find meaning in suffering, you do not put on rose-colored glasses and sing, "Oh well, everything happens for a reason. So, what happened to me in my first marriage, what happened to me with my boss, and

what is happening right now between Sterling and me
all have reasons. So, I am happy because it will all
work out for the best."

Inez: I was wondering about that because I can't see right
now how my abrupt firing at the hands of a ruthless
boss is happening for a good reason.

Sophia: Finding meaning in suffering is very different from
finding a positive reason within the context of what
happened to you. In the latter, you try to see what is
positive within the actual event. You try to see goodness in the injustice. When you find meaning in what
you suffered, you look beyond the event to now. You
try to see clearly and without distortion what you have
learned from what you have endured.

Inez: So, if I say, "This happened for a reason," I may be
trying to put a positive spin on what happened. When
I say, "I have found meaning in suffering," I am trying
to see how I have grown from a bad experience, without calling that experience good.

Sophia: That is a good way of putting it, yes. Bad situations can remain as bad. What you take away from the
experience can be very good. That is what we mean by
finding meaning in suffering. Dr. Victor Frankl, a psychiatrist who was in a concentration camp during
World War II, found that the only people who were
not emotionally destroyed by that horrific experience
were those who found meaning in the atrocity.[1]

Inez: So, then, do I have to begin viewing the injustices
against me in a certain way?

Sophia: That is one thing about Dr. Frankl's approach. He
did not specify a particular content of what you say to
yourself. For him, the fact that you can find meaning is

83

the key. The key is not to find one and only one meaning that all people see.

Inez: But that sounds so . . . relative to me. I can find any
meaning at all as long as I find meaning? What if the
meaning for me from being fired is that the world is a
cold, dark, dangerous place and so I must hide under
the bed?

Sophia: You are correct that you have discovered a meaning, but is it an accurate meaning? Is that who you really
are as a person, someone who cowers under the bed?

Inez: No. I am here talking with you, aren't I? I am not
cowering.

Sophia: Good. Dr. Frankl did not say you should distort
who you are in finding a false meaning from what
you've suffered. He said you should see the truth of
who you have become. If you are not a person who
cowers under the bed, then who are you?

Inez: Well, based on our conversations about this to date,
I am a person who has been emotionally wounded;
who has stood up to injustice; who is worthy of respect
and mercy; and who is special, unique, and irreplaceable and therefore cannot be and must not be shunned,
disrespected, or thrown away.

Sophia: Exactly. And it is your job now to keep this at
the forefront of your thinking and your reasoning
about who you are and who others are. Were you
aware of all of this before you went through all of
your suffering?

Inez: No, because I never gave it much thought.

Sophia: That is Dr. Frankl's point. You now see yourself
in rather wonderful and accurate terms as a consequence of what you have suffered. You have found a

meaning in that suffering—you know who you are and you know who your fellow man and woman in this world are.

Inez: I like this perspective.

Sophia: It will deepen and become richer as you proceed in The Forgiving Life. The second of five parts of the Discovery Phase is discovering your need to seek forgiveness from others.

Inez: As I forgive, I find that I must seek forgiveness from others?

Sophia: Yes, that is a natural outgrowth of forgiving. You realize that you, too, have been imperfect and that you have work to do in that area. You become a more complete practitioner of forgiveness—you forgive and you seek and receive forgiveness from others.

Inez: But, I am not always unfair to those who are unfair to me.

Sophia: Right. I am not saying that you always seek forgiveness from those who have been unfair to you. My only point here is this: As you begin to forgive, your mind is likely to turn to others in your life toward whom you have been unjust. You in all likelihood will then want to do something about this and make amends.

Inez: That makes sense. At first I thought you meant that I always act unjustly toward those who mistreat me.

Sophia: But, you know that is not true and so I would not suggest that to you. The third step is discovering that you are not alone.

Inez: I'm not sure I understand.

Sophia: People realize as they begin the forgiveness process, perhaps for the first time, that it is difficult to just charge ahead on one's own in the forgiving journey. We often need support from others. We need help when we are wounded.

Inez: So, my talking to you is part of this step.

Sophia: Yes, and your talking with me is not the end of this story. You can seek help from another trusted friend or a parent or a counselor. You have a particular spiritual history. For you, seeking the help of God is a good thing because it fits well with your worldview. You see, you are not alone when you forgive, and you should seek good help and support as you proceed and as you wish.

Inez: I do have a tendency to see myself as a rugged individualist who forges ahead on her own. I'll consider this.

Sophia: The fourth step, which may not make much sense to you now because it happens usually near the end of a forgiveness journey, is discovering a new purpose for your life.

Inez: I cannot see how my forgiving Sterling, for example, will lead to a whole new purpose for my life. It seems a bit grand.

Sophia: This was not a part of the forgiveness process in its early formation in the mid-1980s. Those piecing the process together noticed that many of the incest survivors studied by Freedman and Enright[2] expressed an interest, without the researchers even asking, in becoming counselors to other incest survivors. You see, they wanted to give something back to others who suffered a similar fate. Even the survivors themselves seemed surprised by this newly found purpose. I have personally seen this kind of transformation, even among professional psychologists. Many have not had forgiveness on their therapeutic radar because forgiveness therapy had not yet been developed as a discipline when they were in graduate school. Yet, when they began reading about forgiveness, they had a transformation and began incorporating forgiveness into their therapeutic practice. It quite literally turned their practice around, at least for some of them.

Inez: What will be my new purpose?

Sophia: That is for you to discover as you lead The Forgiving Life.

Inez: [*feigning a little pout*] But, I want to know now.

Sophia: [*with a smile*] We are in an age of instant gratification, aren't we? Working through the process of forgiveness takes time, but it is well worth the effort. We have now come to the fifth and final step of the Discovery Phase and to the final step of the forgiveness process itself: discovering the freedom of forgiveness. What do you think I mean by this?

Inez: That I am in a sense set free when I forgive?

Sophia: Yes, and from what are you free?

Inez: Let's see, I know you well enough by now to realize that I should not say, "Freedom from all suffering and from all people who make me suffer."

Sophia: Why do you think I might challenge that?

Inez: Because freedom from "all" suffering is a bit too unrealistic, and I am pretty sure you do not want me to be free from all people who make me suffer.

Sophia: Why not?

Inez: Because of the second step of this Discovery Phase. You will want me not only to forgive but also to seek forgiveness from the person if I hurt him. Oh, yes, and to reconcile if we can.

Sophia: This giving of forgiveness and receiving of forgiveness from the other person and then reconciling is what I call the *triangle of forgiveness.*

Inez: Do you want me to reconcile with everyone I forgive?

Sophia: Only with those with whom it is safe to reconcile.

Inez: Well, I can't exactly reconcile with Enrico. We are divorced and I am remarried.

Sophia: What does it mean to reconcile? How do you understand it?

Inez: Oh, OK. I see that to reconcile is not necessarily to be a wife again to Enrico, but I can reach a certain level of civility and trust with him.

Sophia: Yes, exactly. We reconcile within the proper bounds of our roles. The way you reconcile with a husband is different from how you reconcile with a daughter, and how you reconcile with a daughter is different from how you reconcile with a boss. It depends on the roles we have with each other. And with some people, you would want to keep a safe distance if the person is a danger to you.

Inez: So, am I correct that agape love consists of two different parts? One part is love, which I give for the person's own good because he has inherent worth. A second aspect is the proper way of expressing that love because of the particular roles we have toward each other.[3]

Sophia: Yes, that is a good summary of how we are to give agape love to different people. It is a challenge because if the person is not a danger to you and if he is trustworthy, you should take seriously the possibility of reconciliation, even if you are still angry with him. Let's now get back to the related point that you cannot be free from all people who make you suffer. Why do you think that is?

Inez: I'm feeling that forgiveness is quite a struggle again as I answer this: Because this is a tough world and people who love me and whom I love, despite how good the relationship is, will hurt me from time to time.

Sophia: Yes, and what is your response to that?

Inez: To get out from under the bed and practice forgiveness.

Sophia: And?

Inez: And to ask something of them if we are in a relationship that is to be reconciled.

Sophia: Does this sound reasonable?

Inez: Yes, it does. May I ask a question about the ultimate end of forgiveness?

Sophia: Yes, please, I am interested in why you ask.

Inez: From our conversation so far, it seems to me that forgiveness is something for me. It is like a gift that I give to myself.

Sophia: [*with eyes wide*] Did I give you that impression?

Inez: [*looking concerned at Sophia's concern*] Yes, you have. Why are you startled? Isn't that what forgiveness is? You said that the last step concerns my freedom.

Sophia: Yes, I did say that because that is one of the end points of forgiveness, not what forgiveness itself is. We have to distinguish what forgiveness is from its end point or the consequences of forgiving.

Inez: You just lost me.

Sophia: Let's try an analogy. Analogies, of course, are not meant to prove anything, and they always fail in a certain way because analogies are imperfect representations of what we are trying to know. With that said, here is our analogy. Is there a difference between what Mozart was doing when he was composing his Jupiter Symphony, Symphony No. 41, and what the purpose or end point of writing it was?

Inez: Well, when he was composing it, he was engaged in creativity and production, in making a piece of music.

Sophia: And what was his purpose for doing so?

Inez: I suppose he had multiple purposes: to exercise his genius as an end in itself, to please his patron, to please the concertgoers, to support his young family, and to get rich.

Sophia: He died a rather poor man, and so that last point either was not one of his end points or he failed in reaching that end point. Anyway, can you see the difference between crafting a piece of music and the end point toward which one is striving in crafting it?

Inez: Yes, but what does this have to do with forgiveness?

Sophia: Precisely this: Forgiveness itself is the exercise of a moral virtue: agape love as mercy toward someone who was unfair to you. You said it yourself.

Inez: I did?

Sophia: Yes, you referred to justice as a moral virtue, and you implied the same about forgiveness when you suggested that it is part of the moral virtue of mercy.

Inez: Yes, now I remember.

Sophia: OK, forgiveness, then, is the practice of a moral virtue, and as people do so, they do this for certain ends. What might some of the ends be when people practice the moral virtue of forgiveness?

Inez: As with Mozart and his musical compositions, I suppose there are many: freedom from the burden of emotional wounds [*our final guidepost in the forgiveness process*], aiding the one who was unjust in helping her see what she did, encouraging her to make amends and then reconciling, and I suppose even growing more deeply in living The Forgiving Life.

Sophia: Well said. Can you now see why I am emphasizing the one outcome or end point in forgiving in our context?

Inez: Because I have specifically come to you for advice; your task is to help me. As you help me unburden from the emotional wounds, we are fulfilling an end point for forgiveness, but it is not the only end point.

Sophia: Nor is it necessarily the most important end point. If one of Mozart's end points was the near-perfect exercise of his creative genius, he probably would not see this as the ultimate end. Instead, he might see a nobler end in giving truth veiled in beauty to the world.[4] He might see as another nobler end the sustenance of his family, and an even deeper end for him could have been giving glory to God by his genius.

Inez: I am eager to see where all of this leads for me.

Sophia: By way of summary, in the Discovery Phase you discover the meaning of what you have suffered because of others' injustices; discover your need to seek and receive forgiveness as you practice forgiving; discover that you are not alone when you forgive, but may need others' support; discover a new purpose in life as you apply forgiveness deeply and broadly; and discover the freedom of forgiveness, among a variety of different end points once you forgive.

Inez: Now, before we begin my own forgiveness journey, may we pause for a while so that I can blast

you . . . excuse me . . . I mean, challenge you, regarding what forgiveness is? I have a few questions.

Sophia: I look forward to our exploring the meaning of
forgiveness in our next dialogue.

BACK TO THE BASICS—YOU

You now have a broad overview of the forgiveness process. The point
of Chapters 4 through 6 was to introduce you to the process without
yet asking you to do the work of actually going through that process,
which I begin to ask in Chapter 10. As you survey the material across
these three chapters, what do you see? Do you see a challenge ahead?
Is the challenge something that excites you or terrifies you, or do you
have another reaction to the process of forgiveness? Do you see that
when you extend forgiveness, the process itself ultimately is not
about you, but about reaching out in mercy to those who have
treated you unfairly? Do you see the paradox of forgiveness—as you
reach out in this way, you yourself may begin to heal emotionally?
What do you need to take the next step of exploring who hurt you
and then starting the forgiveness process? Your reviewing material
from the first six chapters may help with those needs.

DO YOU WANT TO BE A FORGIVING PERSON?

Part of being a forgiving person is to know the forgiveness process
and to practice it. As you understand that process more and more
and become comfortable with it, you will find that this is a good
beginning to being a forgiving person. At the same time, practice and
feeling comfortable with this practice is not enough to transform
yourself into a genuinely forgiving person. You will need to begin to
foster a sense of deep connection with forgiveness. It is not unlike
our career example at the beginning of the book. People can spend

their whole lives working at a job or a profession but not really connect in a deep way with it. "I am someone who goes into nursing homes, does what I am told, and gets a paycheck," is one way to see oneself. "I am someone who serves the elderly. That is not just what I do. It is a part of who I am." This thought is much deeper than the first one. That is where we are heading in the next set of chapters: Can you begin practicing forgiveness regularly and deeply enough so that it becomes a part of you?

CHAPTER 7

WHAT DOES IT MEAN TO FORGIVE?

Even though Inez has had a chance to explore what forgiveness is and is not, this process of understanding seems to be ongoing for all of us. How we understood forgiveness last month is different from how we understand it this month, and our understanding is likely to be deeper next year than this year. Be open to new discoveries about forgiveness. To aid your growth in understanding, let us carefully consider Inez's continued development.

> *Inez:* I'm confused. I think I am getting ready to forgive, but I'm not sure exactly what it is I do when I forgive.
>
> *Sophia:* Do you have particular questions about the process model we have been discussing?
>
> *Inez:* No. That is pretty clear to me, but here is my confusion: The process is like a road map, isn't it? It shows us how to get to our destination, which is forgiveness.
>
> *Sophia:* Yes, that is a good description.
>
> *Inez:* Then, let's suppose I take out the road map, the process model of forgiveness, and go on the journey to my final destination, which is forgiveness. Where do I

land? When I reach the final destination of forgiveness, where am I? What am I doing when I forgive?

Sophia: How do you understand forgiveness from one of our earlier discussions?

Inez: I understand the definition of forgiveness this way: In the face of another person's injustice, I try to reduce resentment toward her and try to offer goodness, such as kindness, respect, or even moral love. This is a deliberate choice that I make. When I forgive, I decide to do this. When I forgive, I decide to love; in other words, I try to serve as best I can under the specific circumstances of this particular person and this particular injustice. I offer this love, this mercy, and this forgiveness even if I do not feel much like loving the person who hurt me.

Sophia: I agree with all of this. Does it clear up the confusion?

Inez: No, it actually does not. For example, suppose that I decide to forgive and go ahead with it. Suppose I am successful.

Sophia: Successful? Is forgiveness something that is "all" or "none"? Either a baseball pitcher throws a ball or a strike. There is no in-between? Is that what forgiveness is?

Inez: Somehow, that seems too simple.

Sophia: It is. Forgiveness is one of the many moral virtues, as are justice, patience, kindness, love, and others. It takes lots of time to grow in being able to be a virtuous person.

Inez: OK. I see that, but I am still confused. My confusion concerns what you call psychology—my feelings, my thoughts, how I interact with other people. So, I forgive, I've done it. What is it that I do at the end of this process when I forgive? Do I just sit there and have new feelings? If I sit quietly in the lounge chair and I feel no resentment toward Sterling and also feel warm fuzzies toward him in the form of kindness and compassion, am I forgiving?

EXAMINING THE PSYCHOLOGICAL COMPONENTS OF FORGIVING

Sophia: You've centered on feeling. Is feeling all there is when you reach the destination of forgiveness?

Inez: I don't know, that is my question. It seems by the definition that to forgive is to feel a certain way about the person who caused harm.

Sophia: Let us try to put forgiveness on the foundation it has been on for thousands of years. That foundation is morals.

Inez: I'm not quite sure what you mean.

Sophia: Ever since the Hebrew Bible story of Joseph forgiving his brothers for selling him into slavery, forgiveness has been seen as a moral response to injustice. By this I mean, forgiveness is concerned with human goodness. Goodness concerns others, not just the self.

Inez: So, when I try to forgive Sterling, I'll have good feelings toward him then.

Sophia: Well, yes, but that cannot be the whole story. After all, if morals concern other people, if morals are goodness expressed toward others, then we cannot say that you have a complete moral response if you sit in the lounge chair feeling "warm fuzzies" toward Sterling. What else would you need?

Inez: I suppose I would also need warm thoughts toward him so that I am not hating him.

Sophia: Yes, that adds to our understanding of forgiveness as a moral response, but it still does not go far enough. If forgiveness is moral goodness and goodness is expressed toward the other person, then we need to go even farther down the forgiveness road. Can you see why?

Inez: Because my response is still not directed in any real sense toward Sterling if I continue to sit in the lounge chair having good feelings and thinking good thoughts about him. I need to add doing something toward him.

Sophia: Feeling, thinking, and behaving are all part of goodness. Anything else?

Inez: Isn't that enough?

Sophia: What about approaching all of this with the right motivation? If you are now feeling good about Sterling, thinking good thoughts about him and, let's say for the sake of example, give him a hug, will this count as morally good if you are doing all of this so that he will do a favor for you?

Inez: I see nothing wrong with that.

Sophia: And you would be right, but is this a response of moral goodness or a response of expedience? Is it for him or for you?

Inez: Me.

Sophia: And what is the meaning of a moral response? For whom do we exercise goodness when we forgive?

Inez: Got it. But, I am still confused. Suppose that I cultivate gentle emotions toward Sterling, wish him well in my thoughts, behave in a civil way toward him—all with the right motivation that I want to do this for his good. What exactly am I doing? Am I pardoning him, offering him clemency, absolving him in some way, moving on? Am I tolerating him? Am I ceasing to be disappointed with him? Am I reconciling with him? Can you appreciate my confusion about what, exactly, I am doing when forgiving?

INTERLUDE AS WE GO BACK TO THE BASICS—YOU

It is time for a pop quiz. Please take out a paper and pencil (or your computer) and address how the following are similar to or different from forgiveness, as you understand forgiveness to this point:

- pardoning,
- offering clemency,
- absolving,
- tolerating,
- ending disappointment and being more satisfied with the person,
- accepting the person's apology, and
- reconciling.

Let us now simply think about each concept by asking this question: Is there anything in the meaning of the concept that would distort the full and genuine meaning of forgiving if we accepted it as a synonym of forgiving? Inez and Sophia will wait for you.

BACK TO THE DIALOGUE: DISTINGUISHING CONCEPTS SEEMINGLY SIMILAR TO FORGIVENESS

> *Sophia:* Let's see how you did on the quiz as we take each concept one at a time. When you forgive, are you pardoning the person who acted unfairly?

99

Inez: I would say yes, because when you pardon, you take away a punishment due to a person. This is merciful, as forgiveness is, and it is good.

Sophia: But, is pardoning something that a private individual does, or does pardoning belong to an official who is given the power to pardon? For example, who pardons? Judges? Teachers? Others in authority?

Inez: All of these offer pardon.

Sophia: Why is that? Why is pardon put in the hands of officials?

Inez: Because pardon is usually seen as a disinterested act, one performed by a third party who offers this to someone who broke the rules.

Sophia: Why do you think societies put such decisions into the hands of more objective third parties rather than in the hands of the person who was directly offended?

Inez: I suppose only a disinterested third party can truly pardon because, for example, the mom of a serial bank robber might let her child out of jail—legally pardon— if given the chance. She wants her child back.

Sophia: OK. The decision takes place in a court of law (or in another public venue such as a school) by an official who himself or herself was not the one offended. Yet, when a person forgives, he or she is not in a court of law and certainly is not an innocent bystander (as an official is). Forgiveness is a personal (not official) decision by the one offended.

Inez: But, pardoning is still a moral response because it is an act of mercy.

Sophia: Not always. Pardoning does not always point toward goodness. For example, a judge might pardon a criminal, who committed a lesser crime, to make room in an overcrowded jail for a criminal who is violent. Such expedience is not necessarily goodness; forgiveness, as an act of loving someone who has been unjust to us, is always and without exception an act of goodness. Thus, *pardoning* and *forgiving* cannot be synonyms.

Inez: Good point.

Sophia: How did you judge clemency compared with forgiveness?

Inez: Well, I thought that they are the same.

Sophia: How do you understand giving clemency?

Inez: It happens when a person "throws himself on the mercy of the court." Sterling throws himself at me, a few tears of remorse would be just the right touch, and I say, "I forgive you."

Sophia: Doesn't clemency have certain features of pardon (a magistrate makes the decision)? Thus, clemency is not the same as forgiving because of its shared features with pardoning, which are not necessarily acts of ethical goodness.

Inez: So, any public acts of mercy might be related to forgiveness, but they cannot be the same.

Sophia: Right, because forgiveness is an individual choice to be merciful to someone who was unfair to the one offering forgiveness. What about absolving?

Inez: I said it was the same as forgiveness, but I'm changing my answer. Absolving sounds like a public act by a magistrate. So, I'm saying that is not forgiveness.

Sophia: Good choice for an answer. Besides that, to absolve has a sense that the one absolving is specifically remitting sins. Because neither you nor I are God, we cannot absolve sins. When we forgive, we are not absolving sins, we are having mercy on a person. What about tolerating? Are toleration and forgiveness the same?

Inez: They are very close to the same thing. When I forgive, I offer civility, respect, and even love toward the one who hurt me. I do not condemn, attack, or in any way harm the other. Toleration also deliberately avoids hurting the other person. So, they are synonyms.

Sophia: What do you think of this? To tolerate has two related meanings. First, it means to "put up with" another's unpleasant behavior, as when a friend puts up with another's unpleasant habit of always answering her mobile phone when the two of them are in deep conversation. Because the person with such a habit is not necessarily conscious of it, we can hardly say that all acts of toleration concern unjust behaviors on the part of the other person. Second, to tolerate means to recognize and respect the rights of others. Because a genuine right is never a wrong, such toleration cannot be forgiveness, which occurs in the context of others' wrongs.

Inez: But, when I forgive, can't we say that I am not harming the other? Because tolerance offers this as well, can't we say that forgiveness shares something important with tolerance?

Sophia: Yes, we could say this, but what do you think? Does forgiveness share more with tolerance or more with moral love?

Inez: It shares something with each.

Sophia: But which one shares more with forgiveness?

Inez: I'd say that love has more in common with forgiveness because when we show goodness toward someone who has hurt us, this is a great good and much more than "putting up with" something or someone.

Sophia: Well said.

Inez: Thank you, Sophia. This is kind of fun. I think I am catching on to the depth of forgiveness.

Sophia: I agree. Let's keep probing the idea of forgiveness. Is it the same as ending disappointment with someone and being more satisfied?

Inez: I'm changing my original answer again. I'd say no.

Sophia: Then how does forgiveness differ from ending disappointment and being more satisfied?

Inez: I'd have to say that I can be disappointed with people and with situations in which there was no injustice at all.

Sophia: What might be an example?

Inez: I may be disappointed that Sterling is not making a million dollars a year, but he is a good worker and a good provider, so my disappointment, and his, at his wage is nothing to forgive. We can be disappointed at human imperfection where there is no injustice.

Sophia: What about the other half of the issue—becoming more satisfied?

Inez: When I forgive, I still will not be satisfied with the situation because it was unfair. I hope I will be more satisfied with the person, not because of what he or she did, but in spite of that.

Sophia: We have two more distinctions to make, that between accepting another's apology and forgiving and between reconciling and forgiving. Is there any difference between accepting an apology and forgiving?

Inez: None. If a person has remorse and apologizes, I can forgive. I probably should forgive.

Sophia: So, the other person's apology is a sufficient condition for you to forgive. He apologizes and it is good enough—you forgive.

Inez: Yes.

Sophia: But is the other's apology a necessary condition for your forgiving? In other words, is the apology so very important that without it you will never forgive?

Inez: You've got that right.

Sophia: Why?

Inez: The other's apology is the guarantee that he will not do that again.

Sophia: But we just talked about human imperfection in the context of being disappointed. Even if someone apologizes and has the best of intentions to not be unfair to you ever again, does this mean that she is now morally perfect, never to offend you again?

Inez: I see where you are going with this. An apology is not a guarantee of the future.

Sophia: And if you seek the guarantee?

Inez: I'll never really receive it and so I can't forgive.

Sophia: And what then regarding your ability to open up the road map of forgiveness and go on that journey?

Inez: I'm trapped right where I am. No journey, no final destination. No forgiveness.

Sophia: Whose life is diminished by that?

Inez: Certainly not the one who refused to apologize.

Sophia: Then to forgive is not the same as to get an apology followed by the words, "I forgive you."

Inez: That is one form of forgiveness, right? It's not the only one.

Sophia: You are seeing that forgiveness is an unconditional moral response to injustice. You may offer it at

any time without a prior response from the one who
has injured you.

Inez: That seems more freeing for me than to have to
wait in my house with the forgiveness map all folded
up until a person who offended me knocks on the
door and says certain words to me.

Sophia: We are at our final distinction. Is forgiveness the
same as reconciliation?

Inez: No, and I said no on the quiz. You made this distinction in one of our earlier dialogues, but I am not entirely
sure of how they differ.

Sophia: Forgiving is not part of reconciling, but when
people reconcile, forgiveness is involved. We must be
careful here because reconciling and forgiving are
seen as synonymous with many people who roundly
criticize forgiving as dangerous and ill-advised, especially when there is abuse of some kind. Consider the
research study we discussed earlier, the one involving
incest survivors and forgiveness of their perpetrators.
Were the researchers negligent to work with the women
in forgiving the perpetrators? Might they have put these
women in danger because, on forgiving, they might
want to blindly reconcile with the offenders? I think not
for these reasons: To forgive is to first see that the
other has offended, to see the other's weakness (or even
meanness), and to become more rather than less accurately aware of injustices; and to forgive is to offer
goodness toward an offender, within the limits of balance and safety. Thus, a forgiver might speak kindly
about a person, as the woman did who had the religious ceremony at the cemetery for her father, but not
then come face-to-face with a dangerous person who

105

refuses to change. To reconcile is the process of two or more people coming together in mutual trust (with an emphasis on the word *mutual*) after a process of forgiving and seeking forgiveness. Without mutual trust, reconciliation is not possible. People might tolerate each other, or overlook faults to a degree, but they are not truly reconciled. Forgiveness does not require a prior response by the other person because, if forgiveness is the offer of goodness toward another, one is free to offer that goodness (within wise and balanced boundaries) whenever he or she wishes.

Inez: So, I can forgive my boss and then shun her at the holiday party?

Sophia: We don't want now to misrepresent the distinction between forgiving and reconciling and turn this distinction into some kind of vindictiveness. We want to reconcile when we forgive because we want the best for the other person. And please recall that we reconcile within the proper boundaries of our respective role toward each other. You can be a civil employee with the expectation that the boss will be a civil leader in the company. When we fail to reconcile it is because the other refuses to change. This does not mean that you do not wish him or her well. You do want the person to change, but you will interact only if it is safe.

Inez: I'd like to add something.

Sophia: Yes?

Inez: You've said that forgiveness is a moral virtue, right? It starts within a person and flows out from the person into good behavior for the good of others.

Sophia: Yes.

Inez: Reconciliation cannot be the same as forgiveness because reconciliation is not a moral virtue. It does not originate within a person, but is a set of behaviors between people.

Sophia: Well said.

Inez: You mentioned trust in the context of reconciliation, but you have not mentioned that word in the context of forgiveness. Can I forgive and not trust the person?

Sophia: What do you think? How do you read this?

Inez: I suppose that if someone were a compulsive gambler, I could forgive that person and then not trust him with the checkbook.

Sophia: Right. You would not trust him in that one area, but this is not an excuse to write the person off as having no possibility of being trusted in anything at all.

Inez: OK. That makes sense.

[*Inez looks at Sophia with some confusion in her eyes.*]

Sophia: You still seem confused to me.

Inez: I am no longer confused about the distinctions among forgiveness and the related issues of pardoning, offering clemency, absolving, and the like, but I am confused about exactly what I do when I forgive.

Sophia: You mean besides feeling a certain way about the person; thinking certain thoughts about him; being motivated for his good; and behaving in a civil, respectful, and loving way?

Inez: Yes. Which of these should I be cultivating; civility, respect, or love toward the one who hurt me?

FOLLOWING ETHICAL RULES: WHICH MORAL PRINCIPLE IS AT THE HEART OF FORGIVING?

> *Sophia:* Great question. How do you understand forgiveness relative to these?

> *Inez:* You are asking me which moral principle is at the heart of forgiveness, aren't you?

> *Sophia:* Exactly. What is the moral rule you live by when you forgive? Do you say, "I will practice civility toward her" or "I will practice respect toward her" or "I will practice moral love toward her"? Which should be your guiding principle?

> *Inez:* I say civility because it is the easiest of the three. I can be civil, cordial, and detached but reasonable with people who anger me, but to be loving is an entirely different story. It is too tough, too unrealistic.

> *Sophia:* May we examine your assumption about these three principles?

> *Inez:* I knew you'd ask that. I'm ready to explore them.

> *Sophia:* Suppose you are a soccer coach with high school students. Suppose further that you have a list of rules as follows: Do work in the weight room for 20 minutes a day every other day, or do work in the weight room for 10 minutes once a week, or buy the Get-Ripped-Abs machine for $19.95 that vibrates the purchaser's navel once every other week for the greatest six-pack abs on the planet (shipping and handling extra)? Which of these would you choose?

> *Inez:* Of course, I want excellence from the students. Twenty minutes every other day, as long as they vary the workout, is good. I would avoid extremes—say, 5 hours a day every day at one end and say, the

Get-Ripped-Abs machine at the other extreme. I'd go for excellence.

Sophia: And which is the most excellent way among civility, respect, and moral love as your basis for forgiving others?

Inez: This one is easy to answer and hard to implement. Moral love encompasses civility and respect in its response and so is the most complete. Civility is the least demanding and also the least complete. I can be civil and rather detached from a person. I can even be civil without respecting the person. Even respect does not go far enough. I can respect a person who is homeless by writing out a check to the soup kitchen. That is a somewhat detached way to treat someone who is deeply suffering. Yet, if I love another, I not only must be civil and respectful, I must be more than that. In the soup-kitchen example, I must be personal with the homeless person by going to the shelter, dipping the ladle into the soup, and serving that person. Moral love asks the most of me.

Sophia: How then do you understand moral love?

Inez: It is different from romantic love or brotherly love or the natural love between a mother and her child.[1] It is the kind of love that "goes to the wall" for the other by being in service to him or her without burning yourself out, of course. That would hardly be love if I destroyed myself in the process. I think it is a paradox. As I become personal with another for her good, I can and do experience a kind of refreshment.

Sophia: So, to love in a moral sense is to have the other person's well-being in mind and to give to the other out of a sense of service.

Inez: Yes, because he or she is a person, someone who is special, unique, and irreplaceable. To love is to acknowledge this about the person. It is to enter into their world in a personal and caring way.

Sophia: May we summarize? You asked what the underlying principle is when you forgive. Although civility and respect can be part of this, they are not the most challenging or the most complete. Moral love is complete because it acknowledges the personhood of the other and of the self and responds accordingly, with a sense of personal service and the other's well-being in mind.

Inez: I think I am sounding somewhat like a broken record in this session, Sophia, but I need to press the point about "What am I exactly doing when I forgive?" again.

Sophia: What is unclear to you?

Inez: We have talked about moral principles or moral rules here. Is that all forgiveness is—a rule that I follow? I follow the rule or principle to "morally love those who hurt me" but watch my back and do not reconcile if there is danger. I can't help but think this is incomplete.

Sophia: What is missing?

Inez: Moral rules or principles are certainly one important way to know what forgiveness is. If I say, "I know that moral love is a more excellent principle on which to base my forgiveness," then I have discovered an important rule of forgiveness. Yet, following a rule, any rule, regarding forgiveness, is not the only way to think about forgiveness. Living one's life by rules or principles alone seems so . . . flawed. After all, sometimes rules conflict: Act out of justice when hurt! Forgive out of love when hurt! Forgive out of love, but hate the person in the short run! Does this mean I have broken my own rule?

Do I then condemn myself because I am hurting and am incapable of living up to my rule? How fair is this?

Sophia: We do live by rules, but as you say, rules can conflict, and sometimes, with the best of motives, we cannot act on the moral rules we set for ourselves, which opens us up to moral condemnation, self-condemnation, which is not a good thing. May I suggest another way to think about forgiveness from a moral perspective?

Inez: Yes, please. Save me from a rigid rule-based approach to my life. I cannot hope to follow that rule for each injustice across my whole life.

Sophia: How about this approach: Instead of thinking about forgiveness as a rule, one you come to know and then to follow, what if you thought of forgiveness as a way of life?

Inez: I knew that I should not have asked the "I don't get it" question so much. You've really lost me now.

Sophia: Forgiveness just might be a way of life, the way you choose to live your life. When you do that you know forgiveness is important (it is one of your rules to live by), know that forgiveness is important because it is based on the particular moral principle of love (part of the above rule), are motivated to live this way and not some other way that is not your best self, feel certain feelings such as compassion as you follow the rule, think certain thoughts about the one who hurt you as you live this way, interact with this person in merciful ways and begin to act mercifully with others as well because you generalize this action, strive for greater and greater perfection in the overall expression of forgiveness, and incorporate all of this into your worldview of life: Who are you? Who are the people who hurt you? Who are you to each other? Would it be helpful to think of forgiveness in this more life-encompassing way?

Inez: It all depends on what it will cost me.

Sophia: It will cost you your life. By this I mean you may transform into a person who does not just think about forgiveness and practice forgiveness as a kind of skill. You will become a forgiving person. Forgiveness will become a part of your being.

Inez: Gulp again. I can just hear someone say back to you, "Yes, it will cost me my life. This is going to kill me!"

Sophia: Let us go back to the description of love [*see Chapter 1*] in which you were asked to think about one experience in your life in which you gave and received love in a sweet, remarkable way. You even wrote an essay on the topic entitled "My Unfolding Love Story." Did the experience, which you described in that essay, burn you out?

Inez: No, of course not. We were showing moral love toward each other.

Sophia: But, even if you are the only one showing love, isn't it still love?

Inez: What do you mean?

Sophia: One-way love, from you to another person, is still love, isn't it? It still has the features of gentle emotions, kind thoughts, and serving behaviors, together with good motives. All of this is healthy.

Inez: But I read in books and magazines over and over about "love burnout."

Sophia: Again let us be clear. Are you burning out when you have gentle emotions, kind thoughts, a sense of genuine service (not slavery), and good motives?

Inez: No.

Sophia: I agree, and if this is true, then those who talk about love burnout must be talking about something else.

Inez: Perhaps they are referring to people who behave in a way that others call *loving* but then don't have the complete package, even through no fault of their own. Perhaps their behaviors suggest service and their emotions are resentful. Perhaps they are not balanced in the delivery of their love, not taking time to refresh. Taking care of oneself is part of love, right?

Sophia: Right. An imbalance of love is not genuine love, and so we cannot blame love on what others call *love burnout.*

Inez: And we can't blame those who burn out, can we?

Sophia: Surely not those who made mistakes in understanding what genuine love is and got out of balance, even with the right motive. This shows the importance of what philosophers call *defining your term.* You have to know, and know deeply, what love and forgiveness are before you practice them in a deliberate way, as a self-chosen part of your life. This is why I am delighted that you are pushing yourself so hard today to understand what forgiveness is.

Inez: That kind of clears it up for me, but I am still confused. What am I doing when I become a forgiving person?

Sophia: The ideas I described, about becoming a forgiving person, are what philosophers call a *virtue-ethics approach* to forgiveness. The virtue-ethics approach encompasses the entire person, not just the mind as you think about rules, or not just behaviors as you act in a forgiving way. It, thus, is radically different from a rules-based or principles-based approach to forgiveness.

Inez: To paraphrase Socrates, "May we explore this?"

FORGIVING AS PART OF LIVING A VIRTUOUS LIFE

Sophia: To help you understand how to lead a forgiving life, I would like to outline some of Aristotle's principles for any moral virtue.[2] When you are practicing a virtue, any virtue, whether it is justice, kindness, respect, generosity, or moral love, it has the following characteristics in addition to what we just talked about:

The person knows that the virtue is good or concerned with human welfare. It includes other people and the self. The person knows that forgiveness is good as you practice it.

The virtue originates within the person and is brought forth to others for good. This is done out of *free will*, not coerced.

The person practicing the virtue does so deliberately. He or she is motivated to do good. He or she has what Kant called a *good will*.

The more you practice the virtue, the better you get at expressing it. This requires what I have been calling a *strong will*.

No one is perfect in the expression of any virtue, so you need not be hard on yourself when you fall flat trying to forgive. The point here is this: Get up, dust yourself off, and keep practicing it.

Different people differ in their ability to forgive, so do not expect everyone to be the same.

As people learn to love the virtue they are practicing, they strive for consistency in how they think, feel, and behave. In other words, people try to forgive in the same excellent way each time, although as I said, we are all imperfect.

There are end points toward which forgiveness aims. Of course, forgiveness itself has no consciousness and so it does not strive for a goal, but the one who practices it does. I can think of three goals for forgiveness: practicing it with greater and greater excellence so that I perfect its expression; doing so for the other's good, which can include his repentance and change; and reconciling with the person or people who were unfair to me.

Finally, we should not practice any virtue in isolation from the other virtues. For example, if you practiced forgiveness without a strong sense of justice, how would you know what is and is not fair? If you practiced forgiveness without courage, you might forgive from your position under the bed. As you forgive, you commit to living a virtuous life.

Inez: I've read books that say virtues do not actually exist other than subjectively inside of us. In other words, there really is no objective right and wrong "out there," but only as I perceive it as right or wrong.

Sophia: That is not at all part of the Western idea of virtue and of right and wrong. Why do we have courts of law—to judge those who did wrong or to understand people's thinking when they only think they've done wrong?

Inez: I suppose our judicial system would be very unhappy with a bank robber, identified by 10 witnesses, who then said to the judge, "But you only think I did wrong and all you have to do is change your perceptions."

Sophia: Yes, exactly, the thousands of years of Western legal work would be lost if we thought that way. And where would science be if we denied concrete reality and scientific laws, reasoning that there are no objective laws of science, only internal perceptions of how the world works? Do you think societies that thought this way would be the leaders in scientific investigation or technology?

Inez: Then is it the same with forgiveness? When I forgive, I practice a moral virtue that is centered on actual wrong from another person and not just my internal perception that it was wrong?

Sophia: Think of this in another way. Suppose you are a therapist and I am your client. Suppose further that I come to you because I have been raped. Would you dare to tell me that my sense of the other's wrong is all in my head, and all I have to do is change my perception of that?

Inez: That would not work because it is false. I would be asking you to do something false—to say to yourself that the supposed injustice is not an actual injustice and thus your revulsion to it is not based on anything true but only on a reaction within you.

Sophia: Yes, and that is why we must ground right and wrong in objective truth because we all know down deep that rape is morally wrong, and all involved must stand in that truth if the situation is to be corrected and the victim emotionally healed.

Inez: I'm finally beginning to understand the answer to my question, "What, exactly, do we do when we forgive?" But now I am worried. Can a person forgive too much?

Sophia: Aristotle talked about the balance of the virtues. Each virtue can be distorted in two ways, on either end of a continuum. In the case of forgiveness, if we practice forgiveness as a way of caving in to another's request (by failing to see the injustice and acting without courage), our forgiving will look like "too much," but it is not forgiving in any genuine sense.

Inez: I know why—because caving in is not a sign of goodness at all. The extreme expression of forgiveness as caving in distorts its essence.

Sophia: Yes, and the other extreme is to use forgiveness as a weapon against the other as you constantly remind her that she has needed your "virtuous" forgiveness.

Inez: In this case, rather than my being dominated, I dominate. That, too, is not morally good, and so I am not really forgiving.

Sophia: Right. So, when you ask if you can forgive too much, I ask this: If you truly understand what justice is and practice it properly, can you ever be too just?

Inez: No, as long as I do not distort it and as long as I practice it with other virtues.

Sophia: It is the same with any virtue and so it is the case with forgiveness, as long as we do not get out of balance (dominating or being dominated by the other person) and practice it along with justice, courage, temperance, and wisdom.

THE TRIANGLE OF FORGIVENESS

> *Inez:* OK, please bear with me. I now know that when I forgive, I have certain feelings, thoughts, and behaviors, and with the right motive of my having his best interest at heart, toward Sterling, say, if he is the one I am forgiving.

> *Sophia:* Yes.

> *Inez:* And I now know that when I forgive, I am applying the principle of moral love.

> *Sophia:* Yes, that seems to be the highest reason for forgiving.

> *Inez:* And I further know that forgiveness is a moral virtue. Do I have this right? When I forgive, I am actually practicing agape love (or what we have been calling *service love* or *moral love*). One part of such love is mercy, which is giving more than a person deserves (justice is giving what is deserved). And one part of mercy, when someone is unfair to me, is forgiveness. Moral love is the overarching umbrella and underneath that is mercy and underneath that, in the very specific case of another's injustice toward me, is forgiveness. When I express the virtue, I do so with my very being—I try to love the person and all that this means.

> *Sophia:* Right.

> *Inez:* But what is my goal? What am I trying to accomplish?

> *Sophia:* How do you see it?

> *Inez:* Part of the goal is to feel better, but there has to be more because moral virtues reach out to others for their good. You mentioned in one of our earlier conversations that near the end of a forgiveness process, I will

probably seek forgiveness. In Sterling's and my case, we have hurt each other, and so I am sure I'll seek forgiveness from him. So, is the goal to forgive, feel better, and extend myself to Sterling by asking him to forgive me?

Sophia: These are all good end points, but are they enough? For example, when you forgive Sterling and he is open to your love, how might your forgiving affect him?

Inez: Is part of my forgiving him so that he will see what he has done and actually seek forgiveness from me?

Sophia: Yes, that is a goal, one we do not always reach. If you can get his attention by loving him unconditionally through forgiveness, he may have a change of heart, be sorry for what he has done, apologize, and change.

Inez: I'm liking this . . . but we can't always expect this, can we?

Sophia: No, for the obvious reason that we cannot and do not want to control the other. His response to your forgiveness is up to him.

Inez: But, there is the hope that he will change.

Sophia: Right. Now, let's keep extending this kind of thinking. You said a minute ago that you sometimes hurt Sterling. What is the goal under this circumstance?

Inez: I have to humble myself, realize I have hurt him, and then seek forgiveness in the hope that he will forgive me.

Sophia: Yes. Can you see how giving and receiving forgiveness works both ways?

Inez: Yes, I do. If we can both forgive each other and then seek each other's love, we could soften our hearts toward each other and truly change for the better.

Sophia: Suppose you both did that, what would that mean for your relationship?

Inez: It would mean that we could begin living as a true husband and wife. We could trust each other more.

Sophia: Trust, yes, but without falsely thinking that he (or you) will never do an offensive thing again. Both of you, after all, are human beings, and we all fall flat sometimes.

Inez: Yes, but if he changes then I know he is trying. I know he has my best interest at heart, as I have his best interest at heart. We could be truly reconciled.

Sophia: And what does that mean to be "truly reconciled"?

Inez: We already covered that. It means that we both can trust each other, even if this emerges slowly.

Sophia: Exactly. As you forgive, you make possible what I call the *Triangle of Forgiveness*. By this I mean that there are three aspects—three lines, if you will—to forgiveness: your forgiving Sterling and his forgiving you; his receiving that forgiveness, even asking for forgiveness from you, and changing in a positive way, and your receiving his act of forgiving (and even asking forgiveness from him) and your changing; and he and you both coming together again in mutual trust and reconciling.

Inez: The Triangle of Forgiveness. I like it. This is more complete than my just forgiving and then nothing happens on his end.

Sophia: Yes, such consequences as these complete your forgiveness, but they do not make it any more or any less valuable. You have practiced a tough virtue— forgiveness—and whether or not anyone accepts it, you have done moral good. You can feel good about that, don't you think?

Inez: Yes, of course, but I do like the goal of the Triangle of Forgiveness and hope it happens. I think I am
now ready to forgive Sterling.

Sophia: May we explore that the next time we meet?

BACK TO THE BASICS—YOU

This chapter is filled with detail, and I hope you take some time to
reflect on the detail even if you are in a hurry to get to the heart of
the matter and start forgiving someone. You must first understand
exactly what it is you are doing when you forgive. The material covered here is intended to give you a deep understanding of forgiveness
prior to your practicing it. What is still confusing for you? If you had
to write out a definition of forgiveness now, what would you say?
Can you see the psychology of forgiveness within your definition (it
is made up of thinking, feeling, and behaving toward a person who
was unjust; these are accompanied by the right motivation, seeking
his or her good)? Can you see how forgiveness differs from related
concepts such as pardon and tolerance? On which moral rule will you
base your forgiveness (will you be civil, respectful, and/or loving in
its moral sense)? What is a virtue and what are the virtuous characteristics of forgiveness? What is the Triangle of Forgiveness? Is your
forgiving of another person morally good even if you cannot realize
the Triangle of Forgiveness?

BECOMING A FORGIVING PERSON

Can you now see that to become a forgiving person, you must have
as your goal to become a virtuous person? I can hear some people
making fun of that—goodie-goodie sarcasm. But, that is not my
point at all. I am not suggesting that you become someone who is
sickeningly sweet but instead someone who is solidly grounded in

courage to do what is right, grounded in what mercy is, grounded in an unwavering motivation to do good, and skilled enough to pull this all off. To become physically fit, you need a plan, you need the drive, and you need to be willing to accept whatever physical pain will come your way (within reason, of course) to get in shape. I am asking if you have what it takes to get into forgiveness shape. Let us move on with a possible plan to realize this goal.

Part III

GETTING ORGANIZED

CHAPTER 8

THE FORGIVENESS PLAN

We have come to the point where Inez, and you, now have some decisions to make. Whom will you forgive first? Whom will you forgive next? For one thing, Sophia will be asking herself this: Is Sterling the very best person with whom Inez should begin the forgiveness process? Most forgiveness books center on the client's choice of whom to forgive, but if Inez is to lead The Forgiving Life, then she may want to do some preliminary work, which will be hard work, prior to turning her attention to Sterling. Let us listen as the conversation unfolds between Inez and Sophia.

> *Inez:* Well, I'm ready to forgive Sterling. I don't even
> want him to grovel at my feet any more.
> *Sophia:* That's good. But, I'm wondering. Should we start
> with Sterling?
> *Inez:* Yes, I think so. He has wounded me the most
> recently, and I need to start interacting better with him.
> He's the one.
> *Sophia:* May I ask about your mother?
> *Inez:* [*surprised*] My mother? Why?

Sophia: I'm just wondering if you are angry with her. You said in our initial dialogue that your mom had an authoritarian style.

Inez: A death grip, you mean. She choked the life out of my freedom.

Sophia: You didn't like that and it made you fume.

Inez: Yeah, it did.

Sophia: Does it still?

Inez: Not unless you bring it all up again.

Sophia: The anger seems to still be there, long after you have left home and married and then entered into the new relationship with Sterling. It sounds like this anger is not yet resolved.

Inez: [*silent for a while*] Is this another one of those defenses, those shields that we put up to avoid emotional pain?

Sophia: It is worth exploring. What defense are you using?

Inez: I'm not in denial, that's for sure. I see the overly tough parenting and I see my anger.

Sophia: But, you seem to see that anger only when it is brought up.

Inez: At least I'm seeing it, right? I acknowledge it. I'm angry.

Sophia: Could you be using the defense mechanism of suppression? To suppress is to be aware of something but then push it away as it comes to visit. A person who is using the defense of suppression does not deal with the issue because she is always pushing it away.

Inez: That's my mom and me all right. I think about her, but I try not to think about how harshly she parented us.

Sophia: That's the first time I heard you use the word *harsh* when describing your mom.

Inez: I hadn't thought about it too much, but now that you bring it up, yes, the word *harsh* applies. She seemed to want to discipline in a great big hurry so that she could get back to whatever.

Sophia: Whatever?

Inez: Well . . . yes. Anything but me, it seems.

Sophia: What do you mean?

Inez: She was always so . . . so . . . distracted. She did not have time for me.

Sophia: Again, may I ask what you mean by this?

Inez: I think she wanted us kids to stop whatever conflicts we had as quickly as possible because she did not have the time and energy to get involved. So, she got all authoritarian on us and then off she went to other things.

Sophia: Would you say that she ignored you?

Inez: Sort of. She was not warm. She did not give of herself.

Sophia: She deprived you of love.

Inez: [*wide-eyed and surprised*] No. No. She was a good mom. She was OK.

Sophia: What defense mechanism are you using now, Inez?

Inez: You know, I think that I've ignored this my whole life. My mom was too busy to really, I mean really, reach out and give me love. We did not connect most of the time. She really did not spend that much time with me. Uh-oh.

Sophia: What?

Inez: I don't want to overdo it, but this fits for my dad, too. He was a very nice guy, don't get me wrong, but he was so . . . so . . . busy with his business that he left home early to go to work, came home late, and there was not much left in his gas tank for me.

Sophia: And that makes you . . . what? Fume? Sad? What do you think?

Inez: Sad.

Sophia: What do you want to do about this?

Inez: That makes both my mom and dad candidates for my forgiveness, right? And when I forgive, I am not wagging a finger at them, but instead I am having mercy, right?

Sophia: Yes. And I have another question for you. Did you learn any patterns from your mom and dad, some ways of interacting with other people that you brought into your relationships with Enrico and Sterling?

Inez: Uh-oh.

Sophia: What?

Inez: We're not about to play the blame game toward me now, are we? I say that I learned an authoritarian style from my mom and that I now can't trust because she and my dad basically ignored me and then you blame the divorce on me and my difficulties with Sterling on me?

Sophia: Have I yet to blame you for anything?

Inez: No, but I see it coming . . . and here it is!

Sophia: My point is that we all bring something from our past into our present. We all bring something from our family of origin into our new families. To use a somewhat poetic expression, I call it the *wounded heart.* You are not to blame for that. Everyone in the world, in all likelihood, is walking around with a wounded heart. If our relationships are to be made more whole, we have to attend to our own wounded heart and then help others with theirs.

Inez: But what does this have to do with my mom and dad?

Sophia: If they wounded you, you may be bringing those wounds into your relationship with Sterling. In addition to that, if Sterling has a wounded heart from people in his past, he may be bringing this to you.

Inez: So, from one wounded heart to the other, we then wound each other.

Sophia: Yes, and if you can forgive those who have wounded you and realize the pattern that you now are bringing to your relationship with Sterling, and if he can do the same by examining his own wounds from the past, you both have a chance to heal as individuals and then to heal your relationship. This can have a positive impact on your family as well as on your approach to work.

Inez: [*with a sad look*] My mom's rough edges have become my rough edges. Her wounding me has wounded Sterling. I know he brought some baggage into our relationship. Have his wounds then wounded me? You don't have to answer that. I already know the answer.

Sophia: Would you like to examine the patterns of your wounded heart—for you and for Sterling and the family? Would you like to be set free from these patterns, by first forgiving your mom and dad and then working with Sterling on his wounds so that you can forgive each other?

Inez: I had not even thought about any of this until now. My mom is in another state and I don't see her too often.

Sophia: She need not be present for you to forgive her. You can forgive her from your heart and then decide on the best way to interact with her. You have a certain pattern with Sterling, which you learned in part from your parents. Perhaps if you forgive your mom and dad first and then Sterling, it could help you interact better with him and even with others.

Inez: I see. Yes, that makes sense. If I forgive Sterling and am still fuming at my mom or dad and still interacting with him as they did with me, Sterling and I will go back and forth in our dance of anger and passivity and an inability to trust each other.

Sophia: Great insight.

Inez: [*with a thoughtful look*] OK, I'll forgive my parents and then Sterling.

Sophia: I have another question for you.

Inez: [*with eyebrows raised*] Why do I not want to hear this?

Sophia: [*with a smile*] Might you have established a certain pattern of interaction with Enrico, which spilled over into your new relationship with Sterling?

Inez: Hmm. Let me see. As the relationship with Enrico broke down, so did my ability to trust men.

Sophia: Do you not trust Sterling?

Inez: Not as I think I should.

Sophia: Might it help to forgive your parents first, who wounded your trust, and then Enrico, for hurting your trust even more, and then turn to Sterling? Do you see the pattern here? You have a wounded heart, and those wounds do not come from one source alone. Each person who has wounded you is contributing to the wounded relationship that you now have with Sterling.

Inez: I see where we are going with all of this. You'd like me to do the work of healing my heart from at least some of the serious past injustices before I turn to Sterling. By my doing this, the excess baggage from my past is clearly seen, dealt with, and so does not interfere with Sterling's and my marriage . . . and you'd like Sterling to do the same with his wounds

Sophia: That is the general pattern, yes . . . if you want to lead The Forgiving Life.

Inez: So, do I then have to forgive my brother and sister, my dad, all of my friends from childhood, my teachers, the family dog, and Aunt Harriet for making me kiss her "hello" every time I saw her when I was 6 years old? I'll have to clean up all of the injustices of my past, is that it?

Sophia: Let's draw the line before we get to the dog and Aunt Harriet, OK? And one clarification: We won't actually be cleaning up the injustices of the past, right? We'll be confronting your reaction now to those past injustices. We'll be dealing with your wounded heart, not making the injustices somehow seem fair now.

Inez: Yes, good point. Forgiveness does not change injustices, but it does change my response to them.

Sophia: And please recall that you do not practice any virtue in isolation from the other virtues. As you practice forgiveness, you should practice justice and patience and wisdom, for example.

Here is a general rule to follow as you begin to examine who wounded your heart: You need not forgive everyone who has ever been unfair to you, at least not right away. Focus on those who have actually done some damage, who have actually wounded your heart. As you examine your life, you will remember many people who let you down, insulted you, embarrassed you, and disappointed you in some way. It is legitimate to forgive each of them in time, but for now focus on those who have hurt you deeply enough that you can say, "Yes, that person, by his or her actions, has wounded my heart."

Inez: I'm feeling kind of overwhelmed at the moment.

Sophia: What is it that seems so big to you?

Inez: The mountain of people. When you've lived a while you build up a lot of wounds. Where to begin?

Sophia: We can take it systematically, one person at a time. I recommend that we first make a list of all who have seriously wounded you in your life, from early childhood on to the present time. You need not forgive everyone on that list prior to your turning to forgiving Sterling. Although it may be in your best interest to first forgive certain people, such as your mom and dad or others in your family when you were growing up. These patterns of interactions and the wounds from them can and do make a difference in how we react to other people now.

Inez: Before we do that, I have a question. What if the one who wounded me is a group and not a person?

Sophia: You can forgive a group. What group do you have in mind?

Inez: I have more than one, but as an example, let's suppose that I am ticked off at the company that let me go recently. Can I forgive the company?

Sophia: If a group has been unfair to you then, yes, you can forgive that group. I recommend that you try to make the forgiveness exercise as concrete as possible. Is there someone in the company in particular who wounded you the most?

Inez: Yes, the boss. As you now know, she came to my desk without any warning and escorted me out of the building, with all eyes watching the "ceremony."

Sophia: Well, then, in that case, you might consider forgiving your boss first.

Inez: But, no one came to my defense. All those eyes watching the ceremony? Did anyone complain to the bigwigs of the company or offer sympathy to me? Not that I am aware of.

Sophia: Then your forgiving the group after you've forgiven the boss seems like a good idea. Do you remember any fellow workers in particular who should have supported you? Again, to be concrete, you might try forgiving them first before turning to the company, which is so much more abstract than actual people who were unfair to you within the company.

Inez: OK. I'll try to make this as concrete as possible. And I do have another question: If I can forgive a company, can I forgive a racial group?

Sophia: What do you have in mind?

Inez: As you know, I am not what some these days call "European American" but instead what some call "Hispanic" or even "Latin American." Have you ever experienced racism or ethnic bias in the workplace or in an educational institution? I have. For example, some students look at me as if to say, "What are you doing here, loser!" It is as if I have no chance to succeed here because of my ethnic background and my cultural heritage.

Sophia: Yes, I know what you are talking about. I have had the privilege of talking with many people who have had their heart wounded in this same way.

Inez: Were they able to forgive and move on? Were they able to get the degree?

Sophia: Yes and yes. This requires a pattern of forgiveness similar to your forgiving the corporation or even the family next door. We will start with specific people who have been unfair to you and we can then move slowly to the group that they represent, if you are angry with the group.[1]

Inez: Well . . . we'll have to explore that when the time comes. Sterling is European American, and so I can't say that I am fuming at all people in that group, not at all. Yet . . .

Sophia: Yet, your forgiving the group may be helpful?

Inez: I think so, because of my past. You said that the key test is this: Has the person or group wounded my heart? The answer is yes regarding race and ethnicity.

Sophia: Then we will explore this.

Inez: OK. So far I realize that I need to think about who wounded my heart when I was a child. This could include parents, brothers and sisters, other family members, friends, and teachers. As an adolescent, I can include employers, fellow employees, romantic partners, coaches, and anyone else who has hurt me. As an adult, I can include all of the above and my husbands Enrico and then Sterling, my overbearing boss, and the next-door neighbors. I can include groups, such as the company I used to work for and even members of my church if they have hurt me deeply. I can include racial and ethnic groups, as you just pointed out to me. Why is the room spinning? My head hurts.

Sophia: This can all seem overwhelming. You can't forgive everyone for everything today. This is a long list and a long journey, and that is why we need to take this slowly and systematically.

HOW TO PROCEED

As you can see from the above dialogue, Inez is a bit overwhelmed when she thinks about her whole life and all who have been unfair to her. You may be feeling the same. It is now time to organize your approach to forgiveness, a central step in leading a forgiving life. This is why we have to be careful in how we proceed. I want to be thorough, and at the same time I want this not to be a chaotic or hurried activity for you.

First Issue: Reviewing Your Unfolding Love Story

In Chapter 1, I asked you first to create your Unfolding Love Story before you examined the wounds you have received from others. The important point is to connect you with love, vital to you and your relationships, before moving courageously into an examination of your emotional wounds. Very soon in this chapter, I will ask you to consider the broad landscape of all who have wounded you, in the hope that you will forgive those in particular who have deeply hurt you. In preparation for that, I ask you to read once again that essay in which you and one other person showed agape love to each other. I want you to have a sense of that kind of love as a fortification for you, as a protection, as a strength to which you can refer as you deal with your wounds through forgiveness. As you forgive, you may add to your love story.

Second Issue: Staying in Balance

As we now turn to your issues of being wounded by others, it is important that you stay in balance in two ways. First, please do your best to avoid the psychological defense of denial (see Chapter 4 and this chapter). Such a psychological shield leads us into thinking that we are less resentful than we really are. If a person is very angry at her uncle, for example, and if this feeling is threatening to her (after all, we are not supposed to fume at relatives, right?), then she might put up a shield and deny that she is angry. She might admit to feeling some anger, but she would not admit to the full extent of that emotion if she were in denial.

Second, there is the opposite pattern of psychological defense—displacement (see Chapter 5). Suppose a person is feeling much anger at his mother. If this kind of anger is threatening to him, he might transfer his resentment onto others who are more likely to take it, such as his children. Displacement allows him to express his anger, but it goes in the wrong direction, confusing and hurting his own children. A related psychological defense is projection. In this case, a very resentful person may accuse others of being resentful even though they are not. In this case, he accuses others of being unfair when they are acting in a morally good way. I recommend that you quietly reflect a bit on these defenses to see if you have a tendency to use any of the three before moving to the next section.

CREATING THE FORGIVENESS LANDSCAPE

We are now ready for you to consider all (or many) people who have deeply wounded your heart. First, here is a brief overview of the procedure you will follow, if you so choose, followed by more detailed instructions.

Brief Overview

There are two exhibits in this chapter and one scale, the Forgiveness Landscape Rating Scale, in Appendix B for you to consider. For your ease in photocopying, I have created Appendices B, C, and D, each of which contains one scale related to your forgiving others. Each exhibit and each scale in Appendices B, C, and D are aids in helping you to get organized. The task will be to identify each person who hurt you (Exhibit 8.1); examine the injustices from each person

---

EXHIBIT 8.1. Outline of Possible People Who Have Been Unjust to You

FAMILY OF ORIGIN

The family in which you grew up probably shaped you in both positive and negative ways. Sometimes people and events from our growing-up years leave lasting impressions on us and create lasting patterns, some of which we cherish and others of which we try to overcome. As you reflect on the various people and the wounds they have given you, please keep in mind that we seek to identify and specifically work on the major wounds, not the minor ones.

People in your family of origin: grandfather, grandmother, father, mother, stepfather, stepmother, oldest brother, another brother, oldest sister, another sister, stepbrother, stepsister, uncle, aunt, other family member

PREVIOUS MARRIAGE OR PARTNERSHIP

Some of you have experienced a breakup of a central relationship, and I do not have to tell you about the emotional pain associated with that. It is important to face the injustices and the pain so that you can be set free from them and not bring that woundedness into your current relationship (if you are in one) or into a future relationship.

(continued)

> ## EXHIBIT 8.1. Outline of Possible People Who Have Been Unjust to You (*Continued*)
>
> *People in a previous marriage or partnership:* father of your partner, mother of your partner, partner, son, daughter, partner's son, partner's daughter, other family member
>
> ### CURRENT FAMILY
>
> We now center on the family of which you are currently a part. As with the other families to which you have belonged, I will try to help you assess who may have been unfair to you and your reaction to the unfairness.
>
> *People in your current family:* father of your partner, mother of your partner, partner, son or stepson, daughter or stepdaughter, other family member
>
> ### SCHOOL DAYS FOR YOU
>
> We now turn to your time in school. This area may open your eyes to the issue of denial or suppression of pain from the past. Some people tend to put the pains of their childhood school days into the distant past and try to keep them there, but wounds have a way of affecting us even when we are not paying attention. Here is just one example: Sterling was not particularly athletic as a child and so one student in middle school picked on him whenever they had gym class. Sterling forgot about these incidences in adulthood and subconsciously wanted a great deal of respect from his own students as he taught seventh grade. We all should have respect from others, but this case was different. He had an exaggerated response to students who were having a bad day. He tended to discipline harshly because of his unresolved emotional wounds from when he was in seventh grade. A look of disrespect from one of his students would trigger in him anger from his past. Not knowing this, Sterling had a tendency to be overly angry, displacing his wounds onto students in his class. He needs to forgive the student from his past if he is to be set free and avoid displacing his wrath on his current students.
>
> *People from your school days:* former teacher, administrator, coach, friend or fellow student

EXHIBIT 8.1. Outline of Possible People Who Have Been Unjust to You (*Continued*)

SCHOOL DAYS FOR YOUR CHILDREN OR STEPCHILDREN

Even though I am asking you to center on the injustices your child(ren) or stepchild(ren) experienced in school, this exercise is for you. The unjust treatment of a loved one can trigger hurt or emotional wounds in us. This is sometimes called *secondary forgiveness*—forgiving someone who hurt someone else, thus hurting you.

People from school days of your children or stepchildren: teacher, administrator, coach, your child's or stepchild's friend or fellow student

WORK DAYS

Work can be difficult because we encounter stressed-out coworkers and employers who at times seem to be more concerned about the company than about the dignity of the people who work there. We may encounter unfair wages or working conditions and need to remember that to forgive is not to ignore justice. As we forgive, we may be able to see more clearly the injustices against us, and with reduced anger we may actually realize an even better justice than might have been possible otherwise.

People from your work days: boss, owner, manager, coworker, customer, client, other whom you serve, someone else in the world of work

RELIGIOUS COMMUNITY

What is the old saying—never discuss religion or politics? Why is that? Surely it is because people can and do disagree about these issues. Yet, we also might disagree on which ice cream flavor is best. Why not avoid that topic, too? Religion and politics are filled with emotion because the larger spiritual and community questions and their answers matter a great deal to people. Because they matter, people can get contentious and hurt others with their views, with their intensity, and with their demands. People in religious communities may hurt each other. This is not meant to criticize a

(continued)

> ### EXHIBIT 8.1. Outline of Possible People Who Have Been Unjust to You (*Continued*)
>
> belief system but instead to emphasize that those beliefs are carried out by imperfect people.
>
> *People in your religious community:* religious leader, member of your religious community, coworker on a committee, student (if you were or are involved in religious instruction), other member of your religious community
>
> #### PEOPLE IN YOUR COMMUNITY
>
> When we live in close proximity to others, conflicts at some point will emerge. This can occur with next-door neighbors, with community leaders (politics again), and with community members and groups. Although this category is mentioned last in this exhibit, it is not any less important than other groups. Inez, for example, learned to feel inferior because she often sensed that community members judged her worth by her ethnicity. This left scars, and she wishes to forgive, not as a way to mask justice, but as a way to heal and perhaps even to help heal the community in her own small way. Following are some categories of people involved in communities, but because the idea of "community" is so large, the list may not include all the kinds of people whom you may need to forgive. Please consider people in the "other community member" category if I have inadvertently left off categories of those who hurt you.
>
> *People in your community:* friend, neighbor, community leader, people not known to you who judge you, other community member

(Exhibit 8.2); and then record the person, the injustice, and the degree of hurt you experienced at the time of the injustice (on the scale in Appendix B). Once you have these insights, in the next chapter I will ask you to fill out a forgiveness inventory for each person (which is in Appendix C) so that we can gain further insight into the degree to which you have forgiven or not forgiven this person. Then

EXHIBIT 8.2. Definitions of the Categories for Describing Each Incident of Injustice

Category	Definition
Absent, Emotionally	Person is present but mind seems far away; little love expressed
Absent, Physically	Away from you for long periods
Anger, Displaced	Person is actually angry with another, but takes it out on you
Anger, Excessive	Intense anger expressed verbally and/or physically without actual contact
Anger, Passive	Subtle anger that embarrasses/hurts; not easily detected as anger
Anger, Ridicule	Expressed anger that makes you feel small and judged
Abusive, Emotionally	Extreme and persistent anger; words that damage you psychologically
Abusive, Physically	Extreme physical contact that damages you
Abusive, Sexually	Inappropriate touching and/or physical contact
Excessive Anxiety	Extreme worry displaced onto you
Excessive Punishment	Deserved punishment that goes too far
Excessive Teasing	Joking that goes too far
Excessive Demands	Asking more than what is reasonable
Harsh Judgments	Thoughts/expressions that leave you feeling condemned
Ignoring	Lack of communication
Insensitive	Consistently ignoring your needs
Lack of Love	Failure to express love
Lack of Cooperation	Give-and-take is absent
Lack of Understanding	Failure to see your viewpoint
Poor Decision Making	Decisions are harmful
Selfish	Self-absorbed
Other	Any injustice not specified above

in Chapter 10, we begin your forgiveness journey by having you for-give an important person from your family of origin, the family in which you grew up as a child.

As you consider the series of lists in Exhibits 8.1 and 8.2—focused on those who have hurt you—please note that we are not doing so to rush to a finish line. Instead, I am giving you the oppor-tunity to see your broad Forgiveness Landscape, perhaps for the first time in your life. This insight of seeing all (or most, because you likely will add people as we proceed) of those who have wounded you can be both painful and exciting at the same time. It is painful for the obvious reason that we are dealing with your wounds. It can be excit-ing because, again perhaps for the first time in your life, you will see your opportunity to be free of those wounds. Not only that, but you will have the opportunity to grow in love and to pass that love on to others.

This Approach Is Not for Everyone

Does the thought of filling out scales make you apprehensive? Tired? Unmotivated? If so, then perhaps the systematic procedure I am out-lining is not for you. Under this circumstance, I recommend that you take a less detailed approach. If you want to forgive without refer-ring specifically to the scales, then please only review the scales in this book as something to think about. You might want to write down the names of the people who have greatly wounded your heart because of their injustices but then not do the detailed work that filling out the scales will require. If you have the energy and the resolve to do the detailed work, I encourage you to do so because it will be the most complete approach to forgiveness that you might be able to take. Yet, I realize that people will want to use this book in different ways and that is why I present different options here. With that introduction, let us continue with the description of the detailed approach to forgiving, to leading The Forgiving Life.

More Detailed Instructions

Here, then, is the more elaborated plan. First, carefully and slowly examine the list of people in Exhibit 8.1. I have tried to be comprehensive in listing the possible people who might have been unjust to you (or to your loved ones, such as your children or stepchildren) throughout your life. Of course, because of the variety of people who have likely entered your life, the list will be incomplete, and so you should feel free to add to the list.

We will start within your family of origin because it is often in families that we are wounded significantly for the first time. This will not be true for all of you who read this book. I do wish that I could talk with each of you individually and set up a plan specific to you. Yet, we can come close to that if you realize that some of the people whom I bring up here in this chapter will pertain to you and others will not. You will be skipping many of the people to whom I point you. My intent in pointing you to lots of people is to be as sure as I can that we did not miss anyone in your life in need of your forgiveness. As I said before, we start with your family of origin, the one in which you grew up.

When I list in Exhibit 8.1 a person, such as a grandfather, please think through those instances in which he may have been unjust to you. It is important to reiterate: We are not doing this to blame but instead to have mercy. To help you focus specifically on each person and each incident of injustice, I have listed for you in Exhibit 8.2 the various types of injustices that people typically face. Again, the intent is to be thorough, with the realistic assumption that I cannot be exhaustive in what is on the list. Try to pick out the type of injustice for each time in which you identify a person who has emotionally wounded you. In other words, let's say you have identified your boss as someone who has been unjust to you, and you can recall five specific incidences of her injustice. You should then go through this exercise with your boss all five times: Identify the boss in Exhibit 8.1, identify the specific type of injustice in Exhibit 8.2, and fill out the Forgiveness Landscape Rating Scale in Appendix B for each of these five injustices with your boss. The point is to find out if you should forgive your boss five different times, which may be necessary. (I recommend, if you will be doing this work by hand, that you make sufficient copies of Appendices B–D.)

When you have identified a person from the list in Exhibit 8.1 and then have identified a specific injustice from that person in Exhibit 8.2, please proceed directly to Appendix B and fill out the Forgiveness Landscape Rating Scale specifically for this one person and this one incident that you have identified.

You will then be repeating this pattern of choosing a different person from Exhibit 8.1 who was unfair to you, then choosing the type of injustice from Exhibit 8.2, and then going to the Forgiveness Landscape Rating Scale (see Appendix B) and recording the person, the injustice, and the degree of hurt you experienced at the time the incident occurred. Please continue this pattern until all people are identified and every major injustice from each person is identified and recorded on the Forgiveness Landscape Rating Scale (within reason, of course; you cannot identify every incident of injustice from someone who continually abuses).

Rather than filling out by hand the three scales in Appendices B through D (containing the Forgiveness Landscape Rating Scale in Appendix B and the two other scales that are described in Chapters 9 and 11), you have an online option, which you may find easier to do. That option is described in the next section.

Filling Out the Scales Online

In collaboration with Mind Garden (http://www.mindgarden.com), a major publisher and distributor of psychological scales, we have placed on that website all three of the scales you will be using in this book: the Forgiveness Landscape Rating Scale, the Personal Forgiveness Scale (to which you will be introduced in the next chapter), and the Forgiveness Guidepost Form, a third scale that you will learn about in Chapter 11. The Mind Garden site is ready for you to log on and to do all of this work via the computer (please go directly to the forgiveness materials via http://www.mindgarden.com/forgiveness). The site (for a standard fee) will allow you to fill out the scales a number of times. Mind Garden will do all of the scoring for you and present you with a report of the following:

- the people most in need of your forgiveness;
- the people from "least in need" to "most in need" of your forgiveness;
- your progress in the forgiving process, including your strengths and weaknesses in this process; and
- your degree of forgiveness toward each person entered both before you begin the forgiveness process and afterward.

You also will get a profile of the amount of change you have shown in forgiving people on your list (which will help you to decide whether or not to go through the forgiveness process again with any one person).[2]

BE GENTLE WITH YOURSELF

This can be painful work, and so please do not expect to complete all of your Forgiveness Landscape in one session. This could take days or even weeks to accomplish. You should take breaks from this activity when you are feeling tired or weighed down. Please be sure to have someone available to talk with you periodically as you reflect and make the list. This person should be a confidant who will listen and offer support as you experience the emotional effects of your wounded heart. Please keep in mind that we are heading toward the goal of easing the pain in your heart. This is not some isolated exercise of gaining insight and then that's it—you are left with insight and a wounded heart. On the contrary, this exercise is intended to lessen the emotional pain in your heart as you begin to practice the virtue of forgiveness.

Are you ready to open the door to The Forgiving Life? It may seem stormy out there as you open this door and step out into this new adventure, but the skies will brighten.

YOUR FORGIVENESS LANDSCAPE

Congratulations on completing a challenging task. You now have what we call your Forgiveness Landscape. All of the sheets that you now have on all of the people who have been unjust to you constitute your Forgiveness Landscape. As you go through your ratings, you can see the people who have hurt you the most, compared with others. At the same time, you now have breadth to this landscape. My guess is that you are somewhat surprised by the sheer number of people whom you might want to consider forgiving. That is one of the points of such an exercise—to show you the extent of your wounds and the people involved.

Let us now begin the process of narrowing your list so that we focus specifically on those most in need of your forgiveness within each of our categories (family of origin, previous family, current family, and so forth). Our 0-to-10 scale will help with this narrowing. I ask you to place each of your Forgiveness Landscape Rating Scales in the following order.

First, within each social category (family of origin, etc.), list all of those people to whom you gave a rating of 7 or higher as you rated the amount of hurt. If you are an easy grader and gave most people a rating of 6 or less, please choose those people whom you gave your highest rating of 6. In either case, some of these are the people I will be helping you to forgive in subsequent chapters, if you choose. Of course, you should feel free to forgive others whom you rated lower if you think you should. We can never forgive too much. Do you believe that? You might want to review the dialogue between Inez and the Sophia on this very point in Chapter 7, under the heading Forgiving as Part of Living a Virtuous Life.

In all likelihood, you do have a number of people whom you rated as a 7 or higher in each (or many) of our categories. On which person should you concentrate first? I recommend that we approach this question seriously by doing one more round of diagnosis, this time with an actual forgiveness scale rather than the 0-to-10 scale. Why? That 0-to-10 scale can give us a general ballpark sense of your level of hurt, but it cannot really tell us the degree to which you forgive or don't forgive someone. After all, you can have emotional pain or hurt and still be in the process of forgiving. To be more precise about your degree of forgiveness, we ask you to turn to Chapter 9, become familiar with the Personal Forgiveness Scale, and then turn to Appendix C and fill out that scale on all of those whom you rated as 7 or higher. (If you have five incidents on the same person and all are rated as 7 or higher, then please fill out the Personal Forgiveness Scale for that person five different times. This will help us know the number of times you will have to forgive this person.)

Once you have your forgiveness scores, you will see the people on whom you will need to concentrate the most in your forgiveness journey. Let us begin the process of filling out the Personal Forgiveness Scale in the order of the groups we have discussed in this chapter. We will start with your family of origin, move to your previous family (if that exists for you), then to your current family, then to your school days, and so forth. We will begin the actual forgiveness process—you working on forgiving someone—by focusing on early wounds when you were a child and within your family of origin. We take up this challenge in Chapter 10.

CHAPTER 9

MEASURING YOUR FORGIVENESS

One of the most frequent questions I get is this: "How do I know when I have forgiven someone?" This chapter is intended to help you answer this question, which is so important to so many people.

You now have a list of people from your childhood, adolescence, and adulthood who have wounded your heart, who may have helped shape your personality and character. These are the people who have challenged you. Sometimes, they may be the people who have almost crushed you. They are your opportunity for great personal growth. Of course, we do not seek the suffering so that we can grow, but when that suffering comes, we can see it as an opportunity to grow beyond the wounds, grow beyond our own undesirable patterns with others by forgiving and finding a new way. The people on your list in a certain way form a pathway for you toward greater good. This may seem astounding to you now, but please trust me on this. As you work with forgiveness, you will begin to see new meaning in your life. The people who have wounded you are contributing to that new life meaning for you. I am talking in a paradoxical way—it would seem that our wounds and the people who wound us are all part of a great big package of pain to avoid at all costs. Forgiveness suggests a different response—one of courageously facing what has happened so that you can stand up and make a difference in the world.

I mention all of this because the following exercise itself is challenging and has some pain associated with it, as did the exercises of the previous chapter. This is an extension of that chapter. I have a scale for you to consider, the Personal Forgiveness Scale, which I ask you to fill out for each person on the list in the previous chapter.[1] You will find this scale in Appendix C. I have put it there for your ease in photocopying.

I want to reiterate once again that this systematic exercise will not be for everyone. If you wish simply to think about the degree of forgiveness without filling out a scale each time, then please do so. As a compromise between giving a general subjective judgment (such as "I don't forgive the person," "I am in the process of forgiving," and "I have forgiven the person"), you might ask yourself this question, which is a little more specific than that: On a 0-to-10 scale, how much have I forgiven this particular person for this particular injustice? A 0 = *not at all,* 5 = *in progress,* and 10 = *complete forgiveness.* With these possible options for you, let us keep discussing the more detailed scale as I describe it in this chapter and as you examine it in Appendix C.

This scale, which has 21 items for you to consider, measures the degree to which you forgive someone. A low score represents a low degree of forgiving that person, whereas a higher score represents a higher degree of forgiving him or her. I ask you to fill out the scale for each person because sometimes the results surprise us. For example, you will find that you are far more forgiving toward certain people than you realized. At the same time, you will find that you are far more unforgiving toward certain other people, and on these we wish to concentrate.

In this chapter, we will focus on those whom you rated within one and only one of your social groups, such as your family of origin, or your current family, or your workplace, just to name three examples. You might be overwhelmed if I asked you to fill out the forgiveness scale for each person from all of the social group lists in Chapter 8 all at once. We will be addressing each group in turn (family of origin, previous family, current family, school days, etc.) as we focus on them in the chapters to come. If you are reading this chapter for the first time, we will be concentrating exclusively on the people from your family of origin.

THE PSYCHOLOGICAL DEFENSES

Before you begin filling out the Personal Forgiveness Scale (Appendix C) for each person in one of the social groups from Chapter 8, please consider our discussion of the psychological defenses from the previous chapter. First, you might be using the psychological defense of denial. When the scale asks if you are angry, you might respond *slightly agree* when in your heart of hearts you know, deep down, that the true answer is *strongly agree*. Second, you might be using the psychological defense of displacement or possibly projection. In this case, you might say that you *strongly agree* that you are angry with one of your children, for example, when you are actually extremely angry with your father and you are only transferring that anger onto your child. Please try to avoid both extremes (denial on the one hand and displacement or projection on the other) as you stand with courage in the truth. This will aid your accuracy in how you view the person, and it will aid your emotional healing.

WHEN YOU HAVE IDENTIFIED A PERSON

Please review your ratings of all people from the particular social group on which you are now focusing (again, this will be your family of origin if you are doing this for the first time). Eliminate all of those incidences in which you scored lower than a 7 on the Forgiveness Landscape Rating Scale (to reiterate from the previous chapter, if you are an easy grader and gave most people a rating of 6 or less, then please choose those people whom you gave your highest rating of 6). Place the remaining people and their incidents of injustice in order from the one who hurt you the least (I realize that the person hurt you significantly and so when I use the words *the least,* I mean relative to all on the list) to the one who hurt you the most (highest rating on the 0-to-10 scale). For example, if two people have the same rating, please use your judgment to rank order them. If a person has hurt you 10 times and you gave that person a rating of 7 or higher on, say, eight of the 10 incidences, then please group these eight incidences together for consideration one at a time (i.e., do not follow Person A's least hurtful incident with Person B's least hurtful incident and then go back to Person A's second least hurtful incident). In other words, keep all of Person A's incidents together so that you consider them one after the other. If you choose to fill out the scales online, you will be assisted with this ordering (http://www.mindgarden.com/forgiveness).

To begin filling out the Personal Forgiveness Scale, please choose the one person who hurt you the least. I want you to start filling out the scale without the emotional pain of starting with the most hurtful person. We will work up to him or her. Once you have identified the person, please consider all of the major injustices you experienced from that person. As you begin this exercise of filling out the Personal Forgiveness Scale, you will select only one of the incidents first from this person and focus on that one as you fill out the scale.

After you finish filling out the scale on this one person for each and every incident of injustice against you (that deeply hurt you and that you rated a 7—or 6 if you are an easy grader—or higher on the Forgiveness Landscape Rating Scale), then proceed to the next person and choose one incident on your list from him or her. Exhaust all incidents from this person before filling out the Personal Forgiveness Scale for the next person on your list. Continue filling out the Personal Forgiveness Scale until all people whom you have identified on the Forgiveness Landscape Rating Scale for this particular social group have been rated here. We will consider people in one social group at a time so that you can go about this in an orderly fashion. Before you begin to fill out the scale, please read the information in the following two sections, which will aid you in your responses.

THE STRUCTURE OF THE PERSONAL FORGIVENESS SCALE

Please examine the scale in Appendix C as I describe it to you here. As you will see, there are 21 items. Each of the items can be answered in six ways (*strongly disagree, disagree, slightly disagree, slightly agree, agree,* and *strongly agree*). For example, consider the first item: "I feel warm toward him/her." We are now supposing that you have examined your psychological defenses, your shields against pain and pride that can distort your answer, and can answer honestly. If you sometimes have a little warmth and most of the time you do not, then I recommend that you check *slightly disagree,* which signifies that the warmth is not consistently there, but at the same time, you are not icy cold toward the person, either.

The scale (across the first 18 items) is broken down into three categories: your current feelings toward the person, your current behaviors toward him or her, and your current thoughts about him or her. If the person is not present to you, even if the person is deceased, you can fill out the questions concerning behavior by thinking about how you would interact with him or her if the person were with you now.

If you will be filling out the Personal Forgiveness Scale by hand rather than online, I recommend that you first photocopy sufficient quantities of the scale so that you have the correct number for all people on your list whom you will be rating. As a reminder, you may fill out this and the other scales electronically by going to the Mind Garden website (http://www.mindgarden.com/forgiveness). For any of the social groups (family of origin, previous partnership, current family, and so forth), the task is to focus first on the least hurtful person from that social group who is on your list.

FILLING OUT THE SCALE

You now have one person (and only one unjust incident from him or her) identified. As you fill out the forgiveness scale, take your time and work at your own pace. Try to answer each question as honestly as possible. If you say that you dislike the person, for example, you will not be judged for this. It is your feeling at present, and we are not always in control of such feelings as liking or disliking, especially in the context of being treated unfairly.

Scoring the Scale

After you have completed all 21 items, it is time to add up the scores from each item and create an overall score for this person and the one injustice you have identified. Here is the general rule: The higher the score, the more forgiveness you have. Across all of the first 18 items, you will notice that nine of them are stated positively (I feel warm, I show friendship, I wish him or her well, as examples). You will also notice that nine of the items are stated negatively (I feel angry, I avoid the person, I think he or she is corrupt, as examples). Each of the positively worded items (all of the odd-numbered items, 1, 3, 5, 7, 9, 11, 13, 15, and 17) are scored this way: *strongly disagree* = 1, *disagree* = 2, *slightly disagree* = 3, *slightly agree* = 4, *agree* = 5, and *strongly agree* = 6.

Do you see why we are scoring each of the positive items this way? If you strongly agree that you are warm toward the person, then this item is given the highest score to represent the highest forgiveness. I recommend that you add up all of the positive items first (i.e., all of the odd-numbered items). The total score on these positively worded items will range from a low of 9 to a high of 54.

Now do the adding for each of the negatively worded items. This gets a bit tricky because we will do the exact opposite for scoring than we did with the positively worded items. You will now reverse score each of the negatively worded items (all of the evenly numbered items, 2, 4, 6, 8, 10, 12, 14, 16, and 18). By reverse score I mean that they are scored this way: *strongly disagree* = 6 (notice that for the positively worded items, this would be scored as a 1, the exact opposite of the negatively worded items), *disagree* = 5 (for the positively worded items, this would be scored as a 2), *slightly disagree* = 4 (for the positively worded items, this would be scored as a 3), *slightly agree* = 3 (for the positively worded items, this would be scored as a 4) *agree* = 2 (for the positively worded items, this would be scored as a 5), and *strongly agree* = 1 (for the positively worded items, this would be scored as a 6).

Do you see why we are scoring each of the negative items this way? If you strongly agree that you dislike the person, then this is given the lowest score (a score of 1) to represent the lowest forgiveness. We recommend that you add up all of the negative items together—all of the even-numbered items. The total score on these negatively worded items will range from a low of 9 (representing low forgiveness) to a high of 54 (high forgiveness).

Once you have the total score (across all nine items) for the positively worded items and once you have the total score (across the other nine items) for the negatively worded items, add these two totals together to get your total forgiveness score for this one person. Your total score will range anywhere from 18 to 108.

Scoring Items 19 Through 21

You may have noticed that the final three items, 19 through 21, have not been a part of this discussion. This is because they are not part of your overall forgiveness score but instead are part of what I call *pseudoforgiveness* or forgiveness that is not necessarily the real deal. In other words, sometimes we deny that there was a genuine, deep injustice as we fill out the Personal Forgiveness Scale, and this small three-item scale is intended to help you discern whether you are being truthful with yourself.

For each of the three items, please score them as you would all of the odd-numbered items 1, 3, 5, and so forth through item 17. Please score a 1 for *strongly disagree,* a 2 for *disagree,* a 3 for *slightly disagree,* a 4 for *slightly agree,* a 5 for *agree,* and a 6 for *strongly agree* for each of the items 19, 20, and 21. Then add up the scores for the three items. If the total score is 12 or higher, then you seem to be saying that this, in fact, is not an injustice against you. This indeed might be the case or you might have your psychological defenses up—your shield against pain. What do you think? You can always reflect on this and then take the Personal Forgiveness Scale over again regarding a given person and a given event if you think your shield was up. When that shield is up, we tend to look more forgiving (on items 1 through 18) than we might look when we are not being defensive and possibly denying the extent of the other person's wrongdoing.

Interpreting Your Score on Items 1 Through 18

How did you score across the first 18 items for the first person on whom you filled out the Personal Forgiveness Scale? To give you a "ballpark" sense of all of this, consider the categories of total forgiveness scores in the following paragraphs.

If you scored between 18 and 40, you are low in forgiving this person at this point in time. You have a deeply wounded heart because of this person's unfair treatment of you. This does not mean that you will not raise your score. In fact, I expect you to raise the score if you practice forgiveness, as we will begin to do in the next chapter. This does not mean that you are a bad person. When our hearts are wounded by others, we can react with anger, resentment, frustration, and similar responses. This does not mean that the person to whom you gave this low rating is a bad person. It does mean that you see the wounds he or she gave you and you are responding to that. Please keep in mind that your views of the person may change as you practice forgiveness. Anyone who scores in this low range and is deeply affected by the person's injustice is vulnerable to passing those emotional wounds to other people. As you may be seeing by now, emotionally wounded people tend to emotionally wound others, if they do not do something about those wounds. I am definitely not saying that it is inevitable that you will emotionally wound others. I, however, am letting you know that people are vulnerable to doing so when scoring low, when they are wounded, and when they have not addressed those wounds.

If you scored between 41 and 63, you are still somewhat low in forgiving but obviously are getting closer to a psychological state that is not as angry and therefore perhaps not as vulnerable. Your heart, in all likelihood, is still emotionally wounded, at least to a degree. There is still work to do on negative emotions, behaviors, and thoughts toward the person who was unfair to you. Again, this does not mean that you will not improve. On the contrary, we have seen people continue to improve in forgiveness as they practice the exercises you will practice in the next chapter. Thus, I expect that you will become more positive in your feelings, behaviors, and thoughts toward this person.

If you scored between 64 and 86, you are showing forgiveness, at least to a degree. You may have a minimally wounded heart in need of some forgiveness, but it is not imperative because any adverse psychological effects from the injustice are likely to be minor. We have found in our research that people do not have to score at the very highest levels to experience considerable emotional healing in forgiveness. For example, in the study with incest survivors presented in Table 2.1, most of the courageous participants only reached about the midpoint for the forgiveness scale they were given. They went from a low score to a medium or moderate score on forgiveness of their perpetrator, and that was sufficient for them to progress from excessive anxiety and depression to significantly less and from low self-esteem to higher self-esteem, with the added benefit of greater hope toward their future. So, showing change toward the more positive (within or getting near the 64 to 86 score range) on your forgiveness score on a second or third administration of the Personal Forgiveness Scale is good.

If you scored between 87 and 108 on a first administration of this scale, then you are already forgiving or well on your way to being even more forgiving toward that person. You probably do not need to go through the forgiveness process with that person. I say "probably" in the previous sentence because you surely could go through that process if you wish for even greater forgiveness, but my point is that your score indicates that you do not have a wounded heart regarding this person and this incident. You may be better off turning your attention to another injustice from this person or to a different person who has wounded you emotionally and toward whom you still have unforgiveness.

If this is a score you received after doing the forgiveness work, then my hearty congratulations to you. You are learning how to forgive in a strong and positive way. A key now is to incorporate this kind of forgiving so that it becomes a part of you, a part of your life. As you begin to score in this range across a wide variety of people, you truly are beginning to live The Forgiving Life. How does it feel? For those of you not yet at this place of forgiveness, I encourage you to see it as a goal, one that gives meaning and purpose to your forgiveness journey.

Organizing All of the Scores Within One Social Group

You now may have a number of scores from the Personal Forgiveness Scale for people in one of your social groups. The number, of course, will vary from reader to reader. If you have more than one person on whom you have filled out the scale, then please do your best to order all the people this way: Place on the top of your list (because you will forgive him or her first) the person toward whom you have the most forgiveness. Then comes the person whom you have forgiven the next most, all the way down to the person whom you have forgiven the least. I know this will not be a perfect ordering. For example, for one person, you may have four scores of 85, 84, 81, and then one score of 20. Now suppose there is another person on whom you have three scores of 63, 60, and 55. Toward which one do you have more forgiveness? I would say the second person, even though his scores are on the average lower than the other. Why do I say this? It is because of that very low score of 20. You are better off starting with the person who has scores of 63, 60, and 55. The general rule is this: If you have some very low scores and some very high scores for a particular person, focus mostly on the lower scores and put that person closer to the bottom of your list. Start forgiving those who are easier to forgive.

Please keep in mind that this list you are now creating may not correspond exactly to the ordering from our 0-to-10 scale exercise from the Forgiveness Landscape Rating Scale of Chapter 7. This is because to be hurt and to be forgiving can be different.

To summarize, you need not forgive a person on whom you scored between 87 and 108, the highest quartile, on the Personal Forgiveness Scale because you already have forgiveness for this person.

Of course, if you wish you may go ahead even with these people. You will then order all the other people in this social group as best you can from most forgiven by you to least forgiven by you.

THE SUGGESTED PATTERN YOU CAN USE FOR FORGIVING

In the next chapter, I will help you to forgive. After you have forgiven the first person in a particular social group for one incident (through the exercises of Chapter 10), then please go back to Chapter 10 with this same person and a different unjust incident in mind (if you have one for this person). Keep up this pattern until all incidents for that person are forgiven. I suggest the strategy of starting with the person least in need of your forgiveness as a way to learn the forgiveness process before you jump into it in a deep way. Sometimes we have to start on the "beginner's hill" as we learn to ski, rather than in the Alps. If you have only one person toward whom you rated your level of hurt and forgiveness, then please go ahead with this person as you work through the exercises of Chapter 10.

Next, and only when you are ready, please reread Chapter 10 with the next person on the list within this particular social group— the one now toward whom you have the highest scores as revealed by the Personal Forgiveness Scale. Keep going until you reach the person who might be your greatest forgiveness challenge within the particular social group in which you are working. Having had some practice beforehand may prove helpful for you as you try to forgive the person toward whom you are currently the least forgiving (and toward whom you might have the least interest in forgiving). Forgive him or her for each injustice that you have identified. Please remember that this is a very important person in your life because he or she, in a certain psychological sense, may be living inside you as you carry the wounds inflicted on you.

The Bigger Picture for Your Forgiveness Landscape

We start with the one social group of your family of origin, then progress to a previous partner and family (if you had one), then to your current family (Chapter 13). Then we will turn to forgiveness work from what we are calling "school days" (Chapter 15), when you were a child and from your children's school days, if you have someone to forgive there. Then we turn to your "work days" (also Chapter 15), concentrating on the world of employment, then to your religious community, and then to your social community. We follow the exact pattern that we did in Chapter 8.

As we turn to a new group, I will ask you to fill out the Personal Forgiveness Scale first, organize the scores, and then proceed to forgive, starting with the one toward whom you have the most forgiveness (to help you ease into the forgiveness). All of this work taken together should help you to live The Forgiving Life.

How Much Time Will This Take?

As you are probably beginning to see, on the basis of our definition of forgiveness and Inez's struggle to see the depth of it, as well as the details of the forgiveness process itself (see Appendix A), it takes time to forgive. As you begin, even with the "lighter" forgiveness of those who have not gravely hurt you, it can take weeks to go through the process for the first time with the first person you have identified. So, please be patient with yourself. Try to enjoy the journey. You are walking a path that, I hope, you will come to see as a privilege. It is a privilege because you are growing as a person, deepening love, and casting off resentment.

When you come to the people who have wounded you greatly, the forgiveness process will take even longer. It could take months to forgive. When we worked with the incest survivors, for example, it took each person an average of 14 months to forgive. As you forgive several people who have been unfair, you may find that the process speeds up for you. After all, you are becoming an expert in it. Yet, the time required will vary from person to person, and the degree of hurt (as well as who hurt you) will play a part in the length of your journey.

ARE YOU READY?

If you are reading this chapter for the first time, are you ready to forgive within the family of origin? I will be there with you, in the sense that we will be in dialogue throughout this book, as we proceed. You are not alone in your journey to forgive. If you are reading this for the second time or more, you now know the routine, and so let's keep progressing together. Let us go to Chapter 10 and step onto your forgiveness path.

Part IV

FORGIVING THOSE WHO HAVE HURT YOU

CHAPTER 10

YOUR FORGIVENESS PATHWAY

Welcome to a chapter that will become very familiar to you. This may be the first time you are reading it, or perhaps the 20th time. The more familiar it becomes to you, the greater the indication that you are persevering in leading The Forgiving Life, precisely because you are walking the path of forgiveness over and over. By doing so, you are not obsessing over your wounds, but rather you are healing them. If you have 20 cuts on your leg worthy of attention, would you be obsessing if you tended to each one? No, you would be in denial if you ignored significant cuts and did not allow yourself the chance to heal.

It is now time for you to begin walking the path of forgiveness (perhaps for the first time, perhaps again). I recommend that you see this as part of your Unfolding Love Story, with all of its plots and subplots, twists and turns, triumphs and failures. Stories can be told in many ways, and one of these ways is through the printed word. As you write your story, we begin in your family of origin and then progress through all of your other social groups. Who has wounded you emotionally and whom do you need to forgive, according to your responses in Chapters 8 and 9? Have you developed a pattern of interaction as a result of some of these wounds, which you now bring into your everyday interactions, whether at home, with friends, or at work? To help you break and change this pattern, caused in part by previous wounds to you, I would like you to write your story as I guide you with a series of questions. These questions will become familiar to you as you work through the different people in your life whom you wish to forgive. I will be drawing the questions from the details of the forgiveness process. Please think of this chapter as your basic roadmap for forgiving anyone.

THE WARM-UP

Before we launch into forgiveness, I urge you to please reread your Unfolding Love Story from Chapter 1, in which you first described a loving interaction between you and one other person. I urge you to do this as a way to reconnect with the essence of who you are— someone who needs to give and receive love. With this perspective in place, let us move forward into forgiveness. I encourage you to periodically review that story as you return to this chapter to forgive someone else.

On occasion, I see that some people are concerned that they are about to forgive someone on the Forgiveness Landscape list who actually did not act unfairly. In other words, the one about to forgive is concerned that he or she might be using the psychological defenses of displacement or projection. Perhaps you have such a concern, that you are judging the person wrongly. If so, take heart because the forgiveness process will help you determine that. As you work through the process, you will have a chance to see the truth of these psychological defenses (at least a glimmer of them) in Guideposts 1 and 2 shortly and in Guidepost 12 as you work to more deeply understand the person. Through the process of forgiveness itself you may on occasion conclude that for this person and this particular event, there is nothing to forgive because, for example, there really was an extenuating circumstance or a good and legitimate excuse for the behavior. This does not happen often, but I want you to know of this so that you can go into the forgiveness work with confidence.

On the other hand, are you concerned that all of this focus on others' unfairness will turn you into a judgmental person? After all, the forgiveness process at the very beginning encourages you to emphasize others' faults, not their goodness. It is true that you will concentrate on other people's unfairness as you go through the entire forgiveness process in this chapter and the Triangle of Forgiveness in Chapter 14. Yet, as I have emphasized in this book, please realize that the end point of forgiveness is mercy, not justice. You will not be accusing any person of anything. Instead, you will be offering agape love as you work to understand him or her and to offer compassion.

THE 20 GUIDEPOSTS OF THE FORGIVENESS PROCESS

As you already know from reading Chapters 4 through 6, forgiveness is a process. Each time you walk this path, it will have unique features for you because each of our wounds is unique and requires special care and work. Please expect two things that may be unique each time. First, the amount of time will probably differ in each case: The deeper the wound, the longer forgiveness might take. Please do not expect to rush through the process of forgiveness with any one person. Take heart because forgiveness works. Second, you will not necessarily have to go through all 20 guideposts each time you forgive. As you become more of an expert in this area, you will spend less time on some of the guideposts. For example, when you come to the Decision Phase of forgiveness for, say, the 12th time, you will not have to reflect much on the meaning of forgiveness or whether you want to do so. With these ideas in mind, shall we explore the first phase of forgiveness?

The Uncovering Phase of Forgiveness

As you now know from Chapter 4, this phase comprises eight guideposts and asks you to courageously examine the depths of your wounds that you undeservedly received from this person on your list. I will lead you through each guidepost in turn, but do keep in mind that each one may not be appropriate for you. Feel free to skip those guideposts that are not relevant at present to your situation and to go back and revisit any guidepost even if you are miles down the road to other phases and guideposts. This is not a step-by-step rigid process but one that is flexible according to your needs.

The Uncovering Phase is just that—an uncovering of your wounds, up to eight of them, that you might have received as the other person was unfair to you. I want you to see each wound, rate it on a 0-to-10 scale of severity of the wound for you now, and gain insight into your own situation. The endpoint of all of this is change for the better. As you see your specific wounds, you will be in a better position to take steps to reduce or even eliminate many or all of them.

GUIDEPOST 1: ARE YOU DENYING YOUR WOUNDS OR EXAGGERATING THEM? Because you have filled out the Personal Forgiveness Scale on this particular person, it is unlikely that you are now completely denying the wounds. What may be the case, and what we should explore, is the depth of the wound that you had and perhaps have even now. Might you be suppressing some of the hurt and anger? Inez sometimes deflects her hurt and disappointment with humor. Do you do that? Please keep in mind that it is OK if you do. Psychological defenses are important and protect us from anxiety. My intent in asking this now is to help you to see if you have even more hurt or anger than you realize.

Is it possible that the person's act is not as bad as you thought? I realize that for some of you, this is an absurd question, because we all know without a doubt that abuse, for example, is always wrong, and there are no exceptions. Yet, for others of you, the issue is more subtle than that, so please bear with me. If the actions against you are subtle, not so clearly recognized as wrong, then I urge you to reflect on this question: What, exactly, is wrong in what the other did? Please proceed if you think that the person's actions were, in fact, unfair to you.

I have two more challenges for you regarding defense mechanisms: Are the defenses that you use hurting you in any way? How might they be hurting you? Are the defenses you use hurting others in any way? How might this be the case? Do your best to be specific in your answers. As an example of a defense hurting you, suppose that you are actually much angrier than you are willing to admit. Sometimes this hidden anger presents itself as excessive anxiety. On the other hand, if you are actually much less angry with this person and instead are incorrectly displacing your anger onto someone else, how might this misjudgment be causing possible anxiety to the one whom you see as an offender but may not be?

A central point of all guideposts in the Uncovering Phase is to help you to see how the wounds received in the past can add to your pain in the present. If you have not dealt with the psychological defenses in an adequate way, this can compound the amount of pain that you have. Please do not get discouraged. We are doing the uncovering work so that we can see the wound, cleanse it, and allow it to heal.

GUIDEPOST 2: HAVE YOU FACED YOUR WOUNDS AND ADMITTED THEIR EXISTENCE? To look at your own wounds and to admit they are there is courageous. Many people find this a difficult step. If you are looking at those wounds specifically from this person who has been unfair to you, how hurt are you? How angry are you? Take a look at your ratings on the Personal Forgiveness Scale for some perspective on this. Even if your hurt and anger are somewhat mild, you did not deserve this and so it is unfair to you.

As you reflect on what happened, how long have you experienced the hurt or anger? If you have carried excessive anger for a long period, then you may have resentment for the person. Perhaps you have lived with the resentment for years, which itself is a wound. Sometimes, when we carry wounds for months or years in the form of resentment, we begin to develop symptoms of anxiety or depression. As you look within, are you anxious about the person and what he or she did to wound you? Are you anxious in a more general way, apart from thinking about the unfairness? Forgiveness can help with both patterns of anxiety.

Do you see how the initial wound can lead to more wounds? This is why you need to be gentle with yourself, just as a person who has a deep physical wound needs to practice such gentleness. Forgiveness is one remedy for all of the psychological wounds caused by the injustice.

GUIDEPOST 3: HAVE YOU EXAMINED THE DEGREE OF SHAME OR GUILT YOU MAY BE CARRYING AS A RESULT OF THIS WOUND? Shame, as you now know from Chapter 4, is a psychological characteristic in which you feel belittled by others' judgments of you, a painful situation. In your particular situation with this one person and one injustice, did you experience shame? Try to be as concrete as you can about this. Why or why not do you think you had shame? What happened and how did particular people respond to you so that you either did or did not feel shame?

Please recall our discussion in Chapter 4 of your inner world of pain, what I called *qualia* (because philosophers use the term). You and only you have direct access to that pain, but you can let others know of that pain in an indirect way by using a 0-to-10 scale, with a 0 meaning *no shame at all;* a 5 meaning *a moderate amount of shame;* and a 10 meaning *a very deep, perhaps an excruciating sense of shame.* Suppose that we could measure shame, as we can measure physical pain. On our 0-to-10 scale, how much shame did you experience regarding this one injustice against you when it happened?

Let us fast-forward to the present. How much of the shame from this (and even similar) injustices did you take with you into the present, again on our 0-to-10 scale? Compare the two scores, the one at the time of the injustice and the one now. Has the shame decreased, stayed about the same, or increased? This will give you a sense of the pain that you have been carrying.

As you focus on your present life, has there been any new shame developing for you because of this one person and the one event you have in mind? In other words, are there circumstances now that are the direct result of what happened to you that are leading to more shame? If so, how much shame is this inducing in you on the 0-to-10 scale? Take a moment to reflect in your writing about the source of shame connected to the injustice under consideration here and the new source of shame, focusing on how this has affected you. Again, please be gentle with yourself as you do this kind of reflection.

Let us now take some time to examine any guilt you may be feeling because of the way the person treated you. As you may recall, guilt is different from shame because it originates from within you, not from the glare of others from outside. Guilt is the sense that you have broken your own standards of right and wrong. To examine your guilt, please write down on a sheet of paper as many instances you can recall when you were unfair to others because of your frustration, anger, or resentment toward this one person's injustice that you are considering now. I am not asking you to write down only those times that you might have been unfair back to that person in particular. Instead, I am asking you to consider your displaced anger toward anyone that was a result of this wound you received in your life.

Once you have made the list, please rate on our 0-to-10 scale the degree of guilt you feel right now, which might come from your hurting the person or other people because of your actions or words. A 0 is *no guilt* and a 10 is *extreme guilt*. Your answer will give you a good sense of some work you will have to do later in this book. I will be asking you to seek and try to receive forgiveness from them.

The exercise you just completed can also serve as another indication of the wounds you have brought into your present. Displacing anger onto others wounds them and the one who is displacing.

GUIDEPOST 4: HAVE YOUR WOUNDS AFFECTED YOUR HEALTH? As you know from Chapter 4, Inez was tired from the effects of the injustices that she suffered. In your case, has the particular injustice from this one particular person affected your health in any way? What about overeating? What about a lack of sleep, or headaches, or stomachaches? What about that pain in your neck? (No, I did not say that the person is a pain in the neck.)

Has the struggle with the injustice made you tired? Let us say that you have 10 points of energy to get through each day. How many of those points of energy do you use fighting (even subconsciously) the injustice as an internal struggle? Even if you are giving 1 or 2 points of your energy each day to this, it is too much and could be considered another wound for you.

Have you started a physical fitness program? Do you want to do that? Do you have the energy to do so, and if not, what part does the injustice play in your decisions? I ask these questions because health issues are not so easily connected (in our own minds) to the way people treat us. As you consider these issues over the coming days, you may see clearly whether your health has been affected by the person's actions. To what extent would you say that this person and the event are affecting your health?

GUIDEPOST 5: HAVE YOU BEEN THINKING, OVER AND OVER, ABOUT THE PERSON AND THE EVENT? The kind of thinking I have in mind here can range from the very obvious (such as recurring dreams that are unpleasant) to the subtle (such as occasional thoughts recurring rarely but that are within you over the long haul of your life). Sometimes we are driving down the highway and our mind drifts. Do you ever think about this person and the event when your mind wanders? If so, on the 0-to-10 scale, how often do you have the unpleasant thoughts, with a 0 meaning *rarely,* a 5 meaning *moderately often,* and a 10 meaning *very frequently to the point of distraction*? If a day does not go by without your thinking adversely about the person, this would constitute a 10 on the scale and would suggest a need for some change.

GUIDEPOST 6: DO YOU COMPARE YOUR SITUATION WITH THAT OF THE ONE WHO WAS UNFAIR TO YOU? Sometimes we compare ourselves to the person who hurt us, and we see ourselves as lower than the person. After all, we sometimes conclude that he or she is doing fine in life, but we are struggling. Sometimes we falsely conclude that he or she is of greater (or lesser) worth than us. This guidepost is important to confront because if you conclude, even subconsciously, that he or she is a better person than you are, this could hurt your self-esteem. Some of our research has shown that when people are deeply wounded by others, their self-esteem is damaged.[1] Wounded people too often fall into a pattern of not liking themselves. Please think about that previous statement: Wounded people don't like themselves. Do you see how the injustices people suffer can lead to further wounds, sometimes deeper than the original wound? Your going through the forgiveness process can bolster your self-esteem, as the same research just cited has suggested.

GUIDEPOST 7: HAS THE INJUSTICE CAUSED A SIGNIFICANT CHANGE IN YOUR LIFE? When Inez was released from her position at the insurance company, she had to look for new employment. This was a substantial change to her life and added yet another wound to her. When you consider the person and the situation now under consideration, do you see any changes in your life that were either a direct or indirect consequence of the person's injustice? In what way did your life change that led to greater struggle for you? On our 0-to-10 scale, how great a change was there in your life as a result of the injustice? Let a 0 stand for *no change whatsoever,* a 5 stand for *moderate change in your life,* and a 10 stand for *dramatic change in your life.* Your answer will help you determine whether this is another wound for you. As you can see, the wounds from the original injustice have a way of accumulating and adding to your suffering. We will not be dwelling on these wounds. Our purpose is to identify them so that you can

- have an accurate picture of what has happened,
- decide if forgiveness is a good option for dealing with these wounds, and
- be cleansed of many of these wounds so that you and your relationships are healthier.

GUIDEPOST 8: HAS THE INJUSTICE ALTERED YOUR WORLDVIEW? I have so often seen that as people live with injustices and all of these accumulated wounds, they tend to slowly, and without much awareness, slip into a pessimistic way of viewing the world. A man who is rejected by his partner might decide that no woman can be trusted. A person who is fired from a position as Inez was might conclude that no boss can be trusted. The person might conclude that he or she is a poor worker, again lowering self-esteem. Because this shift in thinking about the world and about relationships (and one's own competence) usually unfolds slowly, the person can actually miss the transformation and be unaware that it even happened.

So, to help you see this shift if it has occurred for you, I ask these questions:

- What was your worldview like before the incident happened? Please take account of age differences between then and now. When you were a child, your thinking was quite different from now. Beyond that, have you become more pessimistic about certain relationships? In what way has your thinking changed?
- If you have become more pessimistic in your general worldview, has the pessimism, shall we say, spread to other aspects of your life? Have you become more pessimistic across the board or is the pessimism, if it exists, centered in certain areas and, if so, what areas?
- Do you like yourself more or less now than before the injustice occurred?
- Do you like others (in general) more or less now than before the injustice?
- Inez has a religious belief and if you do also, then do you like God more or less now than before the injustice?
- On our now-familiar 0-to-10 scale, to what extent do you think your worldview is different (in a negative way) compared with your worldview before this injustice happened? Again, a 0 is *little or no change,* a 5 is *moderate change,* and a 10 is *extreme change in the negative direction.*

SUMMING UP THE UNCOVERING PHASE. You have just had a courageous look at yourself and your wounds. The point of this is not to create even more stress for you. The point is not to lower your self-esteem or to add to a skeptical worldview. Instead, it may be the beginning of healing for you. I want you to see a person—you—who has endured much. I want you to see a person who has the tenacity to acknowledge wounds and to have the determination to change. I want you to see a person who is beginning to say "yes" to the virtues, especially the possibly life-changing virtue of forgiveness. Your worldview now includes the truth that you are exploring forgiveness toward those who have hurt you. Who are you as you pursue this virtue? If you need a break before going to the next section, might I suggest one more reading of the very first entry to My Unfolding Love Story? It may help you to more truthfully answer the question about who you are.

The Decision Phase of Forgiveness

Some people consider this phase the most important and the most difficult because it is the crossroads of forgiveness. It is here that you take courage in hand and commit to the forgiveness path. You commit to change, and change of any kind, especially change as large as forgiveness, is a challenge. With these perspectives in mind, let's take a little walk farther down the forgiveness path.

GUIDEPOST 9: DECIDE THAT WHAT YOU HAVE BEEN DOING HASN'T WORKED. My guess is that you would not be reading this book if you were not emotionally wounded. And, if you have been wounded for a long time, then I also guess that what you have tried in terms of healing has not been completely successful. This is important information because it can help motivate you to commit to forgiveness. So, my question is: Has what you have tried in terms of psychological relief been effective or do you need more? Might that "more" be forgiveness? Why or why not? What have you learned about forgiveness that intrigues you? What have you learned about forgiveness that scares you? What do you need from me to reduce the fear? Do you need more clarity on what forgiveness is? If so, please see Chapters 1, 3, and 7. Do you need convincing that forgiveness works? If so, then please read the scientific evidence in Chapter 2. If you think that forgiveness might be better than some other healing alternatives, then let us keep going together.

GUIDEPOST 10: BE WILLING TO BEGIN THE FORGIVENESS PROCESS. This is one guidepost that is most difficult because here is where you say "yes" to the forgiveness process. It is not unlike being on the hospital gurney about to be wheeled off into surgery, or getting in the car to go to an important job interview, or making the first phone call to the person who will be your true love in life. It is stepping into the unknown for a greater good. This is why I shake my head when people say that forgiveness is a weak act for weak people. On the contrary, it is an act of strength by people who will press on despite apprehension.

As a little review for you, when you say "yes" to forgiveness, you are saying "yes" to the virtue of mercy toward the one who was unfair to you. You are saying "yes" to trying to reduce resentment and you are saying "yes" to being open to goodness toward the one who hurt you. You will not be saying that the injustice was not unjust; you will not be excusing or condoning; you will not be ignoring justice but will exercise both mercy and justice where appropriate; and you may or may not reconcile with the person, depending on his or her readiness to change.

GUIDEPOST 11: DECIDE TO FORGIVE. This guidepost is the first one to ask a forgiveness behavior of you. Are you willing right now to commit to doing no harm to the person you have in mind? By this I mean, are you ready to

- refrain from saying bad things about the person to others? I do not mean that you will never tell a confidant what he or she did. I am asking if you will commit to not condemning the person.
- refrain from subtle revenge, such as a sneer or other action of disrespect?
- respect him or her because all people are worthy of respect, even if this must be given from a distance?

Homework for Guidepost 11. I am a professor. You did not expect to escape from doing some homework, now did you? Growth in the virtues requires practice. For the next day or so, please reflect on this statement at least three or more times: "I will do no harm to (state his or her name, if you know it) because he (she) is a person and all people are worthy of respect."

Work Phase of Forgiveness

Just as the heading suggests, we are about to do some important work on your forgiving the person you are now considering. Hard work can lead to great benefits for ourselves and others, as you know. We start with thinking exercises—how you think about the person. Next, we offer exercises focused on your feelings about the person. We then turn to bearing the pain and finally to a focus on giving a gift to him or her.

GUIDEPOST 12: WORK TOWARD UNDERSTANDING. I will be asking you to more fully understand the one who hurt you; by this I mean, truly getting to know him or her better. You will be looking beneath the surface of who he or she is. You will be looking at the core of his or her personhood. This really is an act of agape love because part of this kind of love is to take the time to get to know the person as deeply as you can. I want you to reflect on this for a little while. You are committing to showing love toward this person by this process of knowing.

Before we begin, please rate as honestly as you can the extent to which you truly think you know this person whom you are about to examine in some detail. A 0 indicates that *you hardly know him or her at all,* a 5 indicates that *you know him or her moderately well,* and a 10 means that *you have deep knowledge of him or her.*

We will now begin to examine the person by asking a general question that should help you with the specific quest for understanding this person. Here is the general (and very important) question: What is a person? This is our basic question because from your answer will come insight into a particular person—the one who injured you. You might want to review the exchange between the Sophia and Inez from Chapter 5 (pp. 69–70 and pp. 74–79) before we continue here.

We need to explore this question if you will be an expert forgiver, one who really knows what it means to forgive. So, please bear with me—forgive me—if this exercise seems a bit off the track. It is not, I guarantee you. I have the following six questions for you about personhood:

1. Is a person a person because of what he or she does—think, love, work, help, and so forth? Inez in Chapter 5 says "of course not" to this question for two reasons. She seems somewhat insulted by the very idea. First, she feels she is not particularly good at each task or each role she has in society. She believes that if she is judged by her abilities and accomplishments, those judging her are using poor judgment. Second, she refuses to be defined by any one role because that cuts off much of who she is as a person. For example, to define her as a student is to cut off her roles as stepmother and as a partner to Sterling. She is far more than one or several roles. To say that we are exclusively or primarily our roles—the functions we have for social groups—is to diminish a person. To say that the one who hurt you is less of a person because of his unfair actions is to diminish him as a person.

2. Is a person a *what* or a *who*? A *what* is a thing. We use things, manipulate them, alter some things at our will. Things have no will. We choose how to use and manipulate things. We even throw things away. A *who* is not a thing and therefore must

not be manipulated, altered against the rational will, nor thrown away—even the person who emotionally wounded you. Things cannot give of themselves to others; persons can. Persons can give of themselves in love to others, and love is at the core of who we are as persons.[2]

3. This next one may seem like a silly question, but it may help you to gain some insight into what the term *personhood* means: Is a person different from a chimpanzee? If so, in what way? Whether you are a person of faith, as Inez is (see Chapter 5), or an agnostic, as Sterling is (as you will see in the next chapter), one answer might go something like this: Chimpanzees do not have the capacity to think as humans do. They cannot reason, they cannot follow deductions in any sophisticated way (e.g., all men are mortal; Socrates is a man; therefore, Socrates is mortal; would not this deduction be lost on a chimpanzee?). Thinking—not the "doing" of thinking but the "capacity" to think—separates us. The one who hurt you surely has the capacity to think, even if his brain was kind of shut off when he hurt you, and so is a person in this sense.

4. Is a person only someone who has the capacity (the potential) to think? What about our capacity to choose—what some call our free will? This capacity differs between us and all other species. We are not bound by instincts as are chimpanzees. Thus, we can choose to be merciful or not by our will. Chimpanzees are likely to show something roughly akin to mercy if there is a payoff. I know that this statement can be debated, but for the sake of your time, let us just say that chimpanzees do not have the full free-will capacity that we as humans have. As a human, the one who hurt you does have the capacity to choose, and she may have chosen deliberately to hurt you. This is wrong, of course. But it was a person who made that decision, and nothing less.

5. What about our capacity to love, in the way that Aristotle and Aquinas have pointed out to us? Does this constitute our personhood? This capacity is far more sophisticated than our capacity to think or to choose because we can think unloving thoughts and choose unloving behaviors. It is also very different from what you are likely to see in chimpanzees (and I am not picking on the chimpanzee or those who study or love them). Sure, some scholars might point out instances of what they call *love* among chimpanzees, but my point is this—you will not see agape love practiced by species other than humans. If you recall, agape love, at our core of who we are, is self-giving, willingly chosen, and practiced even when there is no apparent reward in front of us. It is selfless in that sense. It is not instinctual survival behavior to preserve genes (such as saving a child or a community so that genes are passed to the next generation) but instead is self-chosen and self-giving for the good of another with accompanying emotions (soft emotions, loving emotions) and thoughts consistent with this. The ultimate end of agape love is not materialistic gain to achieve something physically concrete in this world (such as survival of self, survival of others, passing on of genes). Agape love, instead, points to connection (good connection, healthy connection, not some kind of distortion such as excessive dependence) with others as the end in itself, not connection as a means to an end.[3] We find this only in persons and not in species other than *Homo sapiens*. Thus, the capacity for agape love defines personhood and separates us from all other species. The one who hurt you does have the capacity to love in this way, even if love was distantly absent when you were hurt.

6. But is personhood based only on an individual's capacity of any kind, whether it is the potential to think or to exercise free will or even to love? I am asking you to consider whether there

is something more to the person than just his or her individual potential (tendency, predisposition, inclination) to think, choose, and love. An individual capacity is a potential, sometimes an unrealized potential, but each person has the same capacity (not the same amount of skill or level of development, but the same capacity to perform skillfully and to develop if there are no barriers). More fully developed individuals will possess more of these characteristics, but all share in the capacity. Thus, a person is a person because of this characteristic of shared capacity (to think rationally, to choose, and to love in a self-giving way). Each is a part of the same nature, or type, or category. This includes the person who hurt you, the one whom you resent. You both share personhood.

To summarize, what then is a person? First, a person is a *who,* not a *what.* A person is more than skills or roles. He or she possesses certain capacities (rational thinking and so forth), and these capacities constitute the features held in common by all members who are persons. We all share personhood. The one who hurt you is the same kind of being as you are.[4]

On the basis of our theory of love in Chapter 1, all people are persons, in the deepest meaning of the term *person,* because all share in the capacity (with different levels of maturity) of

- needing love,
- giving love,
- understanding love, and
- understanding love's importance.

This theory of love applies to you and to those who have hurt you. The implication, then, is that the one who hurt you has the need for this kind of love, even if he or she does not know it. The one who hurt you has the need to give this kind of love, again even if he or she does not know it yet. The one who hurt you will only thrive if given a chance to give and receive this kind of love, even if for now the person laughs at such an idea. With this perspective in mind of the human person—including the person who was unfair to you— let us ask four questions about him or her as a way to aid your forgiving and work toward understanding.

First question: What was life like for the person who hurt you at the time of the actual injustice? Was he or she confused and frustrated, displacing anger from others onto you? I do not ask this so that you can excuse the behavior. What the person did was wrong, is wrong, and will always be wrong. Nothing changes here with regard to the injustice. Instead, I want you to begin to see the person's vulnerability, his or her weaknesses (not to condemn, but to understand). So, I ask again, in a little different way: Did someone fail to love this person in such a way that he or she was wounded? Can you see a wounded person who wounded you? I call this the *personal perspective.*

Second question, also part of the personal perspective: What was life like for this person when he or she was growing up? You may be able to answer this question when you focus on a person from your family of origin or a close friend or partner, but you may not be able to answer it with other people whom you forgive. If you do have this information and so can answer it, what is your description of this person's childhood? What is his or her story? Were there successes and loves for the person? Who failed to love this person in such a way that he or she brought the wounds to you? Were there wounds of injustice? What were they? Were some of these wounds so deep that he or she became angry in certain ways, or became tired, or even took on a worldview that was distorted and pessimistic? Did this person have the eight wounds from certain injustices—from someone's failure to give love to him or her? Did this lack of love or withdrawal of love toward him or her as a child lead to the same kind of eight wounds you have? If so, who is this person on whom you are concentrating? Is he or she an ogre or a person? What does it now mean to you when you say, "He (she) is actually a person"?

Third question: Can you see this person as a part of the global human community? If he or she is a person, does he or she deserve a little air to breathe in this world? Does he or she deserve a little land to stand on? Does he or she have the right to be treated as a person? If so, why? Why allow him or her to have the basics of life? Is it because all persons have inherent worth and so are worthy of respect? Must respect be earned? If you say "yes," why do you say this? Must you earn respect in society or is it something you naturally deserve because you are a person? If you naturally deserve it, then what about the one who hurt you? This is what I call the global perspective, to see the person as part of the global human village. Such membership does not have to be earned because if you have to fight your way into the global human village, what resources would you have left for a good life after such a continual fight? Can we admit that the one who hurt you deserves the same respect that you deserve?

Fourth question: When we take the cosmic perspective, who is he or she in the largest sense of your own vision of personhood? Can you see the person as special, unique, and irreplaceable as Sterling (next chapter) does with regard to his own father? Can you see him or her as made in the image and likeness of God, as Inez, a person of faith does (again, in the next chapter and as we read in Chapter 5)? Can you see with both Sterling and Inez that here before you is a person—a genuine person—who shares with you the capacity for rational thinking, the exercise of free will, and the need to give and receive love? If so, then who is this person who hurt you? Is this person someone who needs to give and receive love, not because of any actions on this person's part that make him or her deserving of this, but because of this person's built-in personhood? Why are you drawing the conclusions you do?

Please try to write your story of this person, putting together his or her childhood (if possible), his or her world at the time of this particular offense against you, and then the larger picture of this person in a global and cosmic perspective. Who is she (he)? You might want to focus on both your and her (his) inherent worth as you write the essay. By *inherent worth*, I mean the person's unearned, rightful significance or value as a human being. Please draw on your knowledge of personhood as you reflect on his or her inherent worth.

Homework for Guidepost 12. Each day until you turn to forgiving this person for another incident or you turn to forgiving another person, please reflect on these statements at least three times each: "(Person's name, if you know it) and I share a common humanity." "I forgive (person's name) because he or she is a person of worth who is deserving of my agape love, not because of what he (she) did, but in spite of this." "I see (person's name)'s emotional wounds. He (she) and I share this—we are both wounded by others." "I forgive (name)."

GUIDEPOST 13: WORK TOWARD COMPASSION. To begin this guidepost, please first rate your current level of compassion toward the person on our 0-to-10 scale, with a 0 being *absolutely no compassionate feelings*, a 5 being *a moderate level of compassion*, and a 10 being *exceptionally strong compassionate feelings*. Now, after that rating, please take a moment to focus on your own heart as I repeat some questions about the person. This is not a thinking exercise but instead is a feeling exercise, so please concentrate on your feelings as you consider these questions:

- What wounds did he (she) bring into the specific interaction with you? Can you see his (her) wounds and how those were transferred to you? Can you see the love that was withdrawn from him (her)?
- How was he (she) wounded as a child? Did he (she) deserve those wounds? How did those wounds affect him (her)? How

did those wounds lead to a pattern of behavior as an adolescent, as an adult? Can you see his (her) struggle with those wounds? Can you see the struggle because love might have been withdrawn from him (her)?

- Who is he (she) from a cosmic perspective? Can you see that he (she) is actually irreplaceable in this world, even with the wounds he (she) carries? Can you see his (her) specialness despite the wounds that he (she) carries? Can you see the potential for this person who is wounded? Can you see the love struggling to build up in his (her) heart, even if he (she) is unaware of this?

When you concentrate on the region around your heart, do you sense any little beginnings of warmth toward this person, not because of what he or she did, but in spite of this? Any little glimmer of warmth or well-being is the beginning of forgiveness. It is actually the beginning of love, if you allow this to be nurtured in you and to grow, even if very slowly. The characteristics of this warmth will have some of the features of love that we discussed in Chapter 1: happiness (even if just a little bit), connection (in a sense of your shared humanity at least), fulfillment (again, even if just a glimmer at first), completion and timelessness (I recommend that you review these concepts again in Chapter 1), giving yourself away, knowledge of the other, and perhaps the vague beginnings of contentment (but that will come slowly and with practice). Please do not expect too much with these characteristics at first because the growth in virtues is by degrees and by effort and practice. At the same time, please do not expect too little because the virtues, even the heroic ones such as love in the face of injustice, can be won to a greater extent than you might currently think possible. The virtues have a way of surprising us.

Homework for Guidepost 13. Each day until you turn to forgiving this person for another incident or you turn to forgiving another person, please reflect on these statements at least three times each as you concentrate on the area of your heart: "(Name) has been emotionally wounded, and I too have been emotionally wounded." "(Name) has had love withdrawn from him." "I have compassion toward (name)." "I do not condone or excuse what (name) has done. He (she) is more than what he (she) did to me."

GUIDEPOST 14: ACCEPTING THE PAIN. As you may recall from Chapter 5, Inez was afraid of this guidepost because she thought Sophia was asking her to take on even more pain than she already had. And what she had already was a bucket full of pain. As you may recall, Sophia clarified that this exercise does not add pain but asked Inez to work with the pain already inflicted on her. Before we begin, as we have done with the other guideposts, please rate on a 0-to-10 scale your sense of bearing right now the pain that this person caused you. Insight into what I mean can be gained by examining Inez's and Sophia's exchange in Chapter 5 (pp. 71–73). Let a 0 represent your judgment that *you are not bearing the pain well at all,* a 5 mean that *you are bearing the pain to a moderate degree,* and a 10 mean that *you are bearing the pain almost completely* (making room for human imperfection).

It is important for you to consider bearing the pain of others' wounding you because you, as a wounded person who might not bear the pain, run the risk of wounding others. If you can stand up under the weight of the pain, under the weight of the love withdrawn from you, you are giving a great gift to the world. If you think about it, you are taking the bold step of stopping this particular wound toward you from multiplying into many more wounds. You are stopping a cycle of wounding. This, to me, is a life well lived.

As a way to begin getting some insight into this guidepost, I ask you to take some time to examine the life of at least one of your heroes. Who is someone that you greatly admire because of how that person has lived (or is living)?[5] Some high-profile heroes include

Gandhi, Mother Teresa, and Martin Luther King Jr. As is well documented, Gandhi endured beatings for his stance of peace and won freedom for his countrymen of India. Without his bearing the pain, the history of India could be very different. King, in his book *Strength to Love,* bore the pain of rejection, hatred, and fire bombings of his house as he called on people to love one another through forgiveness. His bearing of the pain of racism helped the United States as a community to see a better way. Perhaps lesser known heroes include Amy Biehl, a young peace activist who gave her life in South Africa as she helped bear the pains of apartheid, and Anne Frank, who as a young girl endured being forced into hiding with her entire family because of threats against the Jewish people and was still able to maintain a worldview that acknowledged the good in people. Immaculee Iliba-giza survived ethnic slaughter in Rwanda by hiding with other women in a small room for 3 months. She emerged with a call for people to forgive.[6] Each of these people had love within them; each one deserved to be given love, but that love was withdrawn by some, creating great pain. Yet, out of that withdrawal of love from them, and out of the pain that resulted, came great good.

As you choose a hero from whom to learn, ask yourself this: What injustices did he or she have to endure? Why did this person endure the suffering? What was it inside the person that led to such strength to bear great pain? What supports did this person have to aid in the bearing of the pain? For whom did the person bear the pain—for himself or for others?

Now to the questions for you:

- What can you learn from this person's life to help you bear up under the pain you are now suffering and enduring?
- What strengths do you have inside of you to help you bear the pain?

- As you bear the pain, who will benefit as you endure?
- How will these people benefit?
- Is bearing the pain like this a sign of weakness or great strength?
- As you learn to bear up under the pain of injustice and love withdrawn from you, do you become stronger or weaker?
- As you bear the pain, does your vision of what forgiveness is become clearer or fuzzier?
- What is forgiveness, as you stand under the weight of the pain given to you by the one who was unfair? How has your view of forgiveness deepened?
- Can you become a conduit for good as you bear the pain of this injustice?[7]

Homework for Guidepost 14. Each day until you turn to forgiving this person for another incident or you turn to forgiving another person, please reflect on these statements at least three times each: "I am willing to bear the pain of my wounds so that I do not pass them to others." "I am strong as I bear my wounds and do not pass them to others." "As I bear the pain of my wounds, and do not pass them to (name), I am giving a gift of mercy to him (her)."

GUIDEPOST 15: GIVING A GIFT TO THE ONE WHO WOUNDED YOU. This is one of the paradoxes of forgiveness, as is bearing the pain. Who would ever think of offering a gift to the one who was unfair and who wounded? This is where we can get confused if we are not careful. By way of review, forgiveness as a virtue comes out of love, then mercy as one virtuous expression of love, not justice. We are quicker, I think, to examine the issue of justice—not mercy—when we are wounded. To suggest giving a gift, then, seems to clash with justice, almost pushing justice aside, and that seems both dangerous and highly inappropriate to most of us. Of course, it would be inappropriate and perhaps dangerous, depending on the circumstance, if justice were ignored in the face of mercy. Yet, and again this is by way of review, when we practice any virtue, we should not do so in isolation. Please recall the distortions that befall the virtue of courage when we do not approach it with temperance and wisdom. A person might jump into an ice-filled lake to save a dog even when that person cannot swim. The courage isolated by itself distorts what courage is and could lead to the rescuer's death.

It is no different with love, and mercy as part of love, and forgiveness as part of mercy. You do not throw away your quest for justice, and you are temperate and wise in what gift you select. With these points in mind, how willing are you to give a gift to the person who hurt you? Please rate that willingness on our 0-to-10 scale, with a 0 meaning that *you refuse absolutely to give a gift,* a 5 meaning that *you are moderately willing to give a gift,* and a 10 meaning that *you are eager to give a gift for the other person's sake.*

Presuming that you are willing to take a step, even a small step toward giving a gift to the person, what will that gift be? For example, for some of you, the gift may be a smile toward the one who hurt you—just a smile—but if you have not given one to this particular person in years, this is big. For others, the gift might be a phone call or a visit. If the person is deceased, it might be a kind word to others about him or her. If you are a person of faith, you might pray for the person. The gift will not always look the same for you as you proceed. The gift surely will look different across different people and their particular circumstance of injustice.

Here is an important question for you: For what reason are you giving the gift—for you to make yourself feel better or for the good of the other person? When you give a gift to a child, it may make you feel great, but isn't the gift actually for the child, for his or her benefit? What if the person rejects your gift? You might prepare yourself for this outcome, just in case. If the person to whom you are giving a gift is still very wounded inside, he or she might react with indifference or even anger toward your overture of kindness. Please do not let this discourage you from giving the gift, and please do not let it make you fearful of giving gifts to others in the future. A gift genuinely given with the best of intentions is a very good thing to do. It is even heroic if you think that the other person may withdraw love even more from you because of this merciful act. You might have to bear the pain of giving the gift.

SUMMING UP THE WORK PHASE. You have endured much from the pains of love withdrawn from you. You have now endured much as you have done the work of forgiveness. I have used the words *hero* and *heroic* throughout the discussion of this phase because I am speaking the truth to you. What you have endured is painful, and when you say "yes" to forgiveness—which means saying "yes" to taking a courageous look at the person causing the pain, and "yes" to bearing up under the pain, and "yes" to giving a gift to that person— you are engaging in the practice of heroic virtue.

Please add now to your Unfolding Love Story by continuing to write. What have you learned about forgiveness from doing the work of forgiving? What have you learned about yourself as you have done this work? Who are you as a person? We have spent much time asking about the personhood of the one who hurt you. Let's turn that around by asking: Who are you? Who are you becoming?

Now that you have finished this reflection, I would like to speak for a moment from personal experience in the hope of helping you as you walk this path of forgiveness. I have found that forgiveness is a powerful way of uniting. Forgiveness in essence unites all that is good within you—it makes you whole. Forgiveness unites people, even those estranged for years. Have you noticed that some people in this world seem to want to divide? They may not be doing this consciously and deliberately, but their worldview and their very identity is division. As you practice the uniting virtue of forgiveness, you are likely to encounter opposition—strong, angry opposition. Sometimes this opposition to forgiveness can be intense and surprising because it comes unexpectedly. I am writing this so that you will not be caught off guard if and when this happens, even if it happens unexpectedly. Expect opposition to come unexpectedly! I say all of this so that you can persevere in your work of forgiveness when some around you criticize you or try to throw you off your game. Don't let it happen. The world is filled with too much division, and if you give in to the wounded by rejecting a path to wholeness, then you are not contributing a solution to the major problem of the world, which is division because of a failure to love. Be a hero.

The Discovery Phase

The central point of the Discovery Phase of forgiveness is to learn—about forgiveness, about yourself, about who you are as a person, about your purpose in life, and about other people. The central point is to deepen your story of who you are, about how the world works, and about who others are.

GUIDEPOST 16: FINDING MEANING IN WHAT YOU HAVE SUFFERED. Is suffering a meaningless activity, something to be endured with no apparent good to it, or is suffering a challenge from which to learn and grow? How would you rate your answer to this question on our 0-to-10 scale with a 0 meaning that *there is absolutely no meaning to suffering,* a 5 meaning that *there is some good meaning to derive from suffering,* and a 10 representing your view that *suffering offers a great challenge to grow in love toward others who are suffering.*

Your answer to this question is part of your worldview, your story about how the world works. The answer that there is no meaning to suffering might be part of a pessimistic view of the world.

Such a pessimistic view needs to be taken seriously because the answer could affect your health. Consider, as one example, the clinical observations of the psychiatrist Victor Frankl, whom you met in Chapter 6. As you may recall, he suffered gravely while in a concentration camp during World War II. After his ordeal, he helped other concentration camp survivors to heal from the traumatic experience. He made this sobering observation: Only those who found meaning in what they suffered survived. This experience of Dr. Frankl's is important for us because we might be able to avoid even more suffering by wrestling with suffering's meaning and making the answer part of our Unfolding Love Story.

Let us consider one example of adding meaning to your life because of what you suffered. Did you know that you may be (or in the future may become) someone's hero as they watch you go through this process? Did you ever think about that? Your forgiving presence in the world may aid someone at some time to confront their own wounds and to heal. If you think about it, Gandhi did not become the hero of others by hiding in a dark room when the authorities tried to silence him. Martin Luther King Jr. became a hero to many because he stood up with justice and said, "No!" and he stood up with mercy when he asked people to forgive one another. Amy Biehl was unknown to many, but internet Web sites have made her actions of love known. Her suffering was not in vain. Anne Frank was the same way.

You need not win a Nobel Peace Prize or be recognized widely by others to be a hero. If even one child or one adult watches as you bear up under the pain of injustice and suffer well, they may learn to do the same. And you may never even speak with them or meet them. Your actions alone may be enough to change someone else's life. Have you ever thought about that before? Would your suffering be worthwhile if it helped to transform even one person in this world? That is quite a meaning to your suffering and to your life.

You can be a conduit of good for others. This is a gift to them. Please continue to write your Unfolding Love Story. Who are you? What good has come from your suffering or what good will come from it? The answer could help you to thrive as a person as you live The Forgiving Life.

GUIDEPOST 17: DISCOVER YOUR NEED FOR FORGIVENESS. As we walk the path of forgiveness, we realize we are not on a one-way street, always pointing to our wounds and others' offenses. We eventually come to realize that we, too, have contributed wounds to the world by withdrawing love from others. Ultimately, we are not victims and we are not offenders. We are persons who are wounded and who wound. Even more than that, we are persons who need to receive and to give love. Just as we can be empowered by forgiving, and thus not let the injustices of the past define us, so too can we take steps not to let our wounding of others define us or them. We can learn to seek and receive forgiveness from others, which is one more step in completing the Triangle of Forgiveness (first introduced in Chapter 6). This consists, as we have seen, of forgiving, seeking and receiving forgiveness, and reconciling. We will have much more to say about this triangle in Chapter 14.

GUIDEPOST 18: DISCOVER THAT YOU ARE NOT ALONE. Forgiveness does not occur in isolation. As we have seen, we are persons because of certain individual characteristics such as the capacity to think rationally, make free choices, and practice agape love. At the same time, we are persons because we share our humanity with others, our connections. We do not love in isolation. For the virtue of love to be complete, someone needs to receive that love and reciprocate with love. For us to forgive deeply and consistently, we need others to teach, guide, encourage, challenge, and correct us. For the Triangle of Forgiveness to be complete, someone needs to say "yes" to forgiving and another has to say "yes" to receiving it. Our personhood and our forgiveness are brought out in community.

You are not alone in your forgiveness. You are not alone in the experience of your pain. As we discussed in Chapter 4, when we examined the philosophical idea that we call *qualia,* no one can know exactly what your inner pain feels like, but people can come close to that as you draw close to them and use language, facial expressions, and the expression of emotion to let them know of your pain. Even this very private pain can be shared with others. Because our personhood is, shall we say, caught up in the personhood of others, I urge you to connect in a loving way with at least one other person as you forgive. The shared experience will deepen and enrich the journey.

GUIDEPOST 19: DISCOVER THE PURPOSE OF YOUR LIFE. When Dr. Freedman and I did our study of forgiveness with incest survivors,[8] we were surprised that many of the participants in the study spontaneously stated that they wished to find a way to help other incest survivors to forgive. We were witnessing a shift in the purpose of their lives. They wanted to give something back to forgiveness and to those who suffered as they did. They found a new purpose to their lives. They found a new direction in their lives.

This is not unusual for those who grow in the virtues, whether the virtue is justice, patience, courage, love, or forgiveness. Virtues point toward end points, reasons for exercising the virtues. The more we understand and practice forgiveness, the clearer the end point to this virtue is. One endpoint is the Triangle of Forgiveness or the completion of any one forgiving experience to include the other's receptivity to your overture of forgiving, along with full reconciliation. Another purpose points beyond the specific experience to your life in general. Who are you becoming as a result of forgiving? Who are you becoming as a result of living The Forgiving Life? If our

Theory of Forgiveness is correct, then an important end to which you should be pointing is love. Are you becoming a more loving person, thus exercising more consistently and deeply the truth of who you are? Are you becoming someone who is helping others receive and give love more readily? How might you go about this?

GUIDEPOST 20: DISCOVER THE FREEDOM OF FORGIVENESS. Freedom is usually won after a struggle. As you have seen in this chapter, if you have worked on the issues of each guidepost, forgiveness surely is a struggle because its business is to enter the world of wounds with a stance of mercy for the purpose of healing. As a paradox, forgiveness can heal you emotionally as you look toward the injuring one and respond with mercy. My colleagues and I have seen people's anger, anxiety, and depression diminish or even cease after the struggle to forgive. Forgiveness can heal relationships as people become more open to seeking forgiveness and changing undesirable behavior. Of course, such freedom usually is achieved slowly, and so patience is necessary. That is why I urge you to return to this chapter again and again with different people in mind. Freedom from emotional turmoil may be one of your victories, along with renewed relationships if others are willing to walk the forgiveness path with you.

REMINDER OF THE THERAPEUTIC BENEFITS

Please take a moment to recall the research findings in Chapter 2 (Table 2.1). The people who took part in the various forgiveness therapy programs benefited significantly in their emotional health. We have found that those who followed the same forgiveness path that you just did decreased in such areas as anxiety, depression, and anger. Increases in hope for the future and self-esteem were noted in some of the studies. The improvements, for the most part, continued months after the forgiveness interventions ended. I point this out to encourage you. Doing the important work of forgiving can be very rewarding.

SUMMARY OF YOUR PROGRESS

Congratulations. You've worked through the process of forgiving an important person in your life. You will be returning many times to this chapter, if you so choose, as you continue to forgive everyone in your life who has ever wounded you to such an extent that you need to do the serious work of forgiveness. (Of course, you can and should forgive people for the small injustices of life, and you will not need this chapter to do so. My point here is that you may need my help for the deep wounds.)

Before progressing to the next person on your list (or the same person with a different incident of injustice), let us turn to Chapter 11 to see how you are doing in each of the forgiveness guideposts.

CHAPTER 11

HOW DID YOU DO IN FORGIVING?

You now know the process of forgiveness because you have walked the path. You know the pain of healing, and I hope you are beginning to know the joy of recovery. How did you do this time when you forgave? I ask you now to return to the Personal Forgiveness Scale from Chapter 9 and fill out the scale toward this particular person and the particular event you had in mind as you worked on forgiveness. The point is to help you answer the question "How do I know that I have forgiven?" Please take your time and return to this chapter when you are finished.

Now, please compare your scores from the first time you filled out the scale with your scores this time. Did you change? Was it in a positive direction (more forgiving) or downward to less forgiving? Take heart if you went down; sometimes people get angry when they go through the process for the first time with a particular person because the wounds surface to a greater degree. This can be a positive development because you are less psychologically defensive than before, so going through the process again with this same person may lead to a healthy improvement for you.

If you changed in a positive direction, you should realize that some people still have a profile that suggests much room for forgiveness, but upward change of even 20 points is a good sign of improved forgiveness, and this in some cases can be enough for them to start experiencing some emotional freedom. If you have changed in a positive direction in forgiving and if you are experiencing this kind of emotional freedom, it is not absolutely necessary to turn back to Chapter 10 and begin again with this person and this particular injustice.

If, on the other hand, you have changed little on your Personal Forgiveness Scale score from before to now, and if that score reflected unforgiveness, then I recommend that you try to deepen your forgiveness by revisiting certain sections of Chapter 10.[1]

You might decide either to revisit the same person in Chapter 10 or to start forgiving someone else. To help you in either case, I would like you to rate your success on each guidepost with regard to the person you just forgave. I present you with a description of each guidepost in The Forgiveness Guidepost Form in Appendix D. Please rate your success in dealing with that guidepost on our now-familiar 0-to-10 scale. The point is to have you reflect on how successfully you have mastered that guidepost, with the idea that you may revisit certain guideposts if you have not advanced as thoroughly as you would have liked with them the first time around.

As I present the guidepost and a brief description of it, please make a rating of 0 if you have not even begun to make any progress at all. A 5 means that you have made some progress but have a sense that you are only about halfway toward the goal of success with it. A 10 means that you consider yourself thoroughly successful in mastering that guidepost with this particular person who hurt you in a particular way. Although some of the questions will be similar to those in Chapter 10, you will see that others are quite different. For example, in Chapter 10, when we were uncovering your shame, a 10 represented lots of shame because we needed to see the extent of your wounds. Here in Chapter 11, when I present the 0-to-10 scale on the shame question, I am now interested in how much improvement you have made (in facing and then reducing your shame). Therefore, a 10 now represents the absence of shame in you.

If you are using the online scale (http://www.mindgarden.com/forgiveness) you will get a profile of your average ratings across all people on this Forgiveness Guidepost Form. Otherwise, please make sufficient copies of the form (Appendix D) for your own personal use and calculate the average ratings on your own.

ABOUT THE GUIDEPOSTS

As you return to the guideposts in Chapter 10, either to do further work with this same person and same injustice in mind (or a different injustice from him or her) or to start with another person, please be aware of those guideposts that are particularly difficult for you. As you consult your ratings on the 0-to-10 scale for the guideposts, which ones are currently low, in the 0-to-4 range? As you accumulate more information about how you forgive (across a number of different people you have forgiven), you will see that certain of the forgiveness guideposts pose particular challenges for you (i.e., you score low on these particular ones on the average regardless of whom you forgive). These are the guideposts on which to now focus more of your time and energy. These are your weak areas, and we all have them. Yours will differ from those of other people. At the same time, look at the guideposts on which you scored high consistently across a number of different people whom you are forgiving. These are indications of your forgiveness strengths. Focus on these to give you confidence and renewed energy as you forgive.

WHOM TO FORGIVE NOW?

The answer to this question depends on the progress you are making in this book. Please remember our general approach:

- First forgive the person from your family-of-origin member list toward whom you have the most amount of forgiveness (based on your filling out the Forgiveness Landscape Rating Scale and the Personal Forgiveness Scale). If you scored between 87 and 108 on the Personal Forgiveness Scale, you need not do the work of forgiveness in Chapter 10 because you already have much forgiveness toward him or her. Forgive the person one incident at a time.
- When you are ready, and after reading Chapter 12, then progress to the next person on your family-of-origin member list toward whom you now have the most amount of forgiveness. Forgive this person one incident at a time.
- Continue to work on the material from Chapter 10 for all of the people listed in your Forgiveness Landscape in your family of origin until you reach the person toward whom you originally had the least amount of forgiveness.
- Then turn to previous partner relationship(s) (only if this social group is appropriate for you). Assess your level of forgiveness and then order the people and incidences from most forgiving to least forgiving. Forgive each person here on your Forgiveness Landscape list (toward whom you have some forgiveness to do on the basis of your scores from the Personal Forgiveness Scale).
- Turn next to the material on you current family (which will be in Chapter 13) and follow the pattern.
- Keep this pattern going for "school days," "work days," "worship community," and "social community" (which you will find in Chapter 15).

The point is to systematically work your way through the Forgiveness Landscape until each and every person who has ever wounded you is forgiven. Imagine the relief you will feel. It is waiting for you. The requirements from your end are your free will, your good will, and your strong will to say "yes" to The Forgiving Life.

If you are reading this chapter in the context of your family of origin: I recommend that you pause after you have forgiven one person from your family of origin and before you tackle the difficult task of forgiving the people high on your list (toward whom you are not very forgiving at present) and turn to Chapter 12, where you will watch as Inez and Sterling struggle to forgive a parent. Once you gain more insight into this kind of forgiveness, then turn again to Chapter 10 and continue to forgive all those whom you have on your list from the family of origin.

If you have completed this chapter in the context of your family of origin: After you have forgiven all people for all incidences within your family of origin, it is time to take the next step and turn to your previous family (if this applies to you). On the basis of the information in your Forgiveness Landscape Rating Scale and your scores on the Personal Forgiveness Scale, please order the people (and their injustices against you) from the most amount of forgiveness to the least amount of forgiveness that you have toward them. If you are in the top quartile (by scoring between 87 and 108), your high score means you need not work on forgiveness. Please go to Chapter 10 and start forgiving the person on the top of the list (toward whom you are most forgiving) and work down that list until you have forgiven the person toward whom you are least forgiving. Each time you forgive a person through the exercises of Chapter 10, turn to this chapter. Please remember that it takes time to forgive some people, even weeks or months. Keep this up until you have forgiven all.

If you have completed this chapter in the context of your family of origin and previous family or relationship: After you have forgiven all from your family of origin and your previous family or relationship, it is time to turn to the important issue of forgiving within your current family. Please turn to Chapter 13 for these potentially life-changing forgiveness exercises.

If you are reading this chapter in the context of your partner in Chapter 13: After forgiving your partner for the first incident, and once you have had the chance to work through the material in Chapter 10 and in this chapter, please proceed or return to Chapter 13 and to the section entitled, Include Your Partner Now. If you are reading this chapter in the context of the section entitled Back to the Basics—Your Partner and You (Chapter 13), and if you have now forgiven your partner for each incident in the Forgiveness Landscape Rating Scale, then it is time to pause for a while. Please reflect on this reality: You have forgiven your partner for every wound. You have a clean slate. How amazing is that? Of course, you both will have wounds in the future because human relationships are imperfect, but for now rest in the knowledge that you have given your partner the gift of a clean forgiveness slate. When you are ready, please return once again to Chapter 13, this time to the section entitled The Dialogue Between Your Partner and You.

If you are reading this chapter in the context of other current family members from Chapter 13: After forgiving all current family members, please return to Chapter 13 and to the section entitled Your Unfolding Love Story.

If you are reading this chapter in the context of various social groups from Chapter 15: The task of Chapter 15 is to forgive widely in various social circles so that you can truly lead The Forgiving Life. Please take each social group one at a time as you forgive the people within that group. Consult your Forgiveness Landscape list (Chapter 8), then proceed to assess your level of forgiveness for each person and each incident. Order the people (and their injustices against you) from the greatest amount of forgiveness to the least amount of forgiveness. As a reminder, if you are in the top quartile (by scoring between 87 and 108), you do not need to work on forgiveness because of your high score. Start forgiving the person on the top of the list (most forgiving) and work down that list until you have forgiven the person toward whom you are least forgiving. Each time you forgive a person through the exercises of Chapter 10, turn to this chapter.

After finishing forgiving from your school days: When you have forgiven all in your school days, please be sure to read the section in Chapter 15 entitled After You Have Forgiven. Then turn to the section entitled Your Children's School Days. Please remember that it takes time to forgive some people. Keep this up until you have forgiven all in this group.

After finishing forgiving from your children's school days: Take time to refresh, and when you are ready please turn again to Chapter 15 and read the section on your Work Days.

After finishing forgiving from your work days: It is now time to turn to Chapter 15 and the section Once You Have Forgiven in the Workplace.

When you have completed this chapter in the context of the various social groups from Chapter 15: If you are finished in Chapter 15 with forgiving all of those on your Forgiveness Landscape list, please go to Chapter 16.

CHAPTER 12

FORGIVING YOUR PARENTS

In this chapter, both Inez and Sterling are part of the dialogue. You will see the process of Inez starting to forgive her mother and father. She will be considering her mother's authoritarian approach to parenting and her parents' distancing themselves from her. She was deprived of love that she deserved. For her, this is a trauma, given that we all need love, especially from those who are supposed to be closest to us.

Sterling will begin the process of forgiveness by uncovering his disappointment with and anger toward his father for excessive anxiety, which he inadvertently pushed onto Sterling while he was growing up. After a series of conversations, Inez and Sophia decided to ask Sterling if he would be willing to do this work—healing emotional wounds from parents—along with Inez. This was recommended for three reasons. First, if Inez and Sterling watch each other struggle with wounds from their pasts, they may gain insight into their own relationship. Second, as they see the patterns that they each brought into the marriage, they may be able to aid each other's healing through dialogue and mutual support. Third, seeing each other's emotional wounds may soften their hearts toward each other, which might help them to forgive and reconcile on a deep level.

Because of the importance of this chapter for your growth as a forgiver, I will include commentary on the dialogue throughout. My intent in doing this is to point out subtleties that you might miss if you are new to practicing the virtue of forgiveness. I will try to highlight central features of the forgiveness process as they unfold in the dialogue.

> *Sophia:* We all bring excess baggage into marriages and other important relationships. We have all been wounded, and then we tend to wound others. Can you begin to see each other's wounds from the past and ask: What have I brought into the marriage that wounds my spouse? What has my spouse brought into the marriage that wounds me? How does this sound to you?
>
> *Inez:* Painful.
>
> *Sophia:* The goal, as you both know, is to see each other as vulnerable people in need of growth and support. This should be a beginning foundation for your forgiving each other. As you forgive, you may want to ask for forgiveness for the wounds that you inflicted. The goal of this giving and receiving forgiveness is reconciliation, in a deep, more trusting and loving way. I hope this will help each of you keep forgiveness close within your relationship so that you are ready to forgive, receive forgiveness, and reconcile as you proceed through life together.

> [*Inez and Sterling look at each other but say nothing.*]

> *Sophia:* Shall we start with you, Inez? Are you ready to explore your relationship with your mom and dad when you were young?

Inez: OK. I'll give it a try.

Sophia: Please tell us the story from your childhood. May we start with the loving moments, the memories that fill you with a sense of love? I want you to reconnect with that love first so that you can bring it with you as we discuss your wounds.

INEZ'S STORY OF HER CHILDHOOD

Inez: I can still remember my earliest birthday party, when I was in kindergarten. My mom and dad invited so many kids, and I didn't even know them all. Some were the kids of my parents' friends. I thought that was kind of weird, to invite kids to my party who I didn't even know, but it was because they were trying so hard. Really, it was more sweet than weird. Anyway, I had my eye on this tricycle for the longest time, and at my birthday party, my mom had all the kids stand in a circle around what was to be my present, and when they moved aside, slowly, one by one, there was my beautiful tricycle. Just for me. And it was not inexpensive. My dad had to sacrifice for me to give me that present. My mom was so happy for me. I can still see her with her hands folded up close to her chin, and she had the widest grin. Her eyes used to dance when she was happy. Her eyes danced that day and mine did too, I'm sure.

Sophia: That is a great memory—of the love of your parents and your mom's dancing eyes.

Inez: I keep that memory close to my heart.

Sophia: Let's continue to keep it close to your heart as we slowly explore the wounds. Are you ready for that?

Inez: Well, as you know, we were not rich, with my dad doing the best he could with his machine repair shop in Texas. He could not afford much help, and so he worked very long hours. When he came home sometimes I was already in bed for the night. I know he was tired because he was so quiet and his shoulders, I remember, were kind of round, as if they were so heavy they might roll right out in front of him and tumble to the ground if they were not attached to his back. I used to imagine that as a kid, imagining his shoulders tumbling onto the ground. To me now, it is a sign of his self-giving to us. It is a sign of his love.

Sophia: Did you resent his not being home much?

Inez: No, not so much because I knew he was helping us the best way that he could. I do resent his being too tired for me when he was home. I never really had a connection with him. My childhood is now long gone, and we can't go back and recapture that. I grieve for the loss, the loss of connection with my own father.

Sophia: You can forgive that.

Inez: But what am I supposed to do—make a list of the 2,137 times he could have connected with me but did not? And forgive each one?

Sophia: That would be impractical. Why don't you consider forgiving him for that pattern of being so tired that he ignored you?

Inez: I can do that, but should I? Did he do this deliberately?

Sophia: Probably not, but not all injustices are what people actively do in an intentional way, are they? Aren't some injustices borne out of inaction? If I am late to a meeting and fail to help a child who falls on the sidewalk and hurts his ankle as I hurry by, I am being unjust, aren't I? Your father's inactions hurt you.

Inez: Yes, they did. They were not occasional. They did form what you are calling a pattern, repeated over and over again.

Sophia: Then you can forgive him for that.

Inez: I think I have even more resentment toward my mom. She was hard on us, and when she was not being hard on us she ignored us. I think that she really resented being alone so much. It sapped her strength.

Sophia: Why do you think so?

Inez: Because of the way she took it out on all of us kids and then shrank away from us. I didn't have a real connection with either one of my parents, and now that time of my life is gone. It hurts.

Sophia: We have talked about the psychological defense of displacement, in which a person lashes out at someone who did not even hurt them. They take their pain and throw it like a ball onto others. Did your mom do this?

Inez: Well, let's see, she had a stranglehold on me in terms of time, for example. I could not be a minute late to breakfast or she would yell at me.

Sophia: Did she yell or was she just a bit demanding?

Sophia is making sure that Inez herself is not displacing or projecting before they continue.

Inez: Well, she would yell to me upstairs, and the longer I took the louder she got. When I got downstairs, she would let out her displeasure as she served breakfast, all the time running around the kitchen not even looking at me. She was so . . . so preoccupied much of the

time. She seemed to be kind of dreamy to me, kind of
in a fog. At least that's the way I saw it as a kid.

Sophia: And how do you see it now?

Inez: I see it pretty much the same way, except that now
I see the "why" of it. I see her anger at my dad spilling
over to me. I see her anger at my dad spilling over into
her fatigue, which spilled over to her ignoring me
most of the time, which led to my feeling unsafe.

Sophia: You lacked trust.

Inez: I never quite thought about it that way before, but
yes, one legacy my mom gave me is a lack of trust. It
has hurt me. Yes, Enrico was mean to me, but my lack
of trust was there when we married. I inherited that
from my mom.

Sophia: This is a very courageous insight. You are saying
that your wounds have wounded others. Many people would not have the courage to see this.

Inez: Thanks. Now I see that my mom never really dealt
with the anger of running the household when she
wanted my dad to be there with us.

Inez's mom was angry, one of her wounds from the marriage.
She then became very fatigued and passed all of that anger and
fatigue to Inez in the form of ignoring her. Inez has passed on the
consequence of this—which in her case comes out as mistrust—to
Enrico and now to Sterling. Do you see how wounds can pass from
generation to generation?

Sophia: What other examples do you have of your mom's
anger?

Inez: She used to get on my dad sometimes when he got
home. She wanted him to talk, and he did not have the

energy. She would be very stern with him, almost scolding him. She had a view of how a family should run, and heaven help the one who did not run it her way.

Sophia: Did your mom and dad fight a lot?

Inez: Yeah, not constantly, but I'd say at least once every 2 weeks.

Sterling: [jumping in] That sounds like "constantly" to me.

Inez: I think the marriage was a challenge, with my dad's fatigue and my mom's insistence, anger, and then her fatigue.

Sophia: What about toward you? How often did your mom demonstrate anger toward you and the other children?

Inez: A lot. If I was tired and just daydreamed when I was supposed to be doing my homework, she really let me have it, saying I would not amount to much in this world and how I am lazy and stuff like that. It was OK for her to be dreamy, but not for me.

Sophia: That had to hurt your self-image, being told you were lazy.

Sophia is exploring two aspects of the Uncovering Phase of the forgiveness process here: Guidepost 6, in which Inez feels inferior to her mom, and Guidepost 8, in which Inez's worldview is becoming increasingly pessimistic.

Inez: That's why I'm an overachiever today, at least in part. I am still trying to show my mom that I have what it takes.

Note Inez's low self-esteem, for which she tries to compensate by overwork.

> *Inez:* Sometimes, she would just let loose on McCade, Katina, and me. If the living room was a little messy with papers and glasses, she would really yell at us. Boy, would we jump and get it cleaned up when she did that. We just wanted her to stop. The place was not all that bad most of the time. She was displacing her anger onto us.
>
> *Sophia:* If you had to pick out the one injustice toward you from your mom, the big injustice that wounded you above all else, what would that be?
>
> *Inez:* [*pausing and thinking*] Definitely it was the pattern of ignoring more than the thunder. It made me feel ashamed, not worthy of much . . .

Inez is struggling with the wound of Guidepost 3, shame, of the Uncovering Phase.

> *Inez:* . . . and so burning with anger.

Inez is also struggling with Guidepost 2, deep anger or resentment, of the same phase.

> *Inez:* I definitely was angry and would sometimes yell back at her.

Inez may be struggling with guilt here.

> *Sophia:* It seems clear that you will be forgiving your mom for certain injustices, but you will be forgiving her mostly for a pattern that led to your own anger, your own sense of unworthiness, and your own lack of trust toward others.

Inez: All of that did cut into my self-esteem. I feel that others don't like me, that I am not good enough. I still even have nightmares about my mom.

This is Guidepost 5 of the Uncovering Phase.

Inez: In my dream, I see her with a mouth that is 10 times bigger than normal, and the veins in her neck are popping out as she yells at me. I wake up with my heart pounding. I then continue with this uneasy feeling the next day, occasionally thinking about the dream and about my mom when I was a child. It makes me feel small for most of the day.

Sophia: Do you feel that your very worth is threatened when people yell at you?

Inherent worth is a vital part of forgiveness as we try to see such worth in the one who hurt us and in ourselves. Wounded people often do not see their own worth.

Inez: I'll have to think about that one, but, yes, it seems reasonable to say that.

INTERLUDE

If we look at Inez's situation from the point of view of our forgiveness model, we see the following wounds on which she will need some work:

- a pattern of injustice from her mother in need of forgiving (ignoring and harsh parenting, which led to a definite lack of connection with her mom),
- anger toward her mother,

- shame in need of healing and guilt borne out of her shame and anger,
- thinking about the childhood incidents and having nightmares about them, and
- a negative worldview because she was not trusted and now she has struggles with trust.

Of the eight possible emotional wounds borne out of the injustice (not including the wound of the original injustice itself), she has four of them on which she needs to work.

STERLING DISCUSSES HIS CHILDHOOD

Sophia: Are you ready to tell us of your childhood, Sterling?

Sterling: I grew up in New Hampshire, the firstborn son of parents who immigrated to America from Poland.

Sophia: That must have been difficult for your parents, being new in a very different culture in America.

Sophia is focusing on the parents' wounds so that Sterling can begin to see those wounds.

Sterling: Yes, it was. There were a lot of adjustments they had to make.

Sophia: Can you recall a particular loving incident with your father? I'd like you to reconnect with his love before you enter the world of wounds.

Sterling: Yes, here is one of many examples. I was really interested in sports as a kid, basketball and baseball mostly. I remember my dad checking out books on these topics from our local library and reading them at night so that he could help me. I still remember when he taught me how to throw a curveball. It was pretty cute. He was showing me when I was only 6 years old. Kids should not throw the curve that early, but that warning probably was not in the books my dad read, or at least he missed that part. So, here he is bending over me, trying to get me to hold what for me was this huge ball in my small hand. He wanted me to hold the ball with only two fingers and my thumb, and I kept dropping the ball and he kept picking it up, ever the patient father with me—drop, pick up, drop, pick up. That was a sign of both genuine love and genuine futility all at the same time. It is a precious memory for me.

Sophia: It sounds like you had a happy childhood.

Sterling: Yes, I did.

Sophia: Even when we are surrounded by goodness and happiness, this can be blended with difficulty and wounds. Where were your areas of woundedness?

Sterling: I remember my father showing symptoms of anxiety, which was kind of like other family members in my dad's family of origin. I met some of them when I was a child. They seemed high strung.

Sophia: Could you describe what that means?

Sterling: For example, my dad could be intense, disciplining in a way that was too intense for the situation. If I was acting selfishly, my dad would get overly concerned and send me to my room for long periods of time. He did not yell as much as show high emotional intensity. Although I didn't like these periods of separation from the family while in my room, I did get a certain comfort from the isolation because I then was not directly confronted by my father's worry and intense emotions.

Inez: Do you know what I see? The television is your refuge from the anxieties of the world just as your bedroom was when you were a boy.

Sterling: I had not thought about that until just now. A refuge from anxiety? Perhaps it is.

Inez: And a way to try to refresh from all the fatigue.

Sophia: How do you think the intensity, as you call it, affected you and now affects you emotionally?

Sterling: In looking back on it, I think I had symptoms of stress and anxiety sort of like my dad. I was shy, and I had some ritualized behaviors in getting ready for school, suggesting some obsessive–compulsive symptoms. I had trouble concentrating on class work in elementary school. I averaged a grade of "C," and that did not reflect my true abilities.

Sophia: Is there one incident with your dad on which you'd like to focus as you practice forgiveness toward him?

Sterling: There was one in particular. My brother and I were just being kids, as we were laughing in the living room. I can't even remember what set us off on our laughing binge, but my dad somehow took offense at it. He grabbed me by my shirt and yanked me upwards. I thought I was going to hit the plaster on the ceiling he yanked me so hard, and he had me go to my room . . . for the billionth time. I did nothing wrong that day, I can tell you that.

Sophia: OK, that is a good one on which to work because it is painful and unfair. Is there anything else you would like to add before we start the work of forgiveness toward your dad?

Sterling: As a child, I was a good athlete, which helped me to make friends and to avoid being bullied for my shyness. My dad's reading and informal coaching helped me. While on sports teams in middle school, I was often times the best player but usually let others be the leader. I wish that my dad would have come to watch me play basketball and baseball more when I was in high school, but he was too tired a lot of the time. His intensity left him tired.

One of the father's wounds was diminished energy because of the anxiety that was passed on to him. This fatigue had an effect on Sterling in that he was deprived of his father's presence at his sporting events. Yet, he was not deprived of a meaningful connection with his father, as Inez was with both of her parents.

Sophia: So, his anxiety and resulting fatigue became a barrier between him and you.

Sterling: Yes, it did. I had not thought about it quite that way before, but yes it did, especially as I got older and he began to age.

Sterling: Are you resentful of your dad? I ask in order for us to see if you need to forgive him.

Sterling: Yes, I am resentful—that does not define our relationship, but, yes, it is there. The night of the "yanking" still bothers me. His anxiety and intensity rubbed off on me and I became shy. That was a struggle in childhood. I felt shame, like Inez did, too much of the time. I could not pinpoint the source of it, but I think I basically felt unworthy. After all, if a kid is sent to his room for the smallest thing, he is going to eventually ask, "Who am I and why am I such a pain for others?"

Here is the theme of inherent worth again. Both Inez and Sterling think that they do not have inherent worth. This is going to be a major issue in their forgiving and recovery from their wounds. It will be a major issue in their reconciling with each other.

Sophia: You felt devalued.

Sterling: Yes, and it came out in my schoolwork. I remember one time being distracted in class and the teacher called on me for something and I didn't even hear her. I wasn't being rude, I just didn't hear her. You'd think I swore at her or something, the way she took offense. She called my dad, and when I got home, he got intense and I had just about had it. So, I got intense and had a temper tantrum and here we were in our living room, both bent out of shape. We must have been one sorry sight. That one still hurts when I think about it. I have to forgive him and he probably has to forgive me.

Sophia: How would you say that all of this, your dad's anxiety and your absorbing some of that, impacted your life as an adult?

Sterling: I would have liked to pursue something other than teaching on the local level. For instance, I've always wanted to teach in another country, England or Ireland, but I did not have the energy. Fighting anxiety and stress takes work. And here is another complication for me: I think that my quiet personality led me to seek a teaching career. I wanted to help. I didn't realize when I was studying to be a teacher that being quiet with middle school students would create problems for me. I only found that out when I started teaching, and some of the kids started challenging.

Guidepost 7 of the Uncovering Phase, a significant change in one's life because of being wounded, is an issue for Sterling.

Sophia: It is not easy.
Sterling: No, it is not. I get tired.

This is Guidepost 4 of the Uncovering Phase, the wounds affecting one's health.

Sterling: I can't blame this on my dad and I never would, but he sure did not make it any easier on me with his anxiety, which I learned all too well. He is a good man, and he is also a very hurt man.
Sophia: Has any of this changed how you view the world?

This is Guidepost 8 of the Uncovering Phase.

Sterling: Yes, it has. The world is basically unfair, and we have to do our best to stay afloat even with all of this unfairness bumping up against us every day.
Inez: Sterling, I know I can help you with this. The world is not all gloomy and negative. I'm glad I am able to listen to you talk about your childhood. We can work together to see the world as it is, not how it is colored by our hurts.

INTERLUDE

If we look now at Sterling's situation from the point of view of our forgiveness model, we see the following wounds on which he will need some work:

- a series of injustices from his father in need of his forgiving;
- some anger toward his father;
- shame in need of healing;
- fatigue that gets in his way and in the way of his marital relationship at times as he isolates himself in front of the television;
- a permanent change in his life in that he wanted to pursue overseas teaching but could not bring himself to do it because of anxiety and fatigue; and
- a pessimistic worldview in which he sees the world as an unfair place, as he seems to be looking away from the evidence that there is much in life that also is fair and good.

Of the eight possible emotional wounds (again, not including the original injustices), he has five on which he needs to work.

EXCERPTS FROM THE DIALOGUE WITH INEZ TOWARD FORGIVING HER MOM

Both Inez and Sterling followed the series of questions in Chapter 10, and each struggled to forgive their parent. Let us pick up excerpts of the dialogue (from over five conversations) as Inez forgives. For the sake of simplicity, we will focus on Inez forgiving her mom (not her dad).

> *Sophia:* Inez, you have four significant wounds from your mom's original injustices of intense anger and ignoring you. They are your own anger, shame, nightmares, and a worldview that includes cynicism and mistrust.
>
> *Inez:* Yes, that just about sums it up for me. I have a question for you. Now that I see all of this, and I see my mom's wounds, am I supposed to say, "Oh, I see.

> She is wounded and so it is OK. It is all right that she did all of this"?
>
> *Sophia:* Did the injustices happen? Did they actually occur?
>
> *Inez:* Yes, the injustices did happen. She did yell and she did ignore me.
>
> *Sophia:* Will those injustices still be unjust when you think back on them 40 years from now?
>
> *Inez:* Yes.
>
> *Sophia:* As you are seeing, an injustice does not stop being unjust simply because you understand the person and the injustice and then forgive. What you want to do now is to change your reaction to the injustices. One way to do that is to forgive her, not by condoning her actions or finding an excuse, but by seeing her inherent worth as a person—not because of what she did to you when you were a child and an adolescent, but in spite of this. As you forgive, you reduce your resentment, which is a struggle, and then struggle to offer goodness to her because forgiveness is a virtue and virtues are centered on goodness.

Sophia is bringing Inez into the Decision Phase by reviewing what forgiveness is and is not and by gauging her readiness to forgive.

> *Inez:* I see all of this, and I'm ready to give it a try.
>
> *Sophia:* First question, then, for you: What was going on with your mom when she failed to connect with you? When she basically ignored you? What was in her circumstances and what was in her heart, do you think?
>
> *Inez:* As I see it now, my mom struggled with loneliness and little money as she basically raised the children by

herself. She kind of ran from it all, including the responsibility to simply be with me. The frustration got to her sometimes.

Sophia: What was the source of her frustration?

Inez: My dad's not being home. I think she feared stepping up and so she withdrew. Yet, even though she was disappointed with my dad not being home much, she did not file for divorce or medicate herself with drugs or alcohol. There is a lot that some people do, and my mom did not do any of this.

Sophia: What was life like for your mom when she was growing up? What do you recall?

Inez: I don't know too much because she did not talk often about it, but I do recall that my grandpa worked for the railroad. He was another one who worked his hands to the bone.

Sophia: How did your grandmother react to that?

Inez: I don't really know, but I think she was grateful. I do remember one time my mom said in anger to my dad, "You are just like my dad. You are never around."

Sophia: Perhaps your grandmother was a bit angry, given what your mom said in anger to your dad.

Inez: It is a good point. I wonder if my grandma's frustrations were learned by my mom.

Sophia: Think of your grandma's wounds. Think of her silently raising the children, in a certain sense alone. Now think of that wound transferring to your own mother, who interpreted your father's absence in a certain way that wounded many of you in the family, probably including your dad. What is your view of your mom?

Inez: She was unfair, I won't deny that, but she did not mean to be unfair. She was hurt.

Sophia: She was hurt and in that hurt, she kept going. She did not give up.

Inez: She was doing the best that she could, I guess. Am I now condoning her behavior?

Sophia: How do you see it?

Inez: No, I truly think that she was trying to do her best. She did not intend to put distance between us, but it sure turned out that way. I know that not all people are simply "trying to do their best" when they are unjust. I'm not making some kind of sweeping statement about injustice here. Some people do not do their best and intend to do wrong.

Sophia: Yes, I understand your point. So far, we have explored two things: What life was like for your mom when she was a wife and mother and what life was like for her growing up. You see that her pattern of withdrawal from you was from a position of woundedness. I do not say this to excuse your mom, but instead I say it for greater clarity.

Inez: I understand.

Sophia: I have a third question for you: Who is your mom in an eternal sense?

Sophia is seeing whether Inez has an interest in taking the cosmic perspective toward her mom. This is done within the belief system of each person, respecting that person as he or she is right now.

Inez: Sorry, you lost me.

Sophia: I want you to take the largest perspective possible with your mom on the basis of your faith, on what you believe about people. Who is your mom? Who made her? Where will she go when she dies?

Inez: Oh, I see. You are asking what my big beliefs—my faith—tell me about my mom.

Sophia: Yes. It is one more perspective for you, one that is a part of you. What do you think?

Inez: I was taught as a kid that we are all made in the image and likeness of God. So, that means my mom is that way too.

Sophia: Let's keep exploring this. If you believe this, then who is your mom—even when she was unfair to you because of this pattern we are exploring?

Inez: She is loved by God. She will be in heaven some day, and I hope to be there with her.

Sophia: What is your mom's worth when you take this perspective?

Inez: She is an immortal being. She is awesome. If I could see her in this way as she really is, I'd probably be overcome by her actual beauty.

Sophia: How do you think you should interact with such an "immortal being"? Even when out of her woundedness she did not connect with you as a child?

Inez: With respect and love, that's for sure.

Sophia: Why? Because she does nice things for you? Because she is a nice person? Why?

Inez: Because she is who she is. She is made in God's image and I need to take that seriously if I take my faith seriously.

Sterling: She sure does take that seriously, I can tell you that.

Sophia: To this point we have been thinking about your mom. We have been filtering information about your mom from our minds. How are you thinking about your mom in terms of forgiving her for this ongoing pattern of quick anger and then withdrawing from you when you were young?

Inez: I need to forgive her, but it is hard. She damaged my trust.

Sophia: Did she damage your trust or did her particular choices (of withdrawal) damage that trust?

Inez: OK. Yes, you are right. It was her choices, not her as a person.

Sophia: Give me a little more insight into what you mean.

Inez: I see her as a good person, someone who is vulnerable, someone who was wounded a lot when I was a child. She inherited some of those wounds and kept going. But there must be more to forgiving than seeing my mom as whole person, a good person, and then responding to her.

Sophia: Yes, you're right. We need not filter our forgiveness only through our mind via our brains. We can feel forgiveness. What does forgiveness feel like?

Inez: Sorry again. You lost me for a second time.

Sophia: Let's focus on your feelings toward your mom as you think about your childhood. Quiet yourself and begin to concentrate on the area around your heart as I summarize who your mom is.

[*Inez closes her eyes and becomes very quiet.*]

Sophia: I want you to see your mom as a child. All children deserve love and respect, and she did receive these. Now see her as a child dismayed by her own mom's anger. See your mom-as-child looking up at her own mom with the thought, "What are you doing? Why are you yelling so hard?" See the beginnings of your mom's wounds. Now see your mom as a wife and mother. She wants your dad home and he is not coming and this happens over and over and over. Look into her heart as you concentrate on your own heart. Do you see her wounds from childhood mingling with new wounds from adulthood, compounding her pain?

Inez: I can see that, yes.

Sophia: Now combine all of this with the idea that your mom is loved by God, who sees her wounds and loves her. He sees her imperfections and loves her unconditionally nonetheless. When you concentrate on the area around your heart, how do you feel about your mom, when you see the wounds passed to her by your grandma, when you see her struggling to raise the children under difficult circumstances, when you see her being loved by God in an unconditional way?

Inez: I'm feeling kind of warm inside.

Sophia: Try to label the emotion. What is it you are feeling?

Inez: [*pausing for a while*] I think it is a kind of sympathy for her, not in a sappy way, but in a way in which I see her pain and I want to reach out and give her a big hug . . . and a big kiss . . . which I haven't given her for awhile.

Sophia: Might you be feeling some compassion for her? Compassion is to suffer along with the other person.

Inez: Yes, definitely. Compassion and sympathy.

Most psychologists hope for empathy before sympathy. In empathy, the person feels the same feeling as the other. If Inez's mom is feeling anger, Inez empathizes with her when she (Inez) feels that anger as well. Inez sympathizes with her mom in this way: When her mom is angry, Inez feels sorry for her. Sympathy is a reaction to an emotion, not feeling the same emotion as the other person.

> *Sophia:* Do you also feel any pain?
>
> *Inez:* Well, yes, the old pain of shame and self-doubt. She damaged my ability to trust as we both now know.
>
> *Sophia:* Do you ever throw your pain back to your mom?
>
> *Inez:* Throw the pain back? What do you mean?
>
> *Sophia:* When you feel pain that your mom gave to you when you were a child, what do you do with that pain?
>
> *Inez:* [*looking at Sophia*] I don't want to tell you because I don't want to admit it to myself.
>
> *Sterling:* Maybe I can help you with it. Go ahead.
>
> *Inez:* I think I ignore my mom. I think I withdraw from her. It's like what her pain was when we were growing up. I give the pain right back to her by staying away.
>
> *Sophia:* If you forgive, the process itself will ask you to bear the pain.

Sophia is referring here to Guidepost 14.

> *Inez:* How do I do that?
>
> *Sophia:* Please tell me. How might you consider bearing the pain of your mom's past wounds to you?
>
> *Inez:* I can acknowledge that I am hurt. I can stand up with that pain and not pass it back to her. But if I do that for all of the accumulated arguments, all of the times she ignored me, I am concerned that I will be

crushed by the pain. I'll be like my dad and get round-shouldered. I don't want my shoulders to roll right off of me.

Sophia: You make an important point. Forgiveness does not ask you to take on the pain and live with it forever. Forgiveness is a paradox. As you take on the pain—bear the pain as we say—that pain eventually lifts.

Inez: How long do I have to wait?

Sophia: It is unique to each person. It depends on how familiar you are with forgiveness and how often you have practiced bearing the pain. It depends on the depths of your wounds.

Inez: This kind of scares me, this thought of pain.

Sophia: Before we started our conversations, did you have pain?

Inez: Buckets full. That's why we started to talk with each other.

Sophia: So, because of the injustices you have faced, you have pain.

Inez: Yes. I remember in an earlier dialogue you said that forgiveness is not the origin of my pain. I want to keep that idea fresh.

Sophia: It might help to remember the paradox—as you take on the pain, as you say "yes" to it, then it begins to lift.

Inez: You are referring to the scientific evidence aren't you?

See Chapter 2 for a discussion of this evidence.

Sophia: Yes, and this evidence, of reduced anger and related emotions, has been shown in over 10 studies to date. May I turn in another direction? As you know when we reviewed the process of forgiveness, an important step is to consider giving a gift to the one you are forgiving.

Inez: You don't literally mean a gift all wrapped up, do you?

Sophia: Right. The gift will be different for each person and circumstance. Think of it as a gift of love, given unconditionally to your mom because she is a person, a wounded person, and as you say, a child of God. What gift might you give to her? To forgive is to offer the goodness of a gift.

Inez: Time. Time will be my gift.

Sophia: Could you be more specific?

Inez: Even though I inherited shame as a general pattern in my life, including some sense that I am unworthy, I can bear up under this and give her my time, on the phone and by more frequent visits. She'll like that.

Sterling: She'll love that.

Sophia: As you do that, I have another question for you: What is the meaning of your life? What have you learned from enduring all of the suffering we have been talking about?

Sophia has moved here to the Discovery Phase of forgiveness, Guidepost 16, finding meaning in suffering.

Inez: Wooo . . . that's a big question.

Sophia: It is an important question.

Inez: The meaning of my life? For now, I'll say that my suffering has made me more sensitive to other people's suffering. I can help others lead a better life. To help people like my mom with their wounds. [*Turns to Sterling.*] To help Sterling with his wounds.

Sophia: The self-giving life. How does that sound?

Inez: Before I started studying and applying forgiveness to my own life, I would have said that this kind of life is for suckers, but I would be wrong. As I give of myself, I feel better inside and I can leave something very positive for my mom, and the step kids, and Sterling. Not a bad way to live.

Sophia: Forgiving your mom of course is not a panacea for all of your wounds. As we know, there is still work to do regarding your mom, and the first marriage with Enrico, in which your trust was further damaged. And there is the work with your husband, Sterling. Take heart—you know the pathway of forgiving, and it will become more familiar the more you spend time on this path.

Forgiveness may help to ease the particular wound of trust, but that wound is more likely to be healed as Inez slowly practices reconciliation. The little acts of reconciliation, practiced over and over again, can restore trust. Please see the next chapter for more details on this.

EXCERPTS FROM THE DIALOGUE WITH STERLING TOWARD FORGIVING HIS FATHER

Now let us pick up excerpts of the dialogue (from over five conversations) as Sterling works toward forgiving his father.

Sophia: Just as we reviewed Inez's hurts, let's think about yours. You seem to have carried five wounds from your father's original injustices toward you: anger, shame, fatigue, the lost opportunity to teach overseas, and a worldview that I think you would characterize as pessimistic.

Sterling: Yes, well summarized.

Sophia: As I asked Inez about her mom, I now ask you about your dad: What was going on with your dad when he was so anxious that he yanked you up off of the living room floor and had you go to your room early that night? What were the circumstances of his life, what was in his heart at that time, as best you can recall?

Sterling: I'm now taking a much broader perspective on him, having listened to you and Inez discuss her mom. I want to start with a big picture and then move to that night, OK?

Sophia: Of course.

Sterling: My dad, only in part of course, was a person shaped by his environment, by a Poland that was ravaged by World War II. The wounds of war had to have reverberated across the decades and in a sense went into my dad's heart. He carried the wounds of the war with him.

Sophia: This is an important insight. Your dad was a product of a postwar Europe, a postwar Poland in particular.

Sterling: Yes, and I am not saying anything against my cultural roots at all. Poor Poland was a victim of fascist and communist ideologies, both of which marched through my homeland and destroyed some people's wills. These philosophies crushed many a person's passion for life itself.

Sophia: How did it affect your dad's parents?

Sterling: For one thing, they were humble, and poor. They struggled to make a living. I remember my dad talking of how his father would hoard whatever small amount of money they had. It was a way to stay alive so you did not have to rely on an unreliable government.

Sophia: Would you say that your grandparents, who did the hoarding, were anxious?

Sterling: Yes, of course, that is why they hoarded their small amount of cash. And they were angry. They were victims, and sometimes victims get angry. My dad was anxious because they were anxious. It seems to be a family trait.

Sophia: Your dad did not deserve this.

Sterling: No, he did not. I guess he was a victim of sorts. I kind of think of myself as a victim of my dad's anxiety. I see that he was a victim of the same thing.

Sophia: With this perspective of your dad being a product of a postwar culture, what are your thoughts about him as a dad, when you were growing up, particularly that day he yanked you up almost to the ceiling?

Sterling: He was unfair, but he was being unfair in the context of being hurt. Just like Inez said, she did not deserve it, nor did I. He was actually complaining of his work day as soon as he got home from work. He'd had a bad day and that bad day became my bad night.

Sophia: So, the injustice will stay as it is—an injustice toward you. What will change is your reaction to the injustice and to your father.

Sterling: I understand and like this.

Sophia: So, tell me then about your dad when you were growing up. Talk to me about his injustice and what in all likelihood was going on within his heart.

Sterling: When he sent me to my room, I think he was scared for me. That came out in an intensity that was just too much.

Sophia: What scared him, do you think?

Sterling: Disobedience was considered a tragedy in fascism and communism. The party line and all that. It was ingrained in him. If I disobeyed, I might grow up as an obnoxious adolescent and adult. He was shaping who I was. The major problem is that he was not shaping me, he was trying to control me. He was scared. And I really did not do anything bad that night anyway.

Sophia: When you see a scared dad, who was the product of scared parents who were victims of what you have called harmful ideologies, what is your thought about your dad?

Sterling: I'm surprised that he had the time to read all of those baseball books. Those books are a symbol of his love, to take the time for me when he was hurting inside. He loved me.

Sophia: I'm sure you would have taken that intensity out of your dad's heart, if you could have as a child, but it was not under your control.

Sterling: But my reaction to him now is under my control. I have a certain power to love my dad in a way we have never loved each other. Better late than never, as they say.

Sophia: Are you ready to take the cosmic perspective on your dad?

Sterling: Yes, I am. As you know, I am a humanist. I don't have a faith similar to Inez.

Sophia: Please tell me what it means to you to be a humanist.

Sterling: The end of man is man and so we all have an obligation to be sensitive to and respectful of each person.

Sophia: Why? What does your philosophy say?

Sterling: We are all special, unique, and irreplaceable. All people have great worth because of that.

Sophia: Does your dad, then, have that worth? Is he special, unique, and irreplaceable? Even when he yanked you up by your shirt sleeve that night?

Sterling: Yes.

Sophia: Even if he sent you to your room too often and too long when you were a child?

Sterling: Yes.

Sophia: When you focus on the area around your heart, as Inez did, what does forgiveness feel like?

Sterling: It feels good . . . and it makes me want to make up for lost time with my dad.

Sophia: Are you willing to shoulder all of that pain from all of those nights being sent to your room as a way to forgive your dad?

Sterling: You mean bear the pain so I don't toss it back to him?

Sophia: Yes, bearing the pain knowing the paradox of forgiveness—as you bear that pain then the pain lifts.

Sterling: I'm going to work on it. I can't just will it to happen and then, presto, I do it.

Sophia: Forgiveness is a process, and this will take time.

Sterling: I'm willing to give it time as I work on this.

Inez: I'll help you with it.

Sterling: I'd like that help. Thank you.

Sophia: What gift might you give him?

Sterling: The gift of respect. I will honor him as the head of our family. This is a gift I want to give him. I want to listen to him when he talks and converse with him as two mature adults. I want to acknowledge how special he is and let him know it.

Sophia: As you know from watching Inez and me work on her forgiveness, she has developed a new meaning in life through the suffering she has endured. I challenge you in the same way. What does this forgiveness of your dad mean to you as a person? What does life mean to you?

Sterling: It makes me think that all of my suffering has prepared me to be more responsive to my dad and to others. I see a person's wounds much more now than I did before. What is so challenging about this is the fact that we cannot really see others' emotional wounds. Sure, we can look into their eyes and see sadness, or as Inez did, look at her dad and see shoulders rounded by the weight of the world, but we rarely go that deeply. We miss each others' emotional wounds. I'll try not to do that so much anymore.

Inez: Sterling, will you be willing to see my wounds?

Sterling: I promise you that I will try.

BACK TO THE BASICS—YOU

In Chapter 10, you started with the opportunity to forgive someone from your family of origin. In Chapter 12, you have now had the opportunity to watch two courageous people struggle to forgive a parent. Please continue to write your story by addressing these questions:

1. What were some of Inez's insights that surprised you?
2. What were some of Sterling's insights that surprised you?

3. What can you add to your forgiving of a family-of-origin member from the surprises in Inez's journey? Who is the person you are forgiving? I do not mean, "Is this a parent or a sibling?" I am instead asking that you see the personhood in this individual. Who is she?
4. What can you add to your forgiving of a family-of-origin member from the surprises in Sterling's journey? Who is he?
5. Do you have new insights into what the cosmic perspective is from observing Inez and Sterling? How have your ideas of that perspective changed as a result of watching them?
6. What meaning do you see in the suffering you have endured? How does that meaning in suffering change your Unfolding Love Story? Who are you? Who are you becoming?
7. What other steps must you take to forgive people from your family of origin?

BECOMING A FORGIVING PERSON

You have had quite a workout if you have been doing the kinds of exercises that Inez and Sterling have been doing. Can you see that you are beginning to get into "forgiveness shape"? By this I mean, are you developing more endurance to stay at the task of forgiveness? Are you becoming more familiar with the routine? Is this routine becoming a part of your day and week and month? If the routine is becoming a part of you, is forgiveness finding a place in your heart in a more permanent way? When I ask you, "Are you becoming a forgiving person?" what does that now mean to you?

Are you wondering where to go now? When you are ready, please go now to the next person on your family-of-origin list (or to the same person and another incident of injustice) and proceed just as you have been doing. You will continue to go on the forgiveness pathway in Chapter 10 and then proceed to Chapter 11.

CHAPTER 13

FORGIVENESS BETWEEN PARTNERS AND WITHIN YOUR CURRENT FAMILY

Let us look into the future for a moment. I am supposing that you have or someday will have children. As I have said before, I try to address all of the readers of this book, but in some cases what I am emphasizing does not apply to your particular case. If you do not have or will not have children in the future, you might still benefit from what I am about to say because, in all likelihood, you will leave a legacy with some important children in your life.

As we look imaginatively into the future, we reflect on two scenarios. In the first scenario, we see one of your children (either a biological child or a child whom you have helped or might have an opportunity to help). He or she is an adult and in a group counseling session. The point of this session is to help the members of the counseling group to heal from their emotional wounds of the past. All in the group have been hurt by injustices in the family. These are not just little injustices, when parents have a bad day as we all do. These injustices cut deeply and have wounded your now-grown child (or the now-grown child whom you have influenced). His or her purpose in this counseling group is to find a way to heal the wounds, and it is tough going. Your adult child has responsibilities such as work and family. People in our society do not say, "Oh, you have wounds from your childhood. Let's slow down the pace of your life and let's cut some of the demands on you so that you can heal." Society is rarely that understanding of the unseen wounds and is unlikely to recognize them in your adult child. And so he or she is trying to heal while shouldering all of the other responsibilities of life. Your heart, I know, goes out to your adult child (or to that special child who may not be your own in a biological sense) as you see this.

Now we move to the other scenario. You and your spouse or partner (if you do not have a partner, this may change in the future) have done the hard work of forgiving each other while you have many responsibilities. You are willing to forgive family-of-origin members. You are willing to see the wounds that the two of you brought into your union. You are willing to forgive each other. What effect do you think this will have on your children? Does not common sense tell us that your children are better off now and in the future if you and your partner do the hard work of forgiveness? Your resentments will not be placed on your children's backs to carry into the next generation. Your adult child being in a counseling group surely is no tragedy and can be a sign of great strength. At the same time, your adult child may not have needed the counseling group if you and your partner had not failed to confront your resentments. Forgiveness between you and your partner is a gift you can give to your children and to future generations of great-great-great grandchildren. Do you think the forgiveness struggle—together as partners—is worth this?

The first central task of Chapter 10 was asking you to forgive people from your family of origin who deeply wounded you. One main purpose of this is to prepare you to forgive your partner (or your future partner) and to have him or her forgive you. Peace in your current family is one of the goals here, as is laying a foundation of forgiveness for your children. If I am correct that giving and receiving love is at the heart of who we are as humans, and if forgiveness can restore love, then should we not give forgiveness to your children and to you and your partner? Should not forgiveness be a part of family life if you will experience happiness and emotional well-being as a result? Otherwise, and your own experience is likely to confirm this, tensions build up until conflict becomes a way of life. If this is the case in your family, it is time to break the cycle.

As an aside, if you will be living The Forgiving Life, it is important to continue forgiving all of those whom you need to forgive in your family of origin if you have not yet done so. You have identified those people by filling out the Forgiveness Landscape Rating Scale in Chapter 8 and the Personal Forgiveness Scale in Chapter 9. You can proceed by rereading the process in Chapter 10 and persevering until all on the list are forgiven—and this will take time. And if you have not yet done so, you should then move to the "previous family" (if it applies to you) and follow this same procedure, forgiving all in need of your forgiveness.

The combination of exercises from Chapters 10, 13, and 14 could help you take significant steps in solidifying your marriage or relationship (and if you are single, what you learn from them can prepare you for a future relationship). I cannot overemphasize how important these chapters are for your life. A stable marriage or relationship, with the glue of love at its core, can also contribute to the well-being of each partner, the children, and others outside the family. From your marriage/relationship may come a strength that you can give to fellow workers and even to your work itself and to the community. If love is at the heart of healthy psychology and if forgiveness is part of that love, then you are in a position to aid many people with their own love story as you practice and live out yours.

FORGIVING YOUR PARTNER

When you are ready to turn toward your partner, please be aware that there are four reasons why I have asked you to begin by forgiving one person (and then others) within your family of origin. First,

I want you to get to know the forgiveness process. Second, by doing so, you will become practiced at forgiving—perhaps not to a great extent, but you will have begun. Third, you may forgive more deeply when you see the wounds your partner suffered as a younger person. Finally, you will be able to see the wounds that you both brought into the relationship, which may lead to mutual forgiving and changing of patterns that have led you to wound one another.

As we did for your forgiveness work in your family of origin, let us focus on your initial degree of forgiveness, prior to walking the forgiveness pathway with your partner. You are familiar with the task of filling out the Personal Forgiveness Scale. I ask you to do so now regarding your partner and specifically regarding the incidents you identified in the Forgiveness Landscape Rating Scale. Choose the incident on which you need to forgive the least as your first task of forgiving.

Your First Attempt at Forgiving Your Partner

Now please proceed to Chapters 10 and 11 and forgive your partner for this one (and one only) incident. Once you have done that, please return to Chapter 13. We will then bring your partner into the forgiveness process with you. I ask that you first walk the forgiveness path one time as a kind of trial run, as a way to reduce some resentment as you approach your partner toward a team effort in forgiving.

Include Your Partner Now

To strengthen the marriage bond or your existing relationship if you are not married, I recommend that you bring your partner into the exercises of this chapter. Get to know each other better, as Inez and

Sterling did in the previous chapter. Take the time to see each other's wounds, first from childhood and then in the current relationship. You need not fear this because forgiveness is an antidote to the angers and resentments you both may feel. Forgiveness can stop the resentment and build you up in love. Forgiveness can unite you more deeply and even reunite you if injustices have led to a rift in the fabric of who you are together.

Inez and Sterling's Story

If it is possible, please bring in your partner at this point. Please read together the following dialogue between Inez and Sterling. You might want to summarize this story to date for your partner so that he or she is "up to speed" on what this courageous couple is facing. You already have the specifics of your own story from childhood to share with your partner. We will be encouraging your partner to tell his or her story from childhood, starting with the scenarios of genuine love and then moving on to the conflicts. Please be attuned to those conflicts because, in all likelihood, you are living them out in your marriage. Note also that your partner is experiencing the conflicts and wounds that you have brought into the relationship. The mutual sharing of these stories is intended to spark compassion in you for each other that may not have been there previously. Now to the excerpts of the dialogue, with an emphasis on the following key exchange.

> *Sophia:* Sterling, you have just heard Inez tell her story about her childhood. You have heard about the great love shown by her parents when they so proudly presented her with her first tricycle as a 5-year-old. You have also heard of her mother's angst, her frustration, as she so wished that her husband could be there with

her to help raise the children. Tell me, then, what have you heard so far?

Sterling: [*after a long pause*] I am surprised.

Sophia: In what way?

Sterling: I was not aware of all of the yelling. [*Turns to Inez.*] Your mom is so nice. She is actually sweet. We all have nightmares and I did not connect yours to your mom. I am surprised to learn how much your trust has been damaged.

Inez: Yes, I know, and I think my mom is sweet. She also had a set of lungs on her when I was growing up. And my trust is damaged.

Sophia: Tell me, Sterling, what wounds would you say Inez is carrying from her childhood?

Sterling: For one, she has the wounds of being yelled at . . . a lot. She has shame. She did not have the connection that is so important to her. I think she is afraid to love.

Inez: That's changing. The trust wound, if I can call it that, will not defeat me or us.

Sterling: But I think the biggest wound is how you see family life.

Sophia: Please tell us more about that.

Sophia wants to explore the important issue of Inez's worldview, Guidepost 8 of the Uncovering Phase.

Sterling: How could you trust? If you grow close to someone, they will yell at you and ignore you at the same time.

Inez: I think I trust you, at least some.

Sterling: Like you should? Is it deep or is it on thin ice?

Inez: Actually, thin ice. My mom prepared me for that, yet
she is not the whole story. Some of it definitely comes
from Enrico [*her first husband*] and our divorce, and
some of it comes from us, from how you and I interact.

Sophia: Sterling, tell me how Inez's wounds from childhood are played out now in your home.

Sterling: I can now see why it is so important for you that
I not ignore you. You see it as rejection when I watch
TV, don't you? Like what your mom did and how she
felt when your dad was away at the shop. And I'd better stop with any yelling.

Inez: Yes, you should.

Sterling: It brings you right back to childhood, doesn't it?

Inez: It makes me feel very small and afraid and ashamed.
Besides, even if my mom had never yelled at me, it's
still not good for us.

The dialogue now switches to Sterling, who grew up with an anxious father, who was raised with the stresses of a family of origin
forced to endure a post–World War II reconstruction of their homeland, Poland.

Sophia: Inez, you have heard Sterling's story from childhood, including the great love of his father who read
lots of baseball books so that he could help his son
play the game and be part of a team. You heard about
the anxieties he in a certain sense inherited. How are
you seeing Sterling now?

Inez: I see him as hurt.

Sophia: How does he express that hurt in the home?

Inez: The television is not his means to reject me but his
way of trying to shrink from the stresses of the world

that make him tired. I see him wearing intensity that was placed on him as a child. He has been carrying this intensity for a long time. I see a husband who is courageously going into work every day and is kind of beaten up there in part because of his shyness. I see a struggling man, not a mean man.

Sterling: Thank you. I do not want the television to be my big excuse.

Sophia: What do you mean by that—not using the TV as an excuse?

Sterling: [*to Inez*] As I see it, you are being charitable when you say that the television is my way of escaping my dad's intensity. But there is more. It's hard to explain.

Sophia: Try to put it into words.

Sterling: Inez is right that I don't use the TV as a way to reject her. [*Turns to Inez.*] But you remain right when you challenge me not to use the TV as an excuse to ignore you. When I am angry with your attitude or something you've said to me, I can use the TV to hide.

Inez: I see a sadness in you that I did not see before. Don't get me wrong. I am not saying that you all of a sudden became sad. I am saying that it was in you all along and I did not see it.

Sophia: What do you want to do with this insight, Inez?

Inez: [*turning to Sterling*] I want to help you with the way you see the world and with the way you see us. We can do this.

Sophia: What else do you see when you look into Sterling as a person?

Inez: I see that his yelling is a sign that he is wounded inside. [*Turns to Sterling.*] Because I have a deep wound from my childhood with regard to yelling, I need you to stop that. I do not want you to see this as a threat, but as a call to our being more whole.

Sophia: Sterling, what do you think? How is your yelling connected to Inez's experiences as a child?

Sterling: [*turning to Inez*] It is directly linked to your mom and how it triggers shame and a desire in you to fight back. When you then come at me, I am right back with my dad and his intensity. I then feel shame.

Inez: So, we take turns shaming each other because of our own woundedness.

Sterling: Right.

Inez: No wonder I sulk in the kitchen and you sulk in front of the television. We have to see the sulking for what it is—an attempt to prevent further wounds.

Sophia: So, you are now challenged to talk about this with each other rather than retreating to a seemingly safe place that blocks all communication.

Inez: And makes each of us feel utterly disrespected, which makes us sulk all the more.

Sophia: How do you begin—just begin—to break that cycle?

Inez: We have to change this by first confronting our past, forgiving those who need our forgiveness, and then helping each other in the present. We overreact now because of what we suffered in the past. We need to forgive each other.

Sophia: Sterling, what do you think?

Sterling: I agree. We need to work on forgiving each other. I see her feistiness not as a threat but as part of who she is because it is part of who her mom is. [*Turns to Inez.*] I never saw you as ashamed, but now I see a wounded person who can use a little help and I'd like to be a part of that. I see your wounds and I see your mistrust as being a consequence of those wounds.

Sophia: Then who are you to Inez, and who is she to you?

Sterling: I no longer feel condemned by your mistrust, which I have felt in the past. Sure, I'll have to continue working on this because it hurts when I feel your mistrust, but I have a bigger picture to view now. You are my wife, and I have to treat you with more respect.

Sophia: What about love?

Sterling: That, too.

Inez: Especially that. We owe it to each other.

Sophia: Just as you learned what Sterling calls " feistiness" as a child, he learned to be anxious, but you both have a great foundation for love because you did experience this in your childhoods.

Inez: I'm worried that I will never overcome my mistrust completely.

Sophia: Trust is built up one positive interaction at a time—along with forgiving those who damaged that trust.

Sterling: I don't expect that I will emerge from this as a perfect person either.

Inez: Then we hunker down for the long haul and practice forgiveness regularly, OK?

Sterling: OK.

Inez: Even when you are fatigued?

Sterling: Even then. I promise.

Summary of the Dialogue

In this exchange, which unfolded over weeks, we see some important characteristics of the forgiveness process. First, we see that each person uncovers his and her own pain. Each sees the uncovering of pain in the other. This engenders in them a desire to forgive. As they work toward understanding (Guidepost 12), they see each other now as struggling with strong and negative emotions. They see each other as having struggled with such emotions as children. They see the weaknesses each brought into their marriage. Even more important, they are seeing each other as persons, special and unique persons, deserving of respect and love. They are taking a global perspective on each other. They will begin taking a cosmic perspective on each other soon. For Inez, a person of faith, this will mean training her eyes, mind, and heart to see beyond the surface so that she sees Sterling as made in the image and likeness of God. For Sterling, the agnostic, this means he will begin training himself to see that each life is precious and that Inez's capacity to love makes her very special.

I hope that you saw that each was accepting or bearing pain caused by the other. Inez realizes that Sterling's yelling is a reflection, in part, of his anxiety. Yet, at the same time, she does not lie down and say, "Oh, because you were wounded as a child, go ahead and keep yelling. You just can't help it." On the contrary, she asks justice of him. She forthrightly says that he must not yell. Sterling, now in a position to bear up under the pain that Inez has brought to the marriage, does not see this as a demand or a threat. He sees it for what it is: a call for justice in the marriage. They are giving each other the gift of listening, patience, and a willingness to help the other overcome his or her wounds. These are great gifts of forgiveness.

BACK TO THE BASICS—YOUR PARTNER AND YOU

I ask you now to continue forgiving your partner from your heart for each time he or she has wounded you. This can begin for now without a team effort with your partner, which we take up in the next section. You already have begun forgiving your partner for the one incident in which you scored relatively high on the Personal Forgiveness Scale (prior to your doing the work in Chapter 10 of actually forgiving him or her).

We continue now with the important injustices from your partner (identified previously in the Forgiveness Landscape Rating Scale; see Chapter 8). On which of these incidents should you focus? The answer is in your scores on the Personal Forgiveness Scale (see Chapter 9) for each incident in which your partner hurt you. Please choose the next incident on the list (most forgiving first and then all the way up to the least forgiving) that is not indicative of forgiveness already (in the 87–108 score range on the Personal Forgiveness Scale). I guide you in how to deal with each of these in Chapter 10. Please feel free to begin the dialogue in the next section as you continue to forgive your partner from your heart (which can take place without dialogue, at least for now). This kind of forgiveness (the kind that occurs in the silence of your heart) takes much time, and I do not want you to delay the dialogue as you continue the private forgiveness work.

THE DIALOGUE BETWEEN YOUR PARTNER AND YOU

It is now time for a dialogue between the two of you. My first question is this: To whom are you talking? Yes, you are talking with someone who has certain roles in society and in the family, as we discussed in Chapter 10. So, yes, this is your partner or husband or wife. Yes, this is a worker of a certain kind and a father or mother of children, perhaps. But look farther down the road of personhood: Who is this to whom you are talking? Yes, this is a person who has the capacity to think logically, to freely make decisions, and to love. See even farther now. Is this not someone who shares these exact same capacities as you? Are you not linked in a common humanity as you begin this dialogue? You share humanity. And what is the key, underlying core of our humanity? Our theory of forgiveness says it is to give and receive love, not just any kind of love, but agape love. This is the kind of love that serves, and because it is genuine love, it is not exhausted in the giving as long as you understand that to love also means to exercise all of the other virtues such as justice and patience and a sense of balance (or what is called *temperance*). You share in the need to give and receive this kind of love, and you now have the opportunity to actually exercise this.

You have the opportunity to be gift for and to one another.[1] In this context, I now ask if you will share some honest truths about yourselves with each other.

Points to Help You in the Dialogue

- Are you willing to tell your story of your childhood to your partner? If so, start with a story of love. Let your partner into your heart by sharing one memorable story of love from your childhood.
- Now tell of the injustices, perhaps a pattern of injustices, which you suffered as a child, to such an extent that you became emotionally wounded. Base this on the work you have already done in Chapter 10. You should feel free to include as much information as you wish from the possible eight wounds that typically are associated with one incident of unfairness (Chapter 10).
- Listen to his or her love story from childhood and his or her wounds suffered because of injustices. All the while, you should both remember to whom you are talking—the kind of person each of you truly is.
- Dialogue about how you have brought these wounds into your relationship. What wounds do each of you bring? Work on this until each of you sees the kinds of behaviors and attitudes that are part of a wounded relationship.

- Are you both willing to forgive each other for the wounds you have inflicted on each other? Your task is to label the injustices that each has inflicted on the other and to reduce resentment and offer goodness to each other. You will not be finding excuses by seeing the childhood wounds as an easy out for your current behavior. You will not become each other's door-mat. The goal is to love more genuinely and deeply and to reconcile in those areas needing reconciliation. I want both of you to see, as you develop in the virtue of forgiveness, that your love is stronger than any injustice against you. Talk about what it means to forgive and your current commitment to the forgiveness process.

- As you work toward understanding your partner, tell each other your new story of the other. First, take the personal perspective and retell the other's story to him (her) from the past and now the present. Tell him or her of the wounds you see, of the struggles, of the courage he or she brings to the relationship.

- Now each of you should continue telling the partner's story back to him or her by taking the global perspective. Who is he or she as a person? You began this quietly, in your own mind and heart, before this dialogue. Bring those ideas into the open by sharing this story now with your partner.

- Now please take the cosmic perspective. On the basis of your philosophy of life and/or your faith, tell the other who he or she really is in your eyes. Tell the other person the truth based on this perspective. If yours is a perspective of faith, then bring God into this discussion. How can your faith inform your understanding of the partner and aid you in the forgiving?

- As you feel compassion for your partner, describe to him or her what that feels like and have him or her do the same for you. Describe what a warm heart feels like.

- You are both wounded and have inflicted wounds on each other. Discuss together your avowed commitment to accept the pains of the past so that you do not continue to throw those pains back and forth to each other. It is fine to discuss justice here as well, but we will do so to a greater extent in the next chapter. The point here is to discuss your mutual commitment to accept what has happened as you make a less wounded future together.
- When you are ready, say the words of forgiveness to one another: "I forgive you." Make this mutual so that one of you does not feel small and the center of attention.
- Discuss with your partner what this means: "I am gift to you." Discuss what it means to embody yourself as gift because of the love you will bring into the relationship. Listen as he or she does the same. Discuss with each other the implication of this statement: "My love for you is stronger than any injustice against me."
- Discuss with each other the meaning each of you has found in the suffering that you have endured. Discuss with each other what this dialogue has meant to each of you.
- Commit to working on forgiving on a daily basis together. What can you do as a couple each day to renew forgiveness toward each other? You are not alone in your forgiveness journey.
- What is the new purpose each of you has for your relationship? For your family? Discuss this openly and try to learn about purpose from each other.

Summing Up

The practice of and growth toward perfecting the virtue of forgiveness (and we never reach absolute perfection in the expression of any virtue) does not occur because of one dialogue. Your partner and you have a wonderful opportunity to grow in the virtue of forgiveness together. This is why I suggest a discussion each day that centers on forgiveness, no matter how small or short. You could discuss one struggle you had today with forgiveness—perhaps with someone at work. You could discuss any questions about forgiveness that confuse you today. You could share with your partner how you are seeing him or her from the various perspectives we take in the Work Phase of forgiveness. You should revisit the dialogue and choose a different part of the dialogue each day as a way to keep forgiveness before you. Above all, keep a softened heart for your partner by forgiving him or her each day, even for the smallest things. Keep forgiveness alive in your heart and in your conversation with your partner every day.

THE FORGIVENESS JOURNEY WITH YOUR CURRENT FAMILY

It is now time to turn your attention to others in your current family—the children, others who might be living with you such as an elderly parent, or anyone else. The pattern is now very familiar to you. For each person from your current family listed in the Forgiveness Landscape Rating Scale (Chapter 8), fill out the Personal Forgiveness Scale (Chapter 9), and order the people and the incidents from least in need to most in need of forgiveness. Then proceed to Chapter 10 and work on forgiving each person for each incident. Check out your forgiveness progress by then once again filling out the Personal Forgiveness Scale (for the same issue on which you are working when you forgive) and by examining your effectiveness with each forgiveness guidepost in Chapter 11. Go back to forgiving if it is necessary. This effort is giving your family members a fresh start. Resentment doesn't have a chance to take hold in your family if you persevere in leading The Forgiving Life.

YOUR UNFOLDING LOVE STORY

Before we move to the next chapter, it is time to quietly reflect on the material in this one by extending your own love story. What are you learning about yourself as a person who gives and receives love? What are you learning about yourself as a person who requires the giving and receiving of love? How is your partner any different from this—in terms of attitudes and behaviors and in terms of who he or she is at the very core of being? How can you help each other to be your best selves and to be in the best relationship you can have? I am not looking for perfection here, but at the same time, to grow in virtue is to expect more. If the theory of forgiveness in Chapter 1 is correct, you as a couple will thrive if you acknowledge the importance of love—service or agape love—at the center of who you are in relationship to each other.

INTERLUDE: WHAT IS FORGIVENESS?

I have waited until this point in the book to ask you an important question: What is forgiveness? Yes, you are right that we covered this in Chapter 7. You further are right if you are ready with an accurate definition that includes being treated unjustly and then responding with the cessation of resentment and the offer of goodness toward the one who hurt you. Yet, I am not actually asking this same question again. I am not asking for a dictionary definition of forgiveness, but instead, I am asking a more personal question: What is forgiveness now for you? What does it mean for you now that you have tried it, now that you have accepted it into your heart? Is it still a visitor, coming to you on occasion and in a somewhat formal, detached, guarded way, or is it more than that? Is it a guest in your home, making itself comfortable until it is once again time to leave, or is more than even that?

Is forgiveness beginning to show signs of becoming real in you, taking up residence in you and actually forming a part of who you are? Suppose that forgiveness stopped being a part of this world—that it just flickered out and was gone. Would a part of you now be missing as forgiveness is missing? Would you long for it and try to find it?

Does the next question fit with who you are, or does it still sound a bit unusual to you? Do you have a love of forgiveness? I am not asking if you love the people whom you forgive, but instead I am asking if you love the virtue itself. Would you mourn for it if it just flickered out of this world and was gone permanently?

I ask all of these questions, and will ask them again later in the book, as a way to help you understand the changes that may be occurring in you as you practice forgiveness, accept it as important, embrace it as part of you, see it as a vital part of you, and then develop an actual love of the virtue. Try to be aware of these changes within as you continue to live The Forgiving Life.

We are now ready to continue the forgiveness work within your current family. We will learn more about the Triangle of Forgiveness in the next chapter. As you practice the triangle, you may find that forgiveness and reconciliation both deepen.

CHAPTER 14

COMPLETING THE TRIANGLE
OF FORGIVENESS

Inez and Sterling are making progress in forgiveness. They are doing the work of forgiving their parents. They are both beginning to gently face each other and to work on the process of forgiving each other. It is now time for them to struggle with completing the Triangle of Forgiveness, in which they examine in more depth both receiving forgiveness and working toward reconciliation. Let us pick up the dialogue with Sterling's questions about these important features of forgiveness.

> *Sterling:* I have some questions about the flip side of forgiving, when we seek forgiveness. The other day, I was talking with Inez about something, an argument we had about a month ago that was still bothering me. [*Turns to Inez.*] You were pretty quick about it and you said something like, "If that is still bothering you, I'd like you to forgive me for that." It seemed to me at the time that you were kind of blowing off the whole thing. If I forgive you, then it won't be a bother for you any more when I am upset about it. In other words, isn't the seeking or receiving of forgiveness

supposed to be for the other person, not really for oneself?

Sophia: When you say "for the other person," what do you mean?

Sterling: Well, when we seek forgiveness, isn't it supposed to be because we know we have wounded another person and we feel guilty? As we try to get rid of the guilt, we are doing this for the other, to make things right for her. When I am feeling guilty, I realize that I've hurt someone. My taking steps to rid myself of guilt is good, as long as it includes provisions to aid the one who was hurt by me in the first place.

Inez: [*smiling*] You know, Sterling, you got me on this one. I really was just trying to quiet you so that we could have a little peace in the house. I was not asking for you. I was asking for me.

Sterling: Thank you. That means a lot to me. Do you both see my point—seeking forgiveness can have a false move to it if the one seeking it does so just to quiet the other person down, to stop an uncomfortable conversation, to hide from a challenge.

Sophia: Yes, you have hit on what might be called *false forgiveness,* something that looks like it, but is not it. And please, Inez, do not take offense when I say "false forgiveness." I am not at all referring to you as false. I am saying that we all sometimes use forgiveness for unintended purposes when we are feeling uncomfortable.

Inez: No, I understand. You have to point it out as a general issue.

Sophia: Whenever a person uses forgiving to dominate or allows himself or herself to be dominated by another person, we call that false forgiveness, too. So, whenever a person seeks forgiveness to either dominate (shut down a conversation, for example) or to allow himself or herself to be dominated (seeks forgiveness when nothing was unjust and done only to placate the other person), these are forms of false forgiveness, too, the seeking-forgiveness kind.

Sterling: What about reconciliation? How can that be misused?

Sophia: The same general principle applies: If a person is using the idea of reconciliation to either dominate or to be dominated, then it is a false kind of reconciliation, not reconciliation at all. If someone did wrong, the attempts to reconcile should have the best interests of the offended person at heart.

Inez: What would be some examples of dominating or being dominated when trying to reconcile?

Sophia: Here is an example of dominating with reconciliation. I know a person who began to learn about forgiveness, seeing the distinction between forgiving (a moral virtue arising within a person) and reconciling (two people deciding to come together again in mutual trust). Forgiveness is a virtue and reconciliation is not. Well, once the person realized the distinction, that she could forgive but not necessarily reconcile, she proclaimed to me, "I understand that I can forgive without reconciling, so I forgave my husband and then walked out of the marriage." You see, she did not stick around for even one second to see if reconciliation was even possible. She used forgiveness as a weapon not to reconcile.

Inez: She made it look noble, practicing a moral virtue and letting that supposedly dictate her next move of leaving.

Sophia: Right. The other side of this coin, of course, is being dominated. Here, if a person fails to see the true distinction between forgiving and reconciling, he or she may go right back into a physically harmful relationship, thinking that this is what forgiveness requires.

Inez: So, we have to ask ourselves: When I forgive, am I dominating or being dominated? When we reconcile, is either one of us dominating or being dominated?

Sophia: Yes, those are excellent questions to ask.

Inez: Do you remember my asking you what exactly it is that I do when I forgive?

Sophia: Yes, of course, those were tremendous questions.

Inez: OK, then, what exactly are we doing when we seek or try to receive forgiveness from each other?

Sophia: Here is a sketch of the process of seeking forgiveness, which has parallels in the process of forgiving. We have an Uncovering Phase, a Deciding to Seek Forgiveness Phase, a Working on Receiving Forgiveness Phase, and a Discovering Phase. What do you know of the Uncovering Phase of forgiving?

Sterling: We have the issue of those eight possible wounds from being treated unjustly.

Sophia: Right, and when we seek forgiveness, we have wounded another (we were the one who was unfair), and as a result we feel guilty. As we examine the amount of guilt we have and for what reason, we realize that we have wounded others and ourselves. This uncovering of what we have done can be a great motivator for moving to the next phase, deciding to seek forgiveness. What do you recall about that regarding forgiving?

Inez: We examine what forgiving is and is not and then start slowly, by committing to doing no harm to the other person.

Sophia: It is similar when you seek forgiveness. For one thing, you realize that you will not dominate or be dominated as you seek forgiveness. You realize what seeking forgiveness entails—you need to ask for forgiveness, you need to realize that you will have to gently receive the gift of the other's forgiveness, and you need some humility to do so.

Sterling: And the Work Phase?

Sophia: It is like the parallel phase in forgiving. First, you work to understand, specifically focusing on the wounds you have caused the other. You see the other in his or her woundedness. This sets up feelings in you—gratitude that you may be forgiven, humility as you accept that you did wrong, and a willingness to do your part to change and work toward reconciliation.

Inez: I think I have the idea regarding the Discovery Phase. We probably find meaning in what we have endured to face our guilt, approach the other, and ask for and wait for their forgiving. We realize we are stronger for this, and we make a decision to change our pattern of behavior. The idea of release is there, right? Release from guilt?

Sophia: Yes, you followed the parallels with forgiving very well.

Sterling: But, reconciliation is not so simple. It doesn't just follow naturally from forgiving and seeking forgiveness. I know that from watching Inez. [*Turns to Inez.*] You have been hurt by Enrico and so your trust, which is needed for reconciliation, is tougher for you than for me.

Inez: I have to take reconciliation—with its deep trust—inch by inch.

Sterling: I am being asked to bear the pain from your childhood and from your time with Enrico, then. I admit that we have had our own struggles and that I have been there creating some of them, but I am now realizing that I am being asked to bear the pain from your childhood and your previous marriage. And you are being asked to bear the pain from my past.

Sophia: This is a great insight. You are correct in that. You will have to wait perhaps longer than what you see as reasonable for a full reconciliation with Inez, at least in part because of what happened in her past to damage her trust.

Inez: Sterling, I am sorry for that, I truly am. I cannot help that my trust is fragile.

Sterling: I understand. I really do. Reconciliation, I am realizing, requires patience on both of our parts.

Sophia: Yes, it is part of the process. As you, Inez, continue to forgive your parents, Enrico, and Sterling, and as the two of you practice the entire Triangle of Forgiveness, which includes forgiving, seeking forgiveness, and reconciling, you will grow in trust. It is a struggle and takes time.

Inez: I realize that there are no guarantees when working toward reconciliation. In other words, Sterling may promise not to do something hurtful to me, but then, because he is imperfect, he messes up again. I want some kind of a guarantee here before I do my part to reconcile.

Sophia: Now I'm getting confused. You say that there are no guarantees and then you ask for one. Is that possible?

Inez: Well, maybe I don't really mean a "guarantee." What I'm asking is this: If Sterling is unfair to me and we are trying to reconcile, what do I look for in him that shows me this is genuine reconciliation and not the false variety?

Sophia: You look for the Three Rs.

Inez: Reading, Riting, and Rithmatic?

Sophia: Remorse, repentance, and recompense.

Inez: That's better. Rithmatic is not my strong suit.

Sophia: Remorse is the internal development of sorrow for what I have done. Repentance is the internal act of a good will to change and the use of language to communicate the remorse. The language, for example, may take the form of an apology. Recompense is to make things right. If he yells, is he now trying hard to talk more quietly . . . and not just right now but as a new pattern? Is the recompense for your good and not just for his? In other words, is he doing something to just make himself feel better or to serve your needs in a legitimate way?

Inez: Remorse as sorrow, repentance as both internal good will to change and words spoken to reflect that, and recompense as behaviors to make it right—this is an important checklist for increasing my confidence in the process and for increasing my trust when I see these happening. Thank you, Sophia.

Sophia: Glad to help.

Inez: OK, I now understand that to seek forgiveness has a set of phases similar to forgiving. I understand that to reconcile has the Three Rs Checklist. But here is a complication that we need to address. Let's take an example. Let's suppose that Sterling has yelled at me, which he did last week when he came home tired. As we all know, this is very upsetting to me, even with the progress we are making. Let's continue to suppose that he is seeking forgiveness from me, he genuinely wants to reconcile, and I am forgiving him for this yelling episode.

Sophia: I am with you so far.

Inez: He, then, is on his own journey of seeking forgiveness and reconciling, and I am on my own journey of forgiving. [*Turns to Sterling.*] What if we are not at the same guidepost at the same time? For example, when you asked me to forgive you for the yelling, you were clearly in the Decision Phase of seeking forgiveness. And, I might add, you were doing it well. There was a genuine humility there, which I love to see. You clearly saw that seeking forgiveness is not about you and so you were waiting for me. I could see that you knew that forgiving was my call. You were doing everything right.

Sterling: And . . . ?

Inez: And I was nowhere near the Decision Phase of forgiving. I was in the get-on-the-running shoes-and-run guidepost.

Sophia: You were in the Uncovering Phase, uncovering your anger.

Inez: I was in the fight-or-flight phase and when is the next flight outta here.

Sophia: What part of the Uncovering Phase were you in?

Inez: I was feeling a lot of anger and a lot of shame. I was stewing about it and I was not ready to talk.

Sophia: You have hit on a vital point in the Triangle of Forgiveness. The two of you will not necessarily be on the same parallel phase (or in the same guidepost) as the other when one of you makes a first move in forgiveness. Sterling, you obviously were farther down the seeking-forgiveness road than Inez was down the forgiving road.

Inez: What, then, do we do about that?

Sophia: Talk about it, as you are doing right now. You have both diagnosed where you were on your respective forgiveness paths. Your insights seem accurate to me. Talk with one another about that when you calm down after such an incident. Where are you in the seeking-forgiveness pathway, Sterling? Where are you on the forgiving pathway, Inez? Where are you with respect to the Three Rs? As you see the difference between you, try to have some empathy toward the other. For example, Sterling, you will have to bear the pain of Inez, in this case, not being ready to even discuss the issue. She is in the early Uncovering Phase. Inez, you may have to see that Sterling is eager and ready to genuinely move forward with you, not to dominate or to blow the whole thing off, but to truly seek forgiveness and reconcile.

Inez: It is at that point that we need compassion toward each other, to help each other as best we can where we find the other along the forgiveness path.

Sterling: Well put, my poetic beauty.

Inez: [*smiling at Sterling*] We can do this.

Sophia: And in the "doing," it will not come out perfectly, or even near perfectly every time. That is part of the Triangle of Forgiveness, knowing it is an imperfect system for imperfect people.

Inez: The closeness and mutual trust of true reconciliation comes with time, too.

Sophia: Yes. Remember our discussion of the degree of forgiveness? I made the point that in the incest-survivor study, the brave participants did not get the top marks on the forgiveness scale at the end of the study. The key was that they made progress in forgiving. It is the same with reconciliation. You need not have perfect trust right away to have a good relationship. Let the forgiving emerge. Let the reconciliation emerge.

Sterling: And all the while continue to bear the pain, from what each of us brought into the marriage, from the wounds we have inflicted on each other, and from the fact that we will be on different parts of the forgiveness phases as we work it all through.

Inez: Bearing the pain through forgiveness and taking good steps to correct the injustices, I am beginning to see, is at the heart of a true marriage.

Sophia: Yes, you have to be willing to serve the other in love, to bear pain for the other. Don't you think this is why so many marriages fail—one of the members of this union is unwilling to bear pain on behalf of the other?

Inez: I'm beginning to get it. If one person in a marriage does not understand or refuses to understand what it means to bear the pain through forgiveness, the irony is that even more pain is passed along, within the marriage, to the children, and to whomever is the victim of the displacement that is likely to occur.

Sterling: Important points. "Bear the pain through forgiveness." I'd better put that into my long-term memory bank.

Inez: But what if someone cries "masochism!" to this? After all, if you absorb too much pain, don't you become a punching bag?

Sophia: How do you read this situation? What has been Aristotle's advice for about 2,300 years?

Inez: This I have learned: Never practice any of the virtues in isolation of the others. If we forgive, we also ask for justice.

Sophia: A justice seeker is not a punching bag.

Inez: I have another question. This is not going to happen with Sterling and me. Suppose one member of a marriage forgives, but the other refuses to do their part, refuses to seek forgiveness, to change, to do anything.

Sterling: It sounds like abandonment.

Inez: That is kind of what I had in mind. If one person does all that he or she can in forgiving, and this is flat-out rejected, does this mean that all of the forgiving is not good enough? Does it mean that it is not really forgiving?

Sophia: Tell me, how do you understand forgiving? Let me now put the question to you: What do you mean when you say the word *forgiving*?

Inez: As we know, forgiveness is a moral virtue. It is my call whether or not to exercise this virtue and when I do, it is for other people's good.

Sophia: Let's then put this in a little different context by focusing on a different virtue, say justice. Imagine a very just person, Sheriff Conley, who enters a town in which the residents refuse to be fair. They ignore laws, are not rehabilitated when imprisoned, and laugh at his efforts to have a just community. I ask you: Has this person failed to be just?

Inez: No, but his goals were not realized.

Sophia: Exactly, and that is my point regarding forgiving. Because it is a virtue, a person who cultivates forgiving in his or her heart and mind and then forgives well has in fact demonstrated that virtue, and it can be done very honorably in this way. There is a distinction between what forgiveness is and the outcomes that happen when we forgive. Even if a person rejects your forgiveness, you have been forgiving, perhaps in a very deep way, just as Conley did in that unruly town.

Inez: As I understand it, then, a person can be deeply forgiving, even if others spurn the gift.

Sophia: Yes. Thus, in the case of a very forgiving person whose partner refuses to cooperate, we have the following: the essence of forgiveness, what it is at its core (a moral virtue), was realized, but one of the end points of forgiveness—one of the important goals of forgiveness—was not realized, that of completing the Triangle of Forgiveness.

Sterling: We strive to complete the triangle, but that is out of our control because we need the other person's cooperation to realize that goal. The goal over which we have considerable control, as part of our free will, good will, and strong will, is to forgive regardless of the consequences.

Inez: Well said, my poetic husband.

BACK TO THE BASICS—YOU

What do you have to say to Inez and Sterling? How can you add to the dialogue? Did they go far enough in their seeking forgiveness? Did Sophia quiet their fears sufficiently or would you add more? Do you have any fears or concerns not covered in the dialogue? Do questions arise for you regarding reconciliation? Try to articulate these questions and concerns and try to anticipate Sophia's response.

Do you need to apply the ideas here to your current relationship with your partner? If so, try to complete the Triangle of Forgiveness together, realizing that your partner also may need to work on issues of forgiving, seeking forgiveness, and reconciliation with you. Take each incident one at a time and enter into dialogue, as you did in Chapter 13.

As you strive to make the Triangle of Forgiveness a part of your life together, please keep in mind the points below as guidelines for you as you seek forgiveness:

- In the Uncovering Phase of seeking forgiveness, please be aware of your guilt and any complications from this (fatigue, strained relationships).
- In the Decision Phase of seeking forgiveness, you will need courage and humility; you should be satisfied that you know, to the best of your ability now, what it means to seek forgiveness; you should know what false-seeking forgiveness is and avoid it.
- In the Work Phase, please do the work required of you—apologize, wait, be aware of the other's pain.
- Bear the pain when he or she is not ready to forgive.
- In the Discovery Phase, find meaning in what you and the other have suffered and resolve to make amends.
- Await emotional release.
- In reconciliation, be aware that trust takes time to build up if the hurts were deep or if the person came into the relationship with you already deeply wounded by others.
- Trust can build as you look for and find, in the one who acted unfairly, the Three Rs of remorse, repentance, and recompense.

- Bear the pain of waiting for the other to develop and for the process to unfold.

As you do this work, try to clear the slate of all resentment toward each other, thus becoming gift for one another.

EXTENDING THE TRIANGLE OF FORGIVENESS TO OTHERS

From whom do you need to seek forgiveness? I recommend that you revisit the Forgiveness Landscape from Chapter 8 and take the time to slowly go through the different categories of people, this time with an eye toward those whom you have hurt. I am not suggesting that this be an exercise of identifying every time you were all too human and were a little unjust. I am talking about deep hurt inflicted on others, the kind that you have experienced as a forgiver. Ask yourself this question: Would this person have been so deeply hurt by what I did that I need to approach him or her to ask for forgiveness? If you think his or her level of hurt is a 7 or higher on our 0-to-10 scale, then put that person on your list.

Please keep in mind that the usual end point of forgiving and seeking forgiveness is reconciliation. Is this person someone with whom you wish to reconcile? If not, then approaching him or her with the intent of simply asking for and getting forgiveness is an honorable goal.

Beware of false forms of seeking forgiveness and reconciliation. The general rule, please recall, is this: If someone is dominating and if someone is being dominated by this interaction, then it is not genuine forgiving, seeking forgiveness, and reconciliation. It is time to take a step back and see the truth of what is happening before progressing further.

Please be aware that your practice of forgiving and your leading The Forgiving Life are not dependent on other people's reactions to you. Your expression of the virtue of forgiveness will be completed in the sense that you have done all you could. Your forgiving and/or seeking forgiveness are brought to fulfillment to the extent that others do cooperate, but their rejecting behavior does not take away anything from you as a forgiver or as a seeker of forgiveness.

BECOMING A FORGIVING PERSON

Are you beginning to see how all of the moral virtues are connected? As you forgive, you begin to see how you may have acted unjustly. As you approach a person to ask forgiveness, you now need courage and humility. You begin to appreciate the virtue of justice to an even greater extent because you see how injustice can be so wounding. As you bear the pain, you need patience and wisdom to know when to ask again and when to keep waiting. Most of all, are you seeing how the virtue of moral love, agape love, ties all of this together? As you forgive, you are loving someone who hurt you, again as best you can under your current circumstances. Your love is stronger than any injustice that anyone can throw at you. As you seek forgiveness, you are loving another by bearing pain on his or her behalf. You are not letting your past injustice get in the way of offering love to that person. As you reconcile, even with an acquaintance, you are acknowledging his or her worth as a person and taking a step of trust. You are practicing love. That is at the heart of The Forgiving Life—to develop into a more loving person. Not a bad way to live, don't you think?

CHAPTER 15

SCHOOL DAYS, WORK DAYS, AND OTHER DAYS

Now we turn to the subtle parts of forgiveness. When I ask people about their deepest hurts, without fail the vast majority center these within the family, either on mom or dad or a partner. It is rare for a person to choose someone from their school days as they were growing up. Yet, it is here that we sometimes have wounds deeply hidden from view that have helped to shape our lives today. What I find frequently is this: People have formed their own self-image at least in part from what they experienced in school, and they are completely unaware of this until I ask.

A significant part of who you are may be based on two things: (a) how you were treated by teachers and peers in school and (b) what story you told yourself about all of this. If you were built up in agape love by (even some) staff or peers, your story of yourself may be settled and secure. If you were less fortunate and experienced some or even much rejection, then your story about yourself is likely to have some unnecessarily negative characteristics to it. And we can change this.

Before we launch into the wounds from the past, let us start, as we did with your family of origin, by having you think of one loving experience from your school days. Try to recall one incident in which a staff member or a peer went the extra mile with and for you, befriended you, helped you. Try to experience his or her kindness all over again. Try to sense your happiness as the person reached out to you. Try to get back that sense of fulfillment because you were receiving his or her agape love. Try once again to feel the sense of completeness in you because of what he or she is doing (as you reimagine the true event) for you. Try once again to recapture that sense of contentment that comes from an unexpected giving of such love to you. This is part of your school days, and it is a part of who you are. Please remember this as we explore the wounds from your past.

As we turn to the forgiveness process, I want you to know that doing forgiveness work from days gone by in school is not just for the sake of being a complete forgiver. We are not turning to your school days primarily because to live The Forgiving Life you have to forgive everyone, even if it is not so terribly important for you now. You might begin to see that your school days have had a greater impact on you than you realize.

GETTING ORGANIZED IN PREPARATION FOR FORGIVING

Are you ready to begin forgiving people from your school days? If so, then please review your answers to the Forgiveness Landscape Rating Scale and focus now only on the School Days section and only on those from your own school days (not the school days of your children). Please focus only on those people to whom you gave a rating of 7 or higher on your degree of emotional hurt. As I stated in Chapter 9, if you are an easy grader and gave few people a rating of 7 throughout the Forgiveness Landscape Rating Scale, then please focus on those to whom you gave a rating of 6.

Now take time to slowly and carefully fill out the Personal Forgiveness Scale for each of the people whom you identified in the previous paragraph. Again, this may take time, depending on the number of people you identified. When you are finished with this exercise, please add up the scores and see where you stand, relative to the cut-offs in Chapter 9. As stated in that chapter, you need not forgive those on whom you scored between 87 and 108, the highest quartile. Of course, if you wish you may go ahead even with these people.

You should now place all of the people in order so that you begin forgiving the one person toward whom you have the most forgiveness at the present time. When you are ready, please proceed to Chapter 10 to begin forgiving this person. The challenge is to eventually forgive all on your School Days list. As you turn now to your school days, be sure to refresh, take breaks from the work, and then persevere on the forgiveness path. The directions in Chapter 10 will guide you through forgiving the entire group of people who have hurt you. Before proceeding to Chapter 10, I recommend that you read the next section, which may help you as you forgive.

TWO QUESTIONS TO AID YOUR FORGIVENESS

Question 1. I have a question for you that may be important as you reach Guidepost 12 (work toward understanding) for some of the students on your list. Consider each student on your list one at a time in this section. We begin by focusing on only one student. I would like you to take the personal perspective in which you try to see that person in the context of his or her growing up. Is it possible that his or her behavior toward you was shaped, perhaps in part, by narcissism?

Narcissism is considered today to be a rather pervasive characteristic that can wound others.[1] You will find it expressed perhaps too often in schools, as students are still growing in the virtues and so can slip very easily into a "me first" attitude. Think of narcissism as existing on a continuum from very mild to severe. In general, symptoms of narcissism include an exaggerated sense of one's own importance and a lack of empathy toward others; the person requires excessive admiration from others, has a pervasive sense of entitlement, and shows arrogant reactions to others.

In your school days, you might have been a victim of another's narcissism. If so, I want you to see his or her own pain. Narcissism does not sneak up on a person like a thief in the night but gradually grows in a person over time. If you think about our theory of forgiveness, what in all likelihood is missing—crucially missing—in the life of a student who shows persistent narcissism? Might agape love be missing? Try to see this person in a new and realistic light. See him or her (if this image is true) as searching for love and not finding it. Can you understand and appreciate the wounds this person carried to school every day?

If love is missing for a person, what is that person likely to do? Might he or she strike out at others, wounding them as he or she is wounded? You may have been a victim of a lack of love in a fellow student. As that student (or even staff person) was wounded, so he or she wounded you. You surely do not want their legacy, what they left behind, to now be your legacy.

Question 2. Besides wounds of narcissism, people who have hurt you from your school days may have suffered from excessive anger and even passive anger. Were you ignored? This is passive anger. Were you ridiculed or threatened? These are examples of active, excessive anger, which is actually considered to be pervasive in schools in the United States and in other parts of the world.[2]

We most certainly are not looking for excuses for people's behavior as we take the personal perspective on them. Forgiveness is centered in the important idea that people have free will and therefore have ethical responsibility, even if they are young and still learning. What the person you have in mind did to you was wrong, even if he or she was still learning about right and wrong.

Try now to combine a personal perspective on this one person with the global and cosmic perspectives (again, please see Chapter 10). How are you connected with this person from so many years ago? Are you not connected because of your built-in need to love and be loved (not necessarily by that person, but in general)? Are you not connected because you share a common humanity? Even the very wounded share a common humanity with you. Please take your list of people from your school days and proceed, when you are ready, to forgive them in Chapter 10.

AFTER YOU HAVE FORGIVEN: WHO ARE YOU?

You might now see that you can and will be set free from a school playground that has high walls—walls that did not allow you to climb out of there for many years. How does it look from the other side of that wall? In this context of your forgiving from your school days, I would like you to continue growing as a forgiver by considering a potentially life-changing question: Who are you?

How has this person, and other experiences from your school days, shaped your view of yourself? Are you carrying around a big burden of negative statements about yourself because of how you were treated in school? Do you think your self-esteem, the degree to which you genuinely like yourself, was damaged from all of this love being withdrawn from you? Do you see yourself as a little unworthy?

It is now time to reclaim your own humanity—your own sense of your value. Here are some questions for you to reflect on:

- When you forgive someone, do you try to see his or her inherent worth as a person?
- What does it mean to possess inherent worth? Does a person ever have to earn his or her worth? Why not?

- As you see others whom you have forgiven as possessing inherent worth, are you now willing to say, "I, too, have inherent worth"?
- Are you aware that no one can take that worth from you, under any circumstance?
- Can you now see that any lowered self-esteem that you have been carrying around for years is an illusion? It is false.
- As you continue to offer a deep understanding of other people's worth to them as you forgive them, are you now ready to give this gift back to yourself and to offer yourself that understanding? I have worth, unconditional worth.
- Are you ready to offer this true understanding of inherent worth to yourself even if someone showed narcissistic behaviors toward you or showed excessive anger or even excessive passive anger toward you? Even if you were emotionally beaten down, forgiving helps you stand up again.
- Are you ready to stand in the truth of who you are? You are a forgiver who has been offering love to others in the form of understanding them, being compassionate toward them, and acknowledging their humanity.
- If the negative worldview has contributed to your hurting others, are you ready to seek forgiveness from them? Are you ready to play a part through this seeking in building up their sense of inherent worth?

It is time to acknowledge your own humanity to yourself. And by your free will, your good will, and your strong will, do not ever let this image of who you really are out of your sight.

YOUR CHILDREN'S SCHOOL DAYS

We have a strong desire to protect our children. I hope that your examining your own school days first will help you heal and, at the same time, give you insight into what your children's school days are like. They, too, are faced with others' narcissism, excessive anger, and excessive passive anger. Every day they encounter others who have had love withdrawn from them and who may be taking this out on those around them.

My advice to you is to enter into dialogue with your children about these experiences, not to drag a confession out of them, or to plant seeds of distortion (that school is a dangerous place), or to create phantom problems that are not even there. My point is that you should stand quietly in the truth. If there is a problem, try to see it and not run from it or deny it. If there is a problem, I recommend that you practice forgiving the person who has hurt, or is hurting, your child as a way to have clear thinking on how to solve that problem.[3] Your responses on the Forgiveness Landscape Rating Scale (from Chapter 8) and the Personal Forgiveness Scale (from Chapter 9) will help you decide whether you have people to forgive in this context. If there are people to forgive, please proceed on our familiar journey of turning to Chapter 10.

Just as important is your aid to your child's emotional well-being. You will need to help your child practice forgiveness as you try to solve the injustice. We take up the issues of your children's forgiveness in Chapter 18.

WORK DAYS

Inez's father was round-shouldered because of work. Inez's mother was directly affected by that. Inez and her siblings were then directly affected by how their mother was affected. The work world affected them all both positively (after all, he was a good worker and wage earner) and negatively. What about your own work days? How have they affected and how are they affecting you and others? A common injustice at work tends to be others' passive anger. They do not necessarily "get in your face" but instead ignore you, are subtly angry, and in general give you a sense of your own unimportance (which, as we know, is not true).

As you prepare to forgive all who have hurt you as a worker, you should approach this task with some confidence because you now know our forgiveness routine: You first identify someone from the Forgiveness Landscape Rating Scale and then confirm the extent of your need to forgive that person by completing the Personal Forgiveness Scale. Once you have selected a person to forgive, you carefully go over the questions and issues from Chapter 10. Before proceeding there, I recommend that you read the next section, which may help you as you forgive people in the workplace.

Worldview of Work

What is your worldview regarding work? For example, do you see your work environment as great—can't wait to get to work in the morning? Or, is it more negative than that? If it is more negative, what is your story regarding work? How do you see your fellow workers? Are they, for instance, kind and helpful, or do you see them as "looking out for number one"? If you have a pessimistic story, then what would you say your energy level is at work, on our familiar 0-to-10 scale, with a 0 meaning that you have *virtually no energy at work*, a 5 meaning that you have *your typical, average amount of energy*, and a 10 meaning that you have *a light heart and a spring in your step at work?*

As you forgive people at work for their injustices against you, try to be aware of any shifts in your worldview of work. We often see shifts toward a more positive outlook, not in any distorted way or ideal way, in which you no longer see problems at all. This positive shift occurs toward work in general, not just toward the particular people whom you forgive. One example of this shift in worldview comes from our efforts with teachers in inner-city schools who taught forgiveness education within their classrooms. Over a 2-year period, we asked 52 teachers about their experiences teaching children about forgiveness and how to forgive. They reported that as they taught about forgiveness, they could almost not help putting this into practice as they forgave people in their own lives, even at school. Of the 52 teachers, 95% said that they became better teachers as a result of making forgiveness a part of their classrooms. Still further, 95% of the teachers said that they became better persons as a result of the forgiveness experience in their classrooms, and more than 80% thought that their classrooms as a whole began to function better as a result of focusing on forgiveness with the children. Worldviews become realistically more positive as people forgive in the context of their work. I have seen it with counselors as well. Those who begin to incorporate forgiveness into their work tell me that their practices are refreshed and that they find a new meaning in what they do. With these preliminaries in your mind, please proceed to do the work of forgiveness in Chapter 10.

Once You Have Forgiven in the Workplace

As emotional burdens are lifted, we sometimes can approach life in general and work in particular with renewed energy. I hope this is the case or will be the case for you. One area of change that can contribute to this renewed vitality concerns Guidepost 16 in which you are challenged to find new meaning in what you have endured.

As you forgive people who have been unjust to you in the workplace, can you find it within yourself to be a conduit for good in a place that might be overrun with passive anger and low morale? Surely not all work environments are this way, but too many are. Is it possible for you to make a difference in the hearts of others at work as you bear the pain of injustice and offer agape love through forgiveness to those who bring their own wounds to work with them every day? As they leave for work each day, taking inventory of the necessities to bring with them, no one adds, "Oh, yes, my wounds.

Do I have my wounds with me today? I must bring those to work." Such wounds are rarely conscious, and so many people will bring those wounds without even knowing it and then wound others.

One new meaning for you might be this: Be aware of others' wounds at work. Another might be this: By your forgiving, you may help a person reduce his or her wounds, and you may help prevent further spreading of those wounds to others. The teachers described previously were aware that forgiveness has a way of influencing the entire classroom atmosphere. Your practice of the virtue of forgiveness may help to spread goodness, even if that goodness is small and unrecognized. Yet, some may notice a difference at work. What does this mean to you? What meaning are you getting out of forgiving at work?

OTHERS WHO NEED YOUR FORGIVENESS

As you know from your responses in Chapter 8, you have a forgiveness plan that includes a number of groups and certain people within them. Each person can be forgiven as you consult your Forgiveness Landscape, fill out the Personal Forgiveness Scale, proceed to Chapter 10, and follow the forgiveness path. Relatives, neighbors, religious group members, and others can be a part of your living The Forgiving Life. As you practice, you will improve in the moral virtue of forgiveness. In the following, I discuss some issues that may not be so obvious on the Forgiveness Landscape.

Ethnicity and Racial Issues

Some forgiveness issues are not as noticeable as others. For example, if you recall in Chapter 8, Inez was eager to forgive her academic community for what she saw as injustices centered on ethnicity. She did follow the pathway of Chapter 10 in forgiving certain people for particularly insensitive remarks. This, however, did not end her forgiveness journey regarding ethnicity. She ended up forgiving the large group of "society" because of the norm she sees as established there—the norm that she is judged less favorably than others. The norm, you see, is not just carried by one or two people who wound her. The norm is preserved within the society itself and so she must go there within the forgiveness process, to the society, and forgive even though this is a very abstract entity. This is not a fantasy of hers—thinking that she has been treated unkindly and unjustly because of her ethnicity—but is based on real, concrete behaviors from others, over many incidences starting in childhood and continuing in college. You can forgive a large group such as a corporation or a society by considering that entity as you work through the exercises in Chapter 10. Please remember also to forgive certain people in these entities so that you have both a concrete forgiveness experience (with the certain people) along with the more abstract forgiveness experience (of forgiving the social entity itself).

Forgiving Yourself

One of the most frequent questions I receive concerns the process of forgiving yourself. The short answer is yes, you can forgive yourself, with certain cautions in mind. First, when you forgive yourself, you are both the offended one and the offender. And we rarely offend ourselves in isolation. Thus, you should go and make amends with those who also were offended by your actions. This includes asking for forgiveness, changing your behavior, and making recompense where this is reasonable. After that, as you turn your attention to forgiving yourself, please keep this in mind: What you have been offering to others in forgiving them (gentleness, kindness, patience, respect, and moral love) you can and should offer to yourself. Try this by engaging in the exercises of Chapter 10, with a focus on you.

CHAPTER 16

SURVEYING THE LANDSCAPE FROM THE MOUNTAIN PEAK

How is the view from up there on the mountain peak of forgiveness? It is time for lots of high-fives atop that mountain. You have gone on a great journey. Please sit back and reflect on this vista: You have completed the task of forgiving everyone on your list. This in all likelihood is a unique experience in your life—to have granted yourself the privilege of offering forgiveness to everyone who has ever seriously wounded you in the past.

LOOKING BACK TO HELP YOU LOOK FORWARD

It is time to survey your broad landscape of forgiveness. Please collect all of your scores for all of the people on whom you filled out the Personal Forgiveness Scale. Now please compare your scores on that scale before you began to forgive and after you have forgiven. What does the pattern look like across all of the people? On the average, did you go up on this scale across all of the people? Did you go from low to medium on the average in your forgiveness? Did you go from medium to high on the average? Please remember that the scientific studies generally show that the amount of improvement is more important to your psychological health than reaching the highest level of forgiveness.[1] If your pattern is to gain, let's say, 20 points on the average, but you have gained only 5 points with one particular person, perhaps he or she still needs your forgiveness. You might consider doing some refresher forgiveness exercises with all of those toward whom you showed small improvements.

As an aid to you in the future, when you may have to forgive new people for new injustices, I recommend that you look now at your patterns across all of the Forgiveness Guidepost Forms (Chapter 11) that you have filled out. If you filled out this scale online at Mind Garden (http://www.mindgarden.com/forgiveness), you will now have a profile across all of the people regarding your strong and weak guideposts. By reflecting on your weaknesses, you will learn where you need to focus and practice more. Understanding your strengths is also important because you should emphasize your strengths as you forgive. This may help you to accomplish all other guideposts as your strengths move you closer to the end point of actually forgiving.

Please keep in mind that as you complete the forgiveness pathway with one particular person, this does not necessarily mean that you are completely finished forgiving him or her. Sometimes unexpectedly we wake up and are angry again with the person. This is not an indication of failure. Instead, it is an indication that forgiveness is an imperfect enterprise and so we do revisit the forgiveness process with some people. Be encouraged that if you have already forgiven, then the second or third or 10th attempt will probably be quicker with better results than the time before.

YOUR CONTINUING FORGIVENESS JOURNEY AND UNFOLDING LOVE STORY

You have come through much as a forgiver. You have shown courage by striving to forgive people from your family of origin, your past family (if you had one) and current family, your school days and your children's school days, and your places of employment, among others. When you meet new people in the future, those with wounds who wound you (even if unintentionally), be confident in this: You already know the forgiveness pathway. It is my hope for you that you continue to strive after forgiveness as others treat you in a way that is less than you deserve as a person. Forgiveness is a powerful reminder that you are a person worthy of love and respect, as is each person who wounds you.

Your love story—your story about who you and others are as you continue to grow in the virtue of forgiveness—has been unfolding throughout this book. Near this chapter's end, I will ask you to do more writing on this unfolding story, but for now, I would like you to reflect on a few questions. What are you learning about yourself as a forgiver? What are you learning about other people and their wounds as you become a forgiver? Is the virtue of love growing stronger in you? Typical requirements to keep growing usually include practice (and more practice after that), a clear understanding of the meaning of the virtue, and an environment that encourages and nurtures growth in its practice. You will need the virtue of perseverance as you apply your good will and your strong will to the task of growing as a forgiver. It is so easy to become distracted from this task, to let your mind drift to other, more novel pursuits that provide a pleasant diversion from the stresses of the world. Yet, as you courageously face the need to forgive and practice forgiveness, you will continue to grow in unexpected and delightful ways.

THE FORGIVENESS CHARACTER

One aspect of growth for you is within your character. You know the forgiveness journey, and you have been successful many times in forgiving. My challenge to you now is that there is more. Funny thing about the moral virtues—there is always room for more growth. Aristotle said that moral acts such as justice can only be considered truly just if they are performed by a person with the right character. Although he did not discuss forgiveness in this context, it does follow that forgiving actions can only be considered truly forgiveness when a person of right character performs that act of forgiving. What did Aristotle mean here? He means that there are all kinds of reasons for engaging in acts of forgiveness. For example, a person may forgive the boss to keep a job (expedience). A person may forgive only to feel better, with little concern for the person who is forgiven (self-interest alone). A person might forgive because of peer pressure to do so (conformity).

Aristotle's challenge to you is to cultivate the right reasons for forgiving, the right motivation, the right passions, and the right disposition.[2] The right reasons include the following:

- I forgive because I am having mercy on the one who hurt me. I am aware of this.
- I forgive out of the principle of agape love. I will try to offer this love even to those who hurt me.
- I forgive because I want this agape love to be a part of who I am.

The right motivation includes the following:

- The free will: I choose to forgive and I am not doing so because of any external pressures from others.
- The good will: I am motivated to bring good to the one who hurt me and to others.
- The strong will: I will persevere in this forgiving even if it is difficult.

The right passions include

- feelings of agape love (a softened heart that is in service to others, not some kind of romantic feeling),

- feelings that are appropriate to the person and the situation (not too much or too little of the feelings), and
- a love for forgiveness (you actually love to forgive because you know it is a moral good).

The right disposition includes the following:

- One is not just performing acts of forgiveness, but performing them excellently (getting it right for the right reasons).
- In the performance of the virtue, the forgiver becomes a good man or a good woman (he or she has cultivated a character that is prone to actions and feelings of agape love).
- All of this is done in the context of a balanced life (not dwelling all the time on forgiveness and not ignoring it except on a few occasions a year).

As you bring your knowledge of forgiveness to others, are you doing so with a good character, with a forgiving character?

STANDING IN THE TRUTH OF WHO YOU ARE

In the next chapter, I will be challenging you to bring forgiveness into the world of others—into the hearts of children and teachers, into the heart of businesses and other work places, into places of worship. Before we do that, I would like to pause briefly and ask you to take a broader and deeper perspective on yourself as I ask you some questions that are now familiar to you. They are primarily familiar to you because you have been asking them of other people. The intent of these questions is to develop your forgiveness character. Forgiveness is a paradox in this sense: It seems that the more we give to others in a loving way, the more we get back in return. The questions here are related to those from the previous chapter in which I asked you to reflect on your own inherent worth. Now I will ask you to do so through the more detailed lens of the personal, global, and cosmic perspectives. Here, then, are my questions:

- When you take the personal perspective on yourself (see Chapter 10 for a review), can you see a person (you) who has stood up to being emotionally wounded and is now trying not to wound others?
- When you take the global perspective on yourself, can you see that you are a person and that you are now able to meet other persons in their woundedness and help them to heal emotionally?[3]
- When you take the cosmic perspective on yourself, who are you? If you are like Inez, a person of faith, can you see yourself as made in the image and likeness of God? If you are a humanist like Sterling, can you see that you are special, unique, and irreplaceable and so you should treat yourself with love and respect as you do this for others?
- Please reread what you have written about in your Unfolding Love Story. Now please add to it, deepen it, tell the truth of who you are becoming.
- Who are you?

Your answers, I hope, will strengthen you as you bring your knowledge of forgiveness to others.

Part V

GIVING THE GIFT OF FORGIVENESS TO OTHERS

CHAPTER 17

QUESTIONS AS YOU GIVE FORGIVENESS TO OTHERS

Although looking back can help us see the progress we have made, if we are to continue that progress, then we must also begin looking into the future. Where are we going from here and why? Forgiveness, because it is one of the virtues, challenges us to keep going as we develop more fully as persons. We are never quite finished with our growth in having mercy on others. As you are on that mountain peak surveying your past, present, and future with forgiveness, I want you to see a new adventure awaiting you: giving forgiveness away to others.

I have come to realize that stepping into this realm of giving forgiveness away is not easy. A number of years ago, an enthusiastic person with great intentions approached me with the prospect of giving forgiveness curricula to the teachers in a local school. For several weeks, he and I exchanged ideas about forgiveness education, how and when to teach it, the possible benefits, and related issues. When it came time for him to approach one of the teachers, he completely froze. I mean, he panicked. "I can't do it," he protested with an annoyance that surprised me. How could he now be so agitated with forgiveness when he had been so enthusiastic just days before? And besides, he approached me, not the other way around.

Over the years, I have met people like my friend who are quite hesitant to talk with others about important issues. The fear of stepping on others' toes is so pervasive that it needs some questioning and debate. Why assume that sharing forgiveness is insensitive without examining this assumption? What a waste if we just absorb the assumption without reflection and even some challenge.

How often do you have a chance to leave something of truly lasting value in your society? Life surely need not be led with quiet desperation, as Henry David Thoreau once challenged us. Because I have seen a growing ambivalence in people about sharing what they know is good, at least when it comes to the virtues and related topics, we need to pause here and consider the issue: Are you being The Great Imposer if you discuss forgiveness with others? The best way to present this debate is through dialogue. In other words, I do not want to simply tell you that it is OK to give forgiveness to others. Instead, let us listen to someone who is ambivalent about this, who is not simply assuming that she should (or should not) bring this topic to her own stepchildren and others. Inez shares my friend's hesitations.

You will be meeting Inez and Sophia here for the final time. Inez, as you know, has a chance to teach children about the fine points of forgiveness. How can you go about such an important task well, respecting the child, respecting forgiveness, and respecting the process of education? Let's listen in as Inez begins this adventure and as she brings some serious concerns to the task.

> *Inez:* Today I wanted to discuss your challenge to me of teaching Kailey and Cade, my two stepchildren, about forgiveness.
>
> *Sophia:* You are ready to be an instructor, then?
>
> *Inez:* No, at least not yet. I want to discuss the issue, not plan for the instruction. I'm not convinced yet that this is a good thing.

Sophia: What are your concerns?

Inez: Being Inez-the-Dictator, for one.

Sophia: I don't follow you.

Inez: It feels kind of strange to just waltz into the children's lives and say, "OK, kids, it's time to become forgivers because your stepmom likes the subject." That's so controlling.

Sophia: I have a question for you. Suppose you found a strong nutrition program, one that has scientific backing to it. Would you be a dictator if you started them on that program?

Inez: Yes, if I did not discuss it with them first and get their input.

Sophia: And with a forgiveness education program, you can't get their opinion and permission?

Inez: [*hesitating*] I thought we just went ahead with something like that.

Sophia: Would you just "go ahead" if, say, you found a strong history program or a strong earth science program? Wouldn't you first talk it over? Even in schools, if teachers go ahead with a new curriculum, they pay close attention to how the students respond. If the new approach is boring or ineffective, the teachers adjust, don't they?

Inez: I would hope so.

Sophia: Then why not approach forgiveness education this way? You see, there is no such problem as your being a dictator. You should discuss it with them first; get their opinion; show them the materials; attend to any concerns; and then, if it seems good, go ahead. And don't forget to keep paying attention to the strengths and weaknesses of the program, in part on the basis of the children's reactions.

Inez: So, I am not a dictator then. But, I'm still dogmatic.

Sophia: You are? How so?

Inez: Well, for one thing, I'll be calling the shots about what forgiveness is and is not. They may not agree. They may have different opinions.

Sophia: If one of the children was in a math tutorial with you and his "opinion" was that $2 + 2 = 5$, would you be acting in a dogmatic way by challenging that?

Inez: Of course not, but mathematics and the study of virtues differ dramatically.

Sophia: I admit that the content of study is vastly different, but you seem to be questioning the truth of what forgiveness is and is not.

Inez: No, not exactly. I know what forgiveness is. I accept your definition, but not everyone would.

Sophia: And is that a problem?

Inez: Yes, of course. I am dogmatic if I say, "Here's the way it is, accept it or be banished!"

Sophia: [*with a smile*] But you need not banish someone for getting the wrong answer.

Inez: There you go again, almost equating forgiveness and math. Math has right and wrong answers, but the meaning of forgiveness does not.

Sophia: That is an assumption, a very grand assumption with serious implications.

Inez: And your view that forgiveness has one meaning and only one meaning, across historical time, across cultures, and across people with different experiences, is not an assumption? That, Sophia, is dogmatic.

Sophia: It is dogmatic only if I assume it in the face of contradictory evidence. If the evidence is on my side, and I reject it, what does that say about me?

Inez: It says that you are afraid of the truth.

Sophia: Yes it might say that. To stand in the truth of what forgiveness is—that is hardly dogmatic or dictatorial.

Inez: You'll have to convince me.

Sophia: Before I try to convince you, please tell me of your assumptions regarding the truth of the meaning of forgiveness.

Inez: I can be sure of what forgiveness is for me and that's all. I have thought about it deeply, thanks in part to you, and I am confident—for me—that I know what forgiveness is. I cannot nor should I impose that view on others.

Sophia: You are a relativist, then?

Inez: No. I am sure of what forgiveness is. It is not relative in its meaning for me.

Sophia: But, if someone came up to you and said, "I know what forgiveness is. I've studied it, and for me forgiveness is a three-layer chocolate cake with whipped-cream frosting," then you would have nothing to say to this person?

Inez: After I stifled my smile, I would have a few things to say to the person.

Sophia: But why? If his view of reality is that forgiveness is a chocolate cake and yours is that it is a virtue, practiced in the face of another's unfairness, in which you offer beneficence to that person, who is to say that one is right and the other wrong? To do that, you would have to abandon your position of relativism, in which you are assuming that each person possesses his own unique understanding.

Inez: But, I would rather keep it that way than appear to be dogmatic.

Sophia: Does it seem a bit extreme to you to view yourself as having to be either a chocolate-cake relativist or a dogmatist? Is there no other approach?

Inez: You'll have to tell me. I'm confused.

Sophia: What about a third approach—that of a truth seeker? You seek the truth of forgiveness whatever the outcome as you follow the argument wherever it leads.

Inez: I'm all for that.

Sophia: So was Socrates, but it led to his execution.

Inez: I don't think I'm ready for that.

Sophia: Most people aren't, and that is why they stick with their story that forgiveness is whatever anyone wants it to be as long as they don't impose that view on others and despite all of the evidence to the contrary.

Inez: Are you saying that forgiveness is one and only one thing for everyone in every age and in every culture?

Sophia: For now, I am only asking if we both have the courage to follow the argument wherever it leads, even if it leads to some unpopular conclusions.

Inez: OK, I'm ready for that.

Sophia: Then let's get technical for a little while.

Inez: If by "technical" you mean philosophically precise, then I am with you. Remember, I have a minor in philosophy. So, be prepared.

Sophia: Thank you for the friendly warning. As you know from studying philosophy, the ancient philosophers, such as Socrates, Plato, and Aristotle, believed—no, excuse me—they did not "believe" what I am about to say. They, instead, reached this conclusion by very careful reasoning—that virtues such as justice, wisdom, and courage are absolute, not relative; objective, not subjective; and universal to all people, not situation-specific to a particular circumstance.

Inez: [*wide-eyed*] That was quite a mouthful. I said I have a minor in this stuff, not a PhD. And besides, we spent most of our time in the modern age, with Descartes, Hume, and Kant and not with the dusty old ancients.

Sophia: You mean that the ancients were just set aside?

Inez: They are passé. No one takes their ideas seriously anymore.

Sophia: What is not taken seriously?

Inez: The biggest issue is this: There is no reality apart from my ability to think about that reality. Reality emerges as I am able to grasp it, make sense of it, and make it live within me.

Sophia: I have three questions for you. The answers to them will help us see if forgiveness is primarily objective (existing apart from me, long before I was born and long after I am gone) or subjective (existing because it exists within me—when I go, the idea goes with me).

Inez: I'm ready.

Sophia: First of three questions: Is 1 + 1 = 2 a correct statement even if a 5-year-old cannot understand it?

Inez: But . . .

Sophia: But? This isn't a court of law, of course, but I am tempted to ask, "Would you simply answer the question?" What do you think?

Inez: Yes, on the face of it this seems reasonable. But, I would like to probe this a little.

Sophia: In what way?

Inez: I can prove that 1 + 1 = 3.

Sophia: Be my guest.

Inez: Suppose we define "2" as "2 more than 1." If we do that, then the integer "2," being "2 more than 1" is actually 3. Therefore, 1 + 1 = 3.

Sophia: This sure seems like a magician's trick to me, a slight-of-hand philosophical trick. You simply redefined what "2" means. No one else will buy the definition of "2" as "it is 2 more than 1." You had to redefine what "2" is to make your point.

Inez: I almost had you, though.

Sophia: Perhaps for a second or two, but now to our question: Does 1 + 1 = 2 if we do not fiddle with conventional definitions of these numbers?

Inez: Yes, 1 + 1 = 2. No exceptions.

Sophia: Are you saying that the laws of mathematics exist outside of you? That they exist in every historical period and across all cultures, even if some people do not understand those laws?

Inez: Yes.

Sophia: Then mathematical laws are objective and not subjective. They exist even if someone fails to understand a particular mathematical truth. Do you agree with this?

Inez: I guess I have to for now, but that does not mean I will accept this with regard to the term *forgiveness*.

Sophia: Second question: Would geometric forms exist even if there were no people on the earth to think about them?

Inez: What do you mean?

Sophia: The four-straight-sided, closed-plane objects with four equal sides and four equal (90-degree) angles that are squares exist and have existed long before humans made their appearance on planet Earth.

Inez: So what? What does this have to do with my teaching my stepdaughter and stepson about forgiveness?

Sophia: Please bear with me. If all humans suddenly ceased to exist, and thus no one was around to think about and to draw squares, would squares still have the features that define them?

Inez: This is a trick question, right? It is kind of like the puzzle—if a tree falls in the woods and no one is around to hear it, does it make a sound?

Sophia: Well, no. This is about forms and not sounds or other sensations. Geometric forms such as squares do not consist only of the physical squares that we see or make. Instead, the form of a square is abstract or immaterial and is known through our intellect and not through our senses. We do not invent squares. They exist for us to discover. My question to you: Might forgiveness have characteristics like this in that it has an essence to it that we discover, not invent?

Inez: No. That is ridiculous. Forgiveness cannot be seen in the same way that a triangle can be indirectly seen. If a child draws a triangle, that is a physical—a material—representation of the abstract idea of the triangle. There is no physical counterpart to forgiveness. You cannot represent it in the physical world. No, triangles and forgiveness are very different. This is why I hesitate to teach my stepchildren. They need to figure out forgiveness for themselves.

Sophia: So, the only things in the world that have underlying, abstract essences to them that are objectively real apart from our ability to perceive them are such things as triangles, squares, and other geometric forms?

Inez: For now, I am saying "yes." Except for mathematical laws. I'm saying "yes" to that, too. Math has underlying rules that exist even if I can't understand math.

Sophia: Third question: What about language?

Inez: What about language?

Sophia: Words have meaning apart from people's subtle differences in understanding the nuances of the meaning. For example, you could not understand very clearly any of the discussion of forgiveness that we have had to date unless you and I had a common understanding (for the most part) of what the words mean. This would be the case whether we were speaking in English or whether someone translated the words into Spanish, German, or Chinese. Those who could speak these different languages would still understand the gist of the discussion in the same way.

Inez: What are you trying to say?

Sophia: I am asking whether language is real . . . whether language has meaning apart from the subjective understanding of particular people.

Inez: Yes, it surely seems to be so. Otherwise, you and I could not communicate, we could not translate texts from other languages, and the world would be a very confusing place. Forget about ordering a pizza in Rome, even if I knew Italian. After all, if the waiter and I don't both understand the word *pizza*, I'm more likely to get a fish with an eye staring back at me for dinner than a pizza.

Sophia: Do you see the objective nature of language?

Inez: Yes.

Sophia: Should we go into the issue of grammar? Can you see a structure to grammar that transcends people's subjective sense of sentence organization?

Inez: We studied that in philosophy class. Some of the postmodern writers are frustrated because they can't get rid of grammar and still make their points. Grammar is an embarrassment to people who say that there is no objective reality. They either accept the rules of grammar—that exist apart from them—or they are relegated to talking nonsense.

Sophia: Language and its organization in grammar exist apart from people's subjective understanding of them. People do not invent language or grammar; they discover the rules behind them. Do you see that the word *forgiveness* also has objective characteristics, existing apart from you and me?

Inez: Noooooo. You are assuming again. You don't know if people in Taiwan, for example, would use the same kinds of words that we use when discussing forgiveness.

Sophia: But, you are now making an assumption. You are assuming that I must be wrong.

Inez: Then prove me wrong.

Sophia: We digress from our discussion of whether forgiveness possesses objective, absolute, and universal properties, or subjective, relative, and situation-specific properties, but let us examine the science and then get back to our discussion. Are you familiar with a research instrument to study forgiveness—the Enright Forgiveness Inventory?

Inez: No, I am not.

Sophia: It is similar to the Personal Forgiveness Scale you have been using with me. The Personal Forgiveness Scale only has 18 items in it, whereas the other is longer. It is a 60-item research instrument that asks people to think of one person who has hurt them deeply and then to think about that person in terms of feeling, behaviors, and current thoughts about them. For example, the person considers such statements as these: "I show friendship toward the one who hurt me," "I avoid the person," "I think he or she is worthy of respect," "I feel kindness toward him or her," "I feel negative toward him or her." The more positive the responses, then the more the person forgives.

Inez: OK, I am with you so far.

Sophia: That scale, which represents one slice of forgiveness, has been translated into German, Hebrew, Korean, Portuguese, and Taiwanese.[1] All of these different languages, representing something as subtle and abstract as forgiveness, could present quite a research challenge. In every one of the 14 studies across the wide cultural spectrum (Austria, Brazil, Israel, Korea, Taiwan, and the United States), people agreed that such statements as I just cited in the scale ("I think he or she is worthy of respect," for example) are about forgiveness and not such concepts as condoning or excusing. Those filling out the Enright Forgiveness Inventory were in agreement that the words on the page—the 60 items—were measuring forgiveness and not some other scientific idea.

Inez: What does that prove?

Sophia: It supports the notion that people in vastly different cultures are in common agreement about what forgiveness is. It provides some evidence that forgiveness is not something quirky to each culture.

Inez: Quirky?

Sophia: You know what I mean. This science was done to challenge the notion that people think similarly about what forgiveness is. This science had every opportunity to show us that people from different cultures disagree more than they agree about what forgiveness is. The findings, instead, showed that people in different cultures agree more than they disagree about what forgiveness is.

Inez: This research certainly does not show that forgiveness is unambiguously objective.

Sophia: No, of course not. No science can ever promise to do that for any moral variable, but look how far you and I have come in our discussion. We have shown that there are such objective themes in the world as mathematical laws; there are such objective themes in the world as geometric shapes; there are such objective themes as the meaning of language behind the spoken and written word; there are such objective themes as grammatical laws that cannot be broken if we want to use words in combination that make sense to us regardless of our culture; and the science of forgiveness, which has had every chance to overthrow this notion of objectivity, has not done so, and in fact, even with limited data from six cultures, the evidence is encouraging that when people use the word *forgiveness* they are, for the most part, in agreement about what it is.

Inez: So, are you saying that because there are objective features to the world and that forgiveness as a moral virtue could be one of them, then forgiveness has no subjective properties?

Sophia: No, I would never say that. Remember Aristotle's ideas on the characteristics of the virtues? One characteristic is that people do not all understand forgiveness in the same way because we are all growing in that understanding. We are at different points along the path to understanding. That is subjective because it concerns our own idiosyncratic understanding of what forgiveness is. Yet, we cannot be content with our current learning (our subjective understanding for now) because we should continue growing if we are to live The Forgiving Life.

Inez: So, you are claiming that forgiveness has both objective and subjective features.

Sophia: I am not simply making an assertion about this—blurting it out and that's it. The evidence from rational examination and even the limited science to date surely does not contradict this.

Inez: OK, we have discussed the objective versus subjective nature of forgiveness. What about the next of our three points, that forgiveness has absolute or relative properties?

Sophia: How do you understand the word *absolute?*

Inez: To be absolute to me means that something is unchanging across all of historical time. It never changes, such as $1 + 1 = 2$.

Sophia: And how, then, does the idea of something being absolute differ from something that is objective?

Inez: To be objective means that it is something "out there," independent of me. To be absolute means that it is unchanging. You don't really believe that forgiveness does not change, do you? We are evolved beings. We have changed and, as we have, our expression of the moral virtues has changed.

Sophia: You are sure of that? What is your evidence?

Inez: It only makes sense. If we have become more abstract thinkers as we have evolved, then it only follows that our views of forgiveness have changed.

Sophia: Perhaps, but then we are back to the issue of the objective nature of forgiveness. Has forgiveness itself changed or only our subjective understanding of it?

Inez: Good question. I cannot answer that.

Sophia: We cannot examine the meaning of the word *forgiveness* beyond written history, but when we examine the evidence from over 3,000 years ago, that evidence is strong in favor of the definition we have been using all along. When people forgive, they deliberately try to reduce resentment and offer goodness toward those who have been unjust to them. This is consistent with Hebrew, Christian, and Muslim traditions.[2]

Inez: Aren't all of those part of what we call the monotheistic traditions? All believe in "the one God." Of course they would agree with each other. That proves nothing.

Sophia: Confucianism is not a religion, and many say that Buddhism is not a religion but a philosophy. Neither claims the monotheistic traditions as its origin, but both agree that to forgive is to offer goodness to those who are unfair to us. The definition of forgiveness, although subtly different across these five ancient worldviews, converges significantly across all five.[3]

Inez: So, are you claiming that forgiveness is absolute because of this?

Sophia: No, I am not, but I am saying that these five systems of thought have had every chance to diverge from one another and they have not. There is more in common to their views of what forgiveness is than there are differences. We have to take that seriously, whether we like the conclusion or not.

Inez: We have one more issue, that between a universal view of forgiveness and what you are calling a situation-specific view. In other words, do most cultures think similarly or differently about forgiveness? I think you have answered my major doubt with the science you cited.

Sophia: I do not want to leave you with a false conclusion. I have not cited the cross-cultural evidence to convince you of the cultural universality of forgiveness. The science is not complete, and never will be, to make such a claim. However, the scientific evidence to date does not contradict this view.

Inez: But what about the varied customs for forgiveness across cultures and religions, such as the Hawaiian forgiveness ritual of Ho'oponopono, or the Jewish ritual of Yom Kippur, or the Catholic confessional? All of these are vastly different.

Sophia: Are they? Let's focus not on the specific behaviors of these rituals, which do differ significantly. Let us look beyond the behaviors to what the behaviors represent. Why do people engage in the rituals?

Inez: I suppose to make things right after unfairness.

Sophia: Right. And the one who was unfair hopes for the mercy of forgiveness from the one who was treated unfairly. The one treated unfairly hopes for repentance and change from the one who acted unfairly. The underlying features of forgiveness are preserved in each ritual.

Inez: Then forgiveness is universal.

Sophia: I am not ready to say that completely because we do not know. We could find a culture tomorrow that does the opposite of all of this. Yet, this is so unlikely. Have we ever found any culture that goes against the basic virtues of ours and others' cultures? Have you ever seen a culture that praises murder, or rewards theft, or honors disrespect?

Inez: No, and if I did, I'm not going to book my vacation flight to there too soon.

Sophia: For now, are you comfortable with the idea that there are features of forgiveness that transcend you and your ability to understand it (objective), seem to be unchanging across historical time (absolute), and seem to be held in common across cultures (universal)? At the same time, do you see that forgiveness also has features that are subjective, specific to your under-standing, and in need of your struggle and growth to more fully understand; are relative to you and your circumstance—again, this does not negate the possible absolute character of forgiveness; and are idiosyncratic to culture without negating the universal features that cut across all cultures?

Inez: I'd like to think about it some more.

Sophia: What about your previous desire to help Kailey and Cade learn more about forgiveness?

Inez: There is enough evidence for an objective, absolute, and universal quality to forgiveness that I am ready to help them.

Sophia: Who will be helping them: Inez-the Dictator and Inez-the-Dogmatist, or Inez-the-Truth-Seeker?

Inez: [*with a smile*] I'm not going to answer that one. You already know the answer.

Sophia: Shall we begin exploring the features of forgive-ness education?

Inez: Yes, but I have one more question. Let's suppose that we are wrong. Let's suppose that each culture really is substantially different in its understanding and practice of forgiveness. Let's further suppose that we go into another culture that does not have forgiveness education materials and impose them on that culture. What damage are we likely to do?

Sophia: First, I hope that we would never "impose." Second, let's say for the sake of argument that you are correct. We go into another culture with our understanding of forgiveness and aid teachers in their instruction of forgiveness, which is completely wrong for that culture. What is likely to happen?

Inez: The Teacher-as-Dictator and Teacher-as-Dogmatist ruins the kids while trying to do good.

Sophia: Do you see the assumption here?

Inez: There is no assumption.

Sophia: You are assuming that the teachers are ignorant. You are assuming that the teachers do not have a mind of their own. You are assuming that they uncritically teach something dangerous to the children. You are not giving the teachers or their culture enough credit.

Inez: Oh. I see. If I spoon-feed nonsense to teachers, they are not likely to buy it.

Sophia: What is you experience here? Have you ever known a culture to be so duped? Surely, some subcultures are conquered against their will, but they know the evil of what is happening to them. Would teachers uncritically accept your "dogmatism"?

Inez: No, I have never seen anything like that, and I don't expect to see it either.

Sophia: Are you then ready to help Cade and Kailey?

Inez: I'm ready to start slowly and see what happens.

CHAPTER 18

GIVING FORGIVENESS AWAY TO OUR CHILDREN AND IN OUR COMMUNITIES

In Chapter 13, we talked about giving your children a legacy of love through practicing forgiveness in the home. As you and your partner practice forgiving, you are helping your children to value it, see it in action, and perhaps embrace it for themselves. This chapter is even more direct that that. Why not be explicit about forgiveness with the children? It is one thing to model forgiveness, hold it up as important, and practice it. It is an entirely different matter to hold forgiveness up to the light; examine it; discuss it directly; and help the children know why it is modeled, valued, and practiced in the home. We will be making the understanding of forgiveness explicit in this chapter rather than keeping it implicit, with the children standing on the sidelines and watching the forgiveness drama unfold. They will now be part of the action.

We proceed in two ways in this chapter. First, I discuss some preliminaries with you about being a teacher of forgiveness for children. Second, I describe to you the actual forgiveness curriculum materials (available at http://www.forgiveness-institute.org) which have been developed and tested in schools since 2002. I want you to see what these are like so that you can decide for yourself if you want to use these materials in service to your (or others') children.

SOME BASICS OF FORGIVENESS WITH CHILDREN

I have heard some people say, "But, children can't be taught how to forgive because they are too young to even understand what it is." If you think about it, children's ability to understand forgiveness is actually not a matter of opinion but instead a question that can be scientifically tested. The evidence that children understand and can be taught about forgiveness was presented in Chapter 2. Children as young as 5 and 6 years old can learn about forgiveness, with anger reduction being one common outcome in these studies. So, your teaching can be effective with those children and adolescents whom you choose to help.

It is my opinion, and perhaps this could also be tested scientifically but to date has not, that children will learn better if you as the teacher first practice forgiveness before teaching it. A soccer coach who has never played the game might prove to be less effective than someone who has been immersed in the game. It probably is the same with forgiveness. So, the challenge is for you to be a forgiver first and then a teacher of forgiveness.

As Aristotle taught us, the learning of any virtue is developmental—it takes time; we start with minimal understanding and progress in insight and competence as we practice, practice, and practice the virtue. From my own experience (and the evidence presented in Chapter 2 on scientific investigations of these forgiveness programs in schools), children are able to see that people possess inherent worth. They are able to give and receive love, especially if they are loved. They are able to forgive.

Eventually, children realize that they can generalize their forgiving—if a child forgives her brother, she understands that she can try to forgive her aunt, cousin, or friend. Later, older children and adolescents begin to see, as they practice forgiveness, that it is important to them in their personal lives. They consciously embrace it as a meaningful and even essential activity. In later adolescence and adulthood, some people realize that forgiveness is far more than an activity, far more than something "out there." Now, the developing person realizes that forgiveness is "part of my very identity, part of who I am." It is here that forgiveness is embraced and expressed in many and varied situations, for to do otherwise is to contradict the self.

FORGIVENESS CURRICULA FOR CHILDREN AND ADOLESCENTS

Table 18.1 gives you a list of all the forgiveness curriculum guides available to date. These guides are professionally produced, and each averages more than 100 pages in length. The guides follow the

---

TABLE 18.1. Forgiveness Curriculum Guides Currently Available

Guide	Intended ages
Enright, R. D., & Knutson, J. A. (2010). *I can love! A building block of forgiveness.* Madison, WI: International Forgiveness Institute.	Prekindergarten children, ages 4 and 5
Knutson, J. A., & Enright, R. D. (2008). *The heart of love as the building blocks of forgiveness.* Madison, WI: International Forgiveness Institute.	Kindergarten children, ages 5 and 6
Knutson, J. A., & Enright, R. D. (2008). *The adventure of forgiveness: A guided curriculum for children, ages 6–8* (Rev. ed.). Madison, WI: International Forgiveness Institute.	First-grade children, ages 6 and 7
Knutson, J. A., & Enright, R. D. (2008). *Discovering forgiveness: A guided curriculum for children, ages 6–8* (Rev. ed.).	Second-grade children, ages 7 and 8

(continued)

TABLE 18.1. Forgiveness Curriculum Guides Currently Available (Continued)

Guide	Intended ages
Madison, WI: International Forgiveness Institute.	
Knutson, J. A., & Enright, R. D. (2008). *The joy of forgiveness: A guided curriculum for children, ages 9–11* (Rev. ed.). Madison, WI: International Forgiveness Institute.	Third-grade children, ages 8 and 9
Enright, R. D., & Knutson. J. A. (2010). *Reaching out through forgiveness: A guided curriculum for children ages 9–11.* Madison, WI: International Forgiveness Institute	Fourth-grade children, ages 9 through 11
Knutson, J. A., & Enright, R. D. (2008). *The journey toward forgiveness: A guided curriculum for children, ages 10–12* (Rev. ed.). Madison, WI: International Forgiveness Institute.	Fifth-grade children, ages 10 and 11
Knutson, J. A., & Enright, R. D. (2008). *Be your best self: A guided forgiveness education curriculum* (Rev. ed.). Madison, WI: International Forgiveness Institute.	Sixth-grade adolescents, ages 11 and 12
Knutson, J. A., & Enright, R. D. (2008). *Be your best self: Giving and receiving forgiveness.* Madison, WI: International Forgiveness Institute.	Seventh-grade adolescents, ages 12 and 13
Flesch, A., & Enright, R. D. (2009). *Healing through the heroic gift of forgiveness.* Madison, WI: International Forgiveness Institute.	Eighth-grade adolescents, ages 13 and 14

developmental progression discussed previously, in that the younger children get the basics of forgiveness in preparation for the later middle school years when they as adolescents will be encouraged to practice forgiving, not unlike the progression you have experienced in this book.

The First-Grade Curriculum Guide

I would like now to describe the first-grade (ages 6–7 years or Primary 3 in the United Kingdom) guide to give you a sense of what is in it and the other guides to help you make an informed decision about whether to use them. The curriculum guide consists of 17 lessons. Each is written to take approximately 45 minutes or less, with the intention that you would teach these lessons about once each week. Additional activities in the guide at the end of each lesson are provided for you in case you and the child wish to extend the learning.

The gist of the program is that forgiveness is taught through the medium of story. The children learn that conflicts arise and that we have a wide range of options to unfair treatment through stories such as Dr. Seuss's *Horton Hears a Who, Horton Hatches the Egg, The Sneetches,* and *Yertle the Turtle.* The guide for first-grade children is divided into three parts. In Part 1, you simply introduce five key concepts that underlie forgiveness (the inherent worth of all people, kindness, respect, generosity, and love), without mentioning the word *forgiveness.* In Part 2, the children hear stories in which the story characters display instances of forgiveness through inherent worth, kindness, respect, generosity, and love (or their opposites of unkindness, disrespect, and stinginess) toward another story character who acted unfairly. In Part 3, if the children are ready, you help them, if they so choose, to apply the five principles (inherent worth, kindness, respect, generosity, and love) toward forgiving a person who has hurt them.

Throughout the implementation of this program, you make the important distinction between learning about forgiveness and choosing to practice it in certain contexts. The program is careful to emphasize the distinction between forgiveness and reconciliation. A child does not reconcile with an unrepentant child who bullies, for example.

Exhibit 18.1 gives you an example of Lesson 1 from the first-grade forgiveness curriculum guide. As you will see, this and all subsequent lessons have a "Main Ideas" section for you as the instructor (or for whomever does the teaching). This is followed by the General Objectives section, which gives you a concrete sense of what the child will be learning in this lesson. Next, the Behavioral Objectives section discusses the actual activities in which you and the child will be engaged so that the general objectives can be accomplished. The list of materials follows in the Materials section. These guides require that you visit the local library or order books and DVDs to accomplish the learning. We list for you all of the materials to be used within any one guide. Next comes the Procedures section, which explains what the instructor can do to help the children learn. Then comes the Discussion Questions section, with questions geared to the story and to the specific learning for that day. Finally, there is an Activities section if you wish to extend the learning beyond the discussion questions.

The Other Guides

The other guides—for prekindergarten, kindergarten, and Grades 2 through 8—all follow this format of Main Ideas, General Objectives, Behavioral Objectives, Materials, Procedures, Discussion Questions, and Activities. As we advance up the grade levels, the students get lengthier readings (chapter books, for example, rather than picture books), and the discussion questions require more challenging

---

EXHIBIT 18.1. **First-Grade Lesson 1: A Person Is a Person: Part 1**

THE MAIN IDEAS OF THE LESSON

This is the first of three lessons in Part 1 that will teach about the concept of inherent worth. As the children learn about inherent worth, they will be provided with an important foundation that will help them as they learn to forgive in later lessons.

What does it mean to say that all people have inherent worth? It means that *all people* are of great value (deep worth). They should not be used for others' ends. The deep worth of all people is not based on appearance, possessions, behavior, position in life, place of residence, or other such external differences. These differences certainly contribute to our unique personalities and lifestyles, but they do not determine value. A focus on differences may cause us to miss the fact that all people have deep worth.

How do we get inherent worth (deep worth)? It cannot be earned nor can it be taken away. All people have inherent worth (deep personal value) simply because they are people.

People are not on this earth to be used, manipulated, or disrespected. We are to treat each person as they are—people of deep worth.

GENERAL OBJECTIVES

The children will learn that

All people are of deep worth. A person is a person.

All people should not be used as others' ends.

Inherent worth is not based on personal differences like appearance, possessions, behavior, position in life, place of residence, and so forth.

Inherent worth cannot be earned nor can it be taken away.

All people have inherent worth (deep personal value) simply because they are people.

People are not on this earth to be used, manipulated, or disrespected. We are to try treating each person as they are—people of great worth.

(continued)

317

> **EXHIBIT 18.1.** First-Grade Lesson 1: A Person Is a
> Person: Part 1 (*Continued*)

BEHAVIORAL OBJECTIVES

The children will
Listen to a story written by Dr. Seuss entitled *Horton Hears a Who.*
Participate in a class discussion.
Participate in the A Person Is a Person activity.

MATERIALS

Horton Hears a Who, written by Dr. Seuss
Chalkboard and chalk or paper and pencil

PROCEDURES

The following procedures are to serve as guidelines for you. Please feel free to make adjustments and/or improvements to the procedures, discussion questions, or activities if it will help you to more effectively meet the needs of your children. To maintain the integrity of the curriculum, please make certain that the objectives of the lesson are met.

1. Introduce the Forgiveness Education curriculum. Tell the children, "Today you are being given a special opportunity to begin a journey that will teach you about forgiveness. When we forgive, we begin to see that a person who caused us an unfair hurt has deep worth. We begin to soften our hearts toward that person so that we are not angry at him or her for what he or she did. As we first begin our journey of forgiveness, we will not talk about forgiveness itself, but will learn about some of the things that can help a person to forgive. In the first three lessons, we will talk about the importance of seeing the worth in all people. Then we will discuss love. In Lessons 5

EXHIBIT 18.1. First-Grade Lesson 1: A Person Is a Person: Part 1 (*Continued*)

through 7, we will learn about kindness, respect, and generosity. After that we will begin to talk about forgiveness itself. But, for now, let us turn to today's lesson where we talk about seeing the worth in all people."

2. Introduce the lesson by telling the children that they will be listening to a story written by Dr. Seuss. Dr. Seuss was a popular children's author in the United States. He understood that the happiest children are those who can treat themselves and others well. Dr. Seuss wrote many books that are fun to read and that teach us how to treat people well. We will be reading several of his books and watching one of his videos over the course of this year.

3. Introduce the book written by Dr. Seuss entitled *Horton Hears a Who*. You may want to orient the children to the primary lesson of this book by telling the children, "Listen for the words, 'a person is a person, no matter how small.' As you listen to the story, think about what Dr. Seuss may have meant by these words."

4. Conduct the discussion. The questions can be found in the Discussion section.

5. Have the children participate in the A Person Is A Person activity. See the Activities section for further instructions.

6. Conclude by summarizing the main points of the lesson.
   - What does it mean to say that all people have inherent worth? It means that all people are of great value (deep worth). They are ends in-and-of themselves. This worth is not based on appearance, possessions, behavior, position in life, place of residence, or other such external differences. A focus on differences may cause us to miss the fact that all people have deep worth.
   - How do we get inherent worth (deep worth)? It cannot be earned nor can it be taken away. All people have inherent worth (deep personal value) simply because they are people.
   - It is important that we treat all people as people of great worth.

(continued)

EXHIBIT 18.1. **First-Grade Lesson 1: A Person Is a Person: Part 1 (*Continued*)**

DISCUSSION QUESTIONS

1. What is the story about?
2. Throughout the story, Horton kept saying, "A person is a person, no matter how small." What do you think that means? A person is a person, no matter what he or she looks like, what he or she does in life, and so forth. People have deep worth because they are people.
3. Did Horton know the Whos before he heard them shouting out?
4. How did he know that they were people of deep worth if he didn't know them before? He understood that all people have deep worth regardless of what they look like, where they live, what they can do, and so forth.
5. Did it matter to Horton that the Whos were very small?
6. If size of a person does not matter, what else does not matter when deciding whether a person has deep worth?

ACTIVITY: A PERSON IS A PERSON NO MATTER . . .

You may decide whether to include an activity in the lesson.

A Person Is A Person No Matter . . .

Objective:
The children will list some of the factors that make "a person a person." They will learn that all people have deep worth. They will learn that this deep worth is not based on physical appearance, possessions, career, or other external features. They will learn that people should not be treated as other people's ends and should be treated as people of deep worth.

Instructions:
You will write "A person is a person no matter . . . " on a piece of paper. The children will make a list of the things that do not matter when thinking

> **EXHIBIT 18.1.** **First-Grade Lesson 1: A Person Is a Person: Part 1** (*Continued*)
>
> about a person's deep worth. You may want to classify the various answers. For example, at first your child may focus on a person's possessions (money, houses, and toys); later he or she may focus on physical features (height, weight, appearance), still later on physical strength (health, athletic ability), and perhaps he or she may even focus on one's role in society (firefighter, business person, janitor). If your child misses some of the categories, you may want to ask specific questions to help him or her gain a full understanding of the main ideas of the lesson. For example, if a person is very good looking, does he or she have deeper worth than someone who is not good looking? Why? Why not? If a person is a very healthy person, does he or she have deeper worth than someone who is sick or in a wheelchair? Why? Why not? If a person has lots of money, does he or she have deeper worth than someone who is very poor? Why? Why not? If someone is a mayor of a city, does he or she have deeper worth than a person who cleans? Why? Why not? If someone is a star soccer player, does he or she have deeper worth than someone who cannot play the game? Why? Why not?

answers (seeing all people as part of the human family as we discuss the concept of inherent worth in eighth grade, for example).

THE OVERALL OBJECTIVE

I am hoping for your children that they grow to be virtuous forgivers as they increase their psychological, philosophical, and theological sophistication. I urge you to tie the learning into the worldview and religious outlook that you see as morally good. The overall objective is to equip your children with the expertise to forgive so that when the storms of life hit them as adults, they will have the protection of forgiveness to take out and to use against that storm. Your children might weather the storms better as a result, and others might benefit from what your children do as they forgive in the context of challenge, discontent, and discord. Perhaps your children will contribute to a more peaceful world because of your efforts on behalf of forgiveness with them now.

THE FORGIVING COMMUNITIES

Forgiveness education's main purpose in the long run is to strengthen individuals in the hope that communities are strengthened for greater peace. If forgiveness is basically developed and preserved within a person, what happens when that person passes on? Does the notion of forgiveness pass on as well? The answer seems to be "no" because forgiveness, if these people give it away, becomes preserved in other people. For example, as Inez teaches Kailey and Cade, forgiveness is passed on to another generation. Yet, if we think about this, the two children also have a finite life. Even if they give forgiveness away to others, if the generation that follows them fails to do so, eventually there will be nothing left of forgiveness in a family or a community or even a larger society. We need a larger perspective on forgiveness than this.

We are not seeing far enough if all we see is the moral virtue of forgiveness existing only inside of each individual. How can we preserve the nature of forgiveness across time? Here is an analogy from an entirely different discipline to help us get a grasp on this issue: preserving forgiveness for future generations. Have you read the book, *How the Irish Saved Civilization* by Thomas Cahill?[1] It details how Irish monks painstakingly saved the manuscripts, such as Aristotle's writings, which formed the basis of Western civilization. They did this together while in community with one another. They did this while continental Europe was being overrun by hoards

322

that burned these books and manuscripts. Without their efforts, the manuscripts could have been lost forever.

If you think about it, this was a group effort to save the treasury of Western thought, not an individual effort. The monks were part of an organization that held up education as one of its greatest values. Together while in their monastic communities, they were able to save precious writings for future generations.

They probably saved some manuscripts dealing with forgiveness, too, although this is not my point. What I am trying to get across is that the community itself did the preserving, not an individual or a collection of individuals. For example, the community had to have formed a norm stating that it is worthwhile to preserve the treasury of Western thought. The community had to have a common goal. The community itself had to persevere in that goal long after the first monks started to transcribe the writings of Aristotle and others.

The group serves a different function than the individual does when it comes to forgiveness. The group can establish norms of forgiveness—hold the idea up as important and create a common goal. The group can keep this goal going for many more years than can a person with an average life span of 80 years or so. Groups can keep the idea alive for centuries or millennia.

So, what then do we do about forgiveness if we as individuals have a much shorter life span than a group might have? How do we work with the individual task of forgiveness—to grow in virtue—and the group task—to create a common goal for forgiveness, establish that as a norm in the group, and persevere in all of this for many years?

The School as a Forgiving Community

The Forgiving Community is an idea that can become a reality wherever there is a collection of individuals who wish to unite toward a common goal and go after that goal and preserve that goal for future generations. As an example, recall our discussion of the forgiveness education programs in the Belfast, Northern Ireland schools. One of the schools, because of the lead taken by the school's principal, is now known as a "forgiveness school." If each teacher gives forgiveness instruction to the students behind closed doors, he or she is acting independently, not as part of a cohesive unit. Singing four-part harmony is very different from singing alone because singers have to work as a group to adjust the pitch of their notes so they are in tune.

When all or most teachers in a school commit to teaching forgiveness, they are establishing a norm. The principal and the teachers have agreed that in this particular school, forgiveness is to be valued. Their tasks are to teach forgiveness well at each grade level; to discuss forgiveness among themselves as professional educators so they can learn from and support each other in the delivery of forgiveness instruction; to bring forgiveness beyond instruction from curriculum guides (important as that is) into the arena of the classroom and school discipline; and to involve parents by sending notes home to encourage them to learn about and practice forgiveness in the home, thus advancing the development of this virtue in both school and home.

As previously stated, forgiveness should be brought into the important areas of the school well beyond just instruction. As an example, if two children are having an argument on the playground, a teacher may take them aside and talk with them about what it means to forgive and reconcile. As another example, a teacher may have mercy on a child who is showing bullying behavior (by not punishing him or her) and then challenging that child to now go and have mercy on the child he or she has been bullying. Forgiveness pervades relationships and interactions and helps reduce resentments in the students and between students and teachers. It becomes a part of the life of the community in that school.

This approach could be replicated elsewhere. If such a model for the community works in a school setting, why could it not work in family settings, at work, and in churches and other houses of worship—anywhere that individuals come together for a common purpose?

The Workplace as a Forgiving Community

I can envision this happening in the workplace. Here are the nine steps to making a company into a Forgiving Community:

- First, approach a leader in the organization and discuss the beauty of forgiveness. You should probably use a word different from *beauty* or else you might lose the person right then and there. You could talk of the importance (there is a good business word, *importance*) of forgiveness in reducing resentment. Resentment by many in a workplace probably hampers productivity, as it did for the adolescents' learning when they were overly angry because of certain injustices against them. Their anger put them at risk of doing poorly in school. After they forgave and their resentment went down, their productivity went up with better grades and fewer detentions. This could happen in a corporation, too. At least we could test it out and see.
- Next, hold a workshop for the workers and leaders in which you describe what forgiveness is and is not. I think you could probably do this in half a day or maybe one full day. Introduce the staff to the idea of forgiveness so that they have a very clear idea about it.
- Describe to the leaders and workers the actual scientific findings of studies on forgiveness with adults and with children and adolescents. Give them a chance to see that forgiveness, properly understood and practiced in the company setting, could

eliminate much anger. Do you think there is any resentment in companies? Only kidding with that question because the answer is all too sadly obvious.

- Ask them to try forgiving one person for one injustice within the organization, just to get a sense of the beauty—sorry, I mean the importance—of this virtue.

- To preserve the notion of forgiveness in the company, organize one (even small) group whose task it is to read about forgiveness, discuss it, and find ways of bringing it into the workplace, just as the principal and staff did at the school in Belfast, Northern Ireland. Preserve the norm of forgiveness. Preserve it as a goal. This small group could meet, I would think, as seldom as once a month for an hour to preserve the norm that forgiveness is important.

- Suggest to those individuals in middle management that they encourage workers to forgive one another (as the teachers, who in a sense are "middle managers" at the school, encourage the children to forgive each other when there is tension).

- Suggest to the heads of the company that they meet together once a month for even 15 minutes to preserve the goal of forgiveness in the company, just as the principal keeps the norm of forgiveness strong in the school. If the heads of the company fail to preserve the norm of forgiveness, then the small group of workers could be there as a reminder. If the small group of workers fails to meet and to preserve the goal of forgiveness, then the heads of the company can be there to support them to stay at it. The two groups are a check-and-balance system.

- Consider creating symbols of forgiveness at least in a small, quiet way. As an example, the third-grade forgiveness curriculum has an exercise in which the class makes a forgiveness quilt that can be hung in the corridor outside the classroom for all to see as they walk by. What would be an appropriate symbol for a particular company that serves as a concrete reminder that this is a Forgiving Community? Within the wider community, here is another example: Belfast, Northern Ireland has a culture with many wall murals—messages in art regarding the spirit of the community. What if people within Belfast decided to create some forgiveness murals, as relatively permanent artistic signs of the call for mercy, forgiveness, and compassion within the community?

- Remember that with all of this going, forgiveness does not take the place of efficiency, organization, or profit, just as forgiveness in the school does not overtake discipline and learning, but it does become a part of the overall system, part of the overall goal of good learning. For a company, forgiveness becomes a part of overall good human relations.

Could you see these steps happening, for example, in a family or even a group of families?

Families and Places of Worship as Forgiving Communities

Let's consider groups of families. An initial meeting to share what forgiveness is and how it can be preserved in a group setting could lead to one member of each family coming together once a month to discuss a reading and to talk about the process of forgiveness in the home.

In places of worship, you could follow the corporate model of the pastors or other leaders coming together for even 15 minutes once a month and a small group of members getting together separately from the leaders to discuss forgiveness. Religious instruction for children could consciously and deliberately focus on person-to-person forgiveness for, say, 10% of the yearly instruction time. A commitment of (again, just to throw this out there) five sermons a year on the topic of person-to-person forgiveness could be considered. Creating forgiveness symbols within religious communities would seem to be a natural. Just as in the school in Northern Ireland, forgiveness could be held up as a norm with the goal of preserving forgiveness in this religious setting.

The overall purpose of the group's involvement would be to keep each individual growing in the virtue of forgiveness. The group effort supports individual growth. As certain individuals grow in the virtue of forgiveness, they then become the catalysts in the small groups to encourage sermons, religious instruction, and the persevering in forgiveness. Certain individuals in each generation, then, preserve the group norm and practice of forgiveness.

The Strong Will

Near the beginning of the book, we discussed three important issues for those interested in living the forgiving life: the free will, the good will, and the strong will. These stand in the background and make the development of the virtue of forgiveness possible.

Might introducing forgiveness into communities be a guard, a kind of protection, against a weak will? A strong will is possessed by an individual, as we discussed earlier. That strong will could begin to fade in an individual and, if it does, then that person's commitment to forgiveness may begin to fade. In fact, I've seen it often.

Think of the Forgiving Community as a safeguard against any one person's strong will weakening. If Person A is all fired up about forgiveness and his or her will weakens, there are always others to take up the task of preserving the norm of the importance of forgiveness. There are others to keep the common goal alive in the group, to keep discussing, practicing, and encouraging forgiveness in the community. The group itself is a safety net for any one person's weakness, perhaps similar to what could have happened with the Irish monks as they preserved the thought of Western civilization. We can think of the Forgiving Community as the preserver of a forgiveness tradition in that group or community or society or even nation.

Getting Started

The formation of the Forgiving Community starts in here, inside of your moral self. You need the courage to approach one other person. You then need a strategy. Ask yourself: Will I start with the Family as a Forgiving Community, or the Workplace as a Forgiving Community, or the Place of Worship as a Forgiving Community? You must realize that you are one small person and so you cannot do it all. It will take other individuals to form other Forgiving Communities as well.

We are back to the importance of the strong will. I think it will take strong wills to establish forgiveness in the subcommunities of home, school, workplace, and places of worship. I think it will take even stronger wills to unite all of these subcommunities into an even larger community or societal norm that forgiveness deserves a place in society alongside justice.

There will never be a law requiring forgiveness because it is part of mercy, and societies do not demand mercy. Yet, we have been talking here about group norms (expectations, not laws) that can be a big part of how we interact with one another. For forgiveness to become a norm in society, the various subgroups will have to begin a dialogue with one another and with the leaders on the larger, community level. Only those who are strong in the virtue of forgiveness will be able to pull that off. We are back full circle to the importance of individual instruction on forgiveness so that each heart grows stronger in understanding and practicing it.

CHAPTER 19

YOUR FORGIVENESS LEGACY

We may have come to the end of the book, but your forgiveness journey has just begun. It is my hope for you that you never reach the end of that journey because we never reach the end or perfection of the virtues, including forgiveness. So, no matter what happens to you in this life, you have important work to do.

As you continue to write your Unfolding Love Story, I have a few reminders for you. First, who are you? If you recall from Chapter 6, Inez said, "I am a person who has been emotionally wounded; who has stood up to injustice; who is a person worthy of respect and mercy; and who is special, unique, and irreplaceable and therefore cannot be and must not be shunned, disrespected, or thrown away." At the very core of your being, do you believe this about yourself? Are you a person of worth? Why or why not? Do you have to earn your worth or is it inherent in you—unearned, absolute, and unconditional? Are you a person who loves, even if imperfectly? Even if you have a long way to go in developing agape love, you are on your way when you forgive others. As you love them (as best you can under the circumstances), please continue to see yourself more and more accurately—as someone who is capable of giving and receiving love and therefore someone who can do much good in this world. You are a person of great worth.

Second, who are the people who have treated you unjustly, all of those people in your life who failed to give love, perhaps when you needed it the most? Inez's statement applies to each of them as well. Each person who has hurt you has been emotionally wounded; is worthy of respect and love; is special, unique, and irreplaceable; and therefore must not be shunned, disrespected, or thrown away. Each of these people is far from worthless. Each has great worth. If our theory of forgiveness in Chapter 1 is correct, then your love toward some or all of these people might—just might—fill a gap that helps them to recover their own dignity and sense of worth. Your forgiving them may play a big part in their becoming more loving people to others, many of whom you will never meet. Your love for someone now may make a difference, for example, for a child four generations down the road.

Third, there are more chapters for you to write with the help of others as you continue your Unfolding Love Story. Forgiveness is not finished with you yet. How will you lead your life from this point forward? It is your choice. When that story is finally written, what will the final chapters say about you? The beauty of this story is that you are one of the contributing authors. You do not write it alone, of course, but with the help of those who encourage you, instruct and guide you, and even hurt you. You are never alone when it comes to your love story. It does not matter one little bit where the story was going before you embraced the virtue of forgiveness. What matters now is how you finish that story, how you start to live your life from this point forward.

What do you think? Do you think that most people are deliberately and consciously writing their own love stories, in part on the basis of leading The Forgiving Life? Or, are most people rushing by, not giving much thought to forgiveness or love?

What do you think? Do you think that most people are aware of their legacy, what they will leave behind from this precise moment on, or are they rushing about, not giving a moment's notice to that legacy?

What do you think? Do you think that you can make a difference in a few or even many people's lives by awakening them to the fact that they can rewrite their stories and make them love stories through forgiveness? Do you think you have within you what it takes to change a few or many people's legacies in this world? Do you think you have within you what it takes to form a Forgiving Community, in families, a school, a workplace, or a place of worship?

When I say that much of this is your choice, I am focusing on your free will. When I ask you to see the hurt in all who have hurt you, I am focusing on your good will. I now ask you this: How will you continue the forgiveness journey once you close this book and perhaps put it on the shelf or give it to others? I am asking you here to focus on your strong will. So often in this world we can be distracted from what really matters. The philosopher Blaise Pascal, writing in the 17th century, referred to these distractions as *diversions*.[1] To *divert* is to become sidetracked, to turn away, to so amuse ourselves that we hide from the pain of this world. Modern societies are steeped in diversion, and here is proof: Consider all of your extra income from the past year (left over after paying bills and saving some). Did you spend most of it creating a better world, or did you spend it on entertainment, music, hobbies, and the like? I bring this up not to make you feel bad but to drive home the point. We are in communities that highly value their diversions, and it is hard to escape it all. Diversions could be the very things that make you lose interest over time in leading The Forgiving Life as you—hardly noticing—drift into pleasant pursuits. We have so many ways to distract ourselves, with amusements and delights, that we can truly

333

forget what is important in this world. The fog of pleasure can make it difficult to see.

What do you think? Do you think modern society supports us more in our quest to lead The Forgiving Life or in leading a life of diversion?

Part of your Unfolding Love Story and part of your legacy will depend on how you deal with the diversions of this world as you move forward. You will have many, many opportunities to put down the writing of your love story and look elsewhere. Few people will even realize what you are doing if you drift away from forgiveness and take up a spirited hobby. And there is nothing wrong with hobbies as long as they do not become substitutes for your continuing love story.

Few will catch on that you have put your love story on the shelf as you pursue some seemingly harmless pastime that will not help to change the world, no matter how small that part of the world is. This is why you need the strong will—to fight to continue developing your love story and giving others a change to do likewise.

What does your common sense tell you now that you have struggled after forgiveness? Is it worth the effort? Has it begun to change you into a more loving person? Are your eyes now more trained on love so that you see it more easily and give it away more readily? Is it worth the struggle to now keep it—to hold it tightly— in your mind, in your heart, in your actions, and in your relationships? Is it worth the effort to not hold it so tightly within you so that you can willingly give it away to others?

To grow in any virtue is similar to building muscle in the gym through persistent hard work. We surely do not want to overdo anything, including the pursuit of fitness. Yet, we must avoid underdoing it, too, if we are to continue to grow. It is the same with forgiveness. We need to be persistently developing our forgiveness muscles as we become forgivingly fit. This opportunity is now laid out before you. What will you choose? Will you choose a life of diversion, comfort, and pleasure, or the more exciting life of risking love, challenging yourself to forgive, and helping others in their forgiveness fitness?

Think of this book as your fitness guide and I as one of your gym instructors. To which chapter would you like to turn as a way of increasing your strength, endurance, and happiness? If your will is strong enough to continue, I will help you develop your legacy.

PROCESS OF HOW PEOPLE FORGIVE SOMEONE WHO WAS UNJUST

PRELIMINARIES

Who hurt you?

How deeply were you hurt?

On what specific incident will you focus?

What were the circumstances at the time? Was it morning or afternoon? Cloudy or sunny? What was said? How did you respond?

PHASE I—UNCOVERING YOUR ANGER

How have you avoided dealing with anger?

Have you faced your anger?

Are you afraid to expose your shame or guilt?

Has your anger affected your health?

Have you been obsessed about the injury or the offender?

Do you compare your situation with that of the offender?

Has the injury caused a permanent change in your life?

Has the injury changed your worldview?

PHASE 2—DECIDING TO FORGIVE

Decide that what you have been doing hasn't worked.
Be willing to begin the forgiveness process.
Decide to forgive.

PHASE 3—WORKING ON FORGIVENESS

Work toward understanding.
Work toward compassion.
Accept the pain.
Give the offender a gift.

PHASE 4—DISCOVERY AND RELEASE FROM EMOTIONAL PRISON

Discover the meaning of suffering.
Discover your need for forgiveness.
Discover that you are not alone.
Discover the purpose of your life.
Discover the freedom of forgiveness.

APPENDIX B: FORGIVENESS LANDSCAPE RATING SCALE

Social Group for the person you are rating here (Family of Origin, Work Days, etc.). Please make your selection from Exhibit 8.1.

_____

    Person (grandfather, boss, and so forth). Please make your selection from Exhibit 8.1. _____

    Note: Please feel free to fill out this rating scale for the same person if there are other incidents of injustice from him or her toward you. If a person, for example, was unjust to you six different times and you wish to consider forgiving him or her for each incident, then please fill out this form six times for that person.

    Incident of Injustice (such as "Absent, Emotionally," "Anger, Excessive," "Ignoring," etc.). Please make your selection from Exhibit 8.2. _____

    Please rate the amount of emotional hurt you experienced at the time of the injustice regarding this person and this incident. Rate your degree of emotional woundedness (at the time of the incident) on a 0-to-10 scale. Please circle the appropriate level of hurt (at that time) for this one person and this one event:

    0 = _no hurt or emotional wounds whatsoever_

    1 = _a barely detectible amount of hurt or emotional wounds_

2 = *extremely mild hurt or emotional wounds*

3 = *very mild hurt*

4 = *mild hurt*

5 = *a medium amount of hurt or emotional wounds*

6 = *more than a medium amount of hurt or emotional wounds*

7 = *an amount of hurt or emotional wounds that approaches severe*

8 = *a severe amount of hurt or emotional wounds*

9 = *a very severe amount of hurt or emotional wounds*

10 = *most extreme hurt or emotional wounding possible*

APPENDIX C

PERSONAL FORGIVENESS SCALE

We are sometimes unfairly hurt by people, whether in our families, in friendships, at school, at work, or in other situations. We ask you now to think of someone who has hurt you unfairly and deeply—someone who has wounded your heart. For a few moments, visualize in your mind the events of that interaction. Try to see the person and try to experience what happened.

1. How deeply are you hurt right now by this person and this incident? (circle one)

No hurt	A little hurt	Some hurt	Much hurt	Very great hurt
I	2	3	4	5

2. Who hurt you?

Parent	Spouse	Child	Friend of the same gender	Friend of the opposite gender	Employer

Reproduced by special permission of the Publisher, MIND GARDEN, Inc., www.mindgarden.com from the Enright Forgiveness Inventory by Robert D. Enright and Julio Rique. Copyright 2000, 2004 by International Forgiveness Institute. Further reproduction is prohibited without the Publisher's written consent.

Other (specify):

3. Is the person living?

Yes	No

4. How long ago was the offense?
(Please write in the number of days or weeks, etc.)

____days ago	____months ago
____weeks ago	____years ago

5. Please briefly record from Exhibit 8.2 what the specific injustice was. Feel free to describe what happened when this person hurt you (as a way for you to remember as you practice forgiveness):

_____

_____

_____

_____

_____

_____

Now, please answer a series of questions about your current attitude toward this person. We do not want your rating of past attitudes, but your ratings of attitudes right now. All responses are confidential, so please answer honestly.

This set of items deals with your current feelings or emotions right now toward the person. Try to assess your actual feeling for the person on each item. For each item, please check the appropriate box matching your level of agreement that best describes your current feeling.

I feel _____ toward him/her. (Place each word in the blank when answering each item.)

I feel . . .	Strongly Disagree	Disagree	Slightly Disagree	Slightly Agree	Agree	Strongly Agree
1 warm						
2 negative						
3 kindness						
4 dislike						
5 happy						
6 angry						

This set of items deals with your current behavior toward the person. Consider how you do act or would act toward the person in answering the questions. For each item, please check the appropriate box matching your level of agreement that best describes your current behavior or probable behavior.

Regarding this person, I do or would _____. (Place each word or phrase in the blank when answering each item.)

I do or would do . . .	Strongly Disagree	Disagree	Slightly Disagree	Slightly Agree	Agree	Strongly Agree
7 show friendship						
8 avoid						
9 aid him/ her when in trouble						
10 ignore						
11 do a favor						
12 not speak to him/her						

This set of items deals with how you currently think about the person. Think about the kinds of thoughts that occupy your mind right now regarding this particular person. For each item please check the appropriate box matching your level of agreement that best describes your current thinking.

I think he or she is _____. (Place each word or phrase in the blank when answering each item.)

I think he or she is . . .	Strongly Disagree	Disagree	Slightly Disagree	Slightly Agree	Agree	Strongly Agree
13 of good quality						
14 corrupt						
15 a good person						

Regarding this person, I _____. (Place each word or phrase in the blank when answering each item.)

Regarding this person, I . . .	Strongly Disagree	Disagree	Slightly Disagree	Slightly Agree	Agree	Strongly Agree
16 disapprove of him/her.						
17 wish him/her well.						
18 condemn the person.						

In thinking through the person and event you just rated, please consider the following final questions.

	Strongly Disagree	Disagree	Slightly Disagree	Slightly Agree	Agree	Strongly Agree
19 The person was not wrong in what he or she did to me.						
20 My feelings were never hurt.						
21 What the person did was fair.						

APPENDIX D: THE FORGIVENESS GUIDEPOST FORM

Social group for the person you are rating here (family of origin, work days, etc.). Please make your selection from Exhibit 8.1 _____

    Person (grandfather, boss, etc.). Please make your selection from Exhibit 8.1 _____

    Incident of Injustice (such as "Absent, Emotionally," "Anger, Excessive," "Ignoring," etc.). Please make your selection from Exhibit 8.2 _____

UNCOVERING PHASE

1. Have you avoided dealing with your anger? In other words, might you still be denying the extent of your anger (or frustration, or sadness, or some other emotion)? 0 = *you are completely avoiding facing your anger;* 10 = *you are no longer avoiding the anger even a little bit.*

2. To what extent have you faced your anger? 0 = *not at all;* 10 = *completely.*

3. Are you feeling shame? 0 = *yes, to a very great extent;* 10 = *no, not at all.* Are you feeling guilt? 0 = *yes, to a very great extent;* 10 = *no, not at all.*

4. Is the anger affecting your health? 0 = *it is affecting your health now to a very great extent;* 10 = *it is not affecting at all your health right now.*

5. Are you thinking over and over about the injury? 0 = *yes, to a very great extent;* 10 = *no, not at all.*

6. Do you now compare your situation with that of the one who wounded you? 0 = *yes, to a very great extent;* 10 = *no, not at all.*

7. Is the injustice causing a significant change in your life now? 0 = *yes, to a very great extent;* 10 = *no, not at all.*

8. Is the injustice influencing your worldview? Are you now more negative in how you approach life and how you think about the world? 0 = *yes, to a very great extent;* 10 = *no, not at all.*

DECISION PHASE

9. Have you concluded that what you did prior to working on forgiveness has not worked so well? I ask to be sure that forgiveness is what you want to work on. 0 = *no, I am not at all sure that I want to work on forgiveness in particular;* 10 = *yes, I am completely sure that I want to work on forgiveness in particular.*

10. Are you willing to begin the forgiveness process? 0 = *no, I am sure that I do not want to start forgiving;* 10 = *yes, I am completely confident that I want to forgive.*

11. Decide to forgive. 0 = *I am not at all sure that I want to do no harm to the one who was unfair to me;* 10 = *I completely commit to doing no harm to the one who was unfair to me.*

WORK PHASE

12. Work toward understanding. Here I ask whether you have taken the personal, global, and cosmic perspectives on the person who was unfair to you. Do you see the person as a person and do you understand what that word *person* means? *0 = no, I have a very long way to go before I take these perspectives and see him or her as a person; 10 = yes, I have done the work, taken these perspectives, and see him or her as a person.*

13. Work toward compassion. *0 = no, I have no compassion whatsoever for the person; 10 = yes, I have great compassion toward him or her.*

14. Accept the pain. By this I mean that you are shouldering the pain of the injustice and not throwing that pain back to him or her in a psychological sense. I further mean that you are not tossing that pain onto others, wounding them. *0 = I am not bearing the pain well at all and so I might, even unintentionally, wound others because of my pain; 10 = yes, I understand what it means to accept the pain and I am not wounding others because of my pain.*

15. Giving a gift to the one who wounded you. *0 = no, I do not intend to give a gift of any kind to this person; 10 = yes, I have given a gift to him or her and I have thought carefully about the kind of gift that would be best for this person.*

DISCOVERY PHASE

16. Discover the meaning of suffering. This is not an action but an insight. *0 = I see no meaning whatsoever in what I have suffered from this person, my suffering is meaningless; 10 = I have given this much thought, and I have found great meaning in my suffering from what this person did to me.*

17. Discover your need to be forgiven. By this I mean that you realize that you have offended others and have needed or now are in need of their forgiveness. 0 = *no, I have not needed nor do I need others' forgiveness;* 10 = *yes, I fully realize my need to be forgiven by others and I have asked for that forgiveness.*

18. Discover that you are not alone. By this I mean that you see your connection with others. These others can help you on your forgiveness journey. 0 = *no, I am not aware that I need others' help to forgive;* 10 = *yes, I am well aware of my need for others as I walk the path of forgiveness.*

19. Discover the purpose for your life. Purpose is action oriented. You are pointing toward what you do in life, toward what you should be doing in life. 0 *no, I have not figured out at all my purpose in life;* 10 = *yes, I fully understand my purpose in life.*

20. Discover the freedom of forgiveness. By this I mean that you have experienced emotional relief and may even be mending a relationship, if this is possible for you. 0 = *no, I have experienced no freedom of forgiveness;* 10 = *yes, I have experienced tremendous freedom of forgiveness.*

NOTES

PREFACE

1. From *Forgiveness Is a Choice* (p. v), by R. D. Enright, 2001, Washington, DC: American Psychological Association.
2. *No Future Without Forgiveness,* by D. Tutu, 2000, New York, NY: Image.

CHAPTER 1. A THEORY OF FORGIVENESS IN BRIEF

1. The endnotes in this chapter (and only this chapter) are intended more for psychologists, philosophers, and other academics than for general readers because we are discussing the subtle points of theory here. If you are puzzled by any of my statements in the text, then these (perhaps difficult) endnotes may be worth your time. Psychologists and philosophers sometimes make a distinction between forgiveness and what they call *forgivingness.* I am not talking about forgivingness when I challenge you to lead The Forgiving Life. Forgivingness is like an attitude, a trait, or a disposition in which a person "has a tendency to forgive" or "generally forgives" or sees

himself or herself as "someone prone to forgive." Suppose someone has a "disposition toward working in a soup kitchen" but then never actually goes there or never dips the ladle into the soup. What exactly do we have here? If someone has a "disposition toward forgiving," is it possible that he or she could show the same inertia as our absent-from-the soup-kitchen person who also has a disposition? As we will see in this book, forgiveness properly understood is not only a disposition and certainly not a disposition considered independently from all the other characteristics of a virtuous life. Forgiveness as a virtue encompasses a much more complete approach to the world by including motivations ("I want to forgive"), thinking ("I see the one who hurt me as a person of worth"), feelings ("I have compassion toward him or her"), actions ("I forgive you"), as well as attitudes or dispositions ("I like forgiveness and like to practice it"). The Forgiving Life leads people to practice all of this over and over and eventually to develop a strong identity: "I am a forgiving person," not because one has a new disposition alone but because one truly practices forgiveness in all of its depth and loves doing it.

2. See *Agape: An Ethical Analysis,* by G. Outka, 1977, New Haven, CT: Yale University Press. To work and to love within psychoanalysis is mentioned on the American Psychoanalytic Association's website (http://www.apsa.org/About_Psychoanalysis.aspx); see also *A General Theory of Love,* by T. Lewis, F. Amini, and R. Lannon, 2001, New York, NY: Vintage.

3. Those who hold to materialist theories such as Democritus in ancient Greece, E. O. Wilson in biology, and B. F. Skinner in psychology would argue that free will is an illusion because we are formed not by our free-will choices, but instead by forces

that are strictly composed of matter such as atoms colliding or natural selection, or by social forces outside the individual person such as economic structures or rewards and punishments. See *Consilience,* by E. O. Wilson, 1999, New York, NY: Vintage, and *Beyond Freedom and Dignity,* by B. F. Skinner, 1971, New York, NY: Bantam. I acknowledge that matter and social forces influence us, but they alone do not or even primarily shape us. If there is no free will, then you cannot say whether one thing is morally right and another morally wrong. If you reflect on it, you cannot say someone did wrong, moral wrong, if he is not responsible for his behavior. The legal system, for example, implicitly rejects materialism every time it says "The defendant is guilty." The defendant is not guilty if his genes or the principles of operant conditioning made him behave as he did. Would any materialist continue to be a materialist if his or her daughter was raped and the defense attorney said, "Rape is not morally and legally wrong. Society reinforces men for being aggressive, and he was only responding to this conditioning. My client therefore is innocent of all charges, and I ask dismissal of them all"? Either you accept free will as legitimate (and morally condemn rape, for example) or you lose your moral voice in standing up against moral atrocities. Even if you said that rape is not advised for this or that reason, you could not use moral language to defend your position. To avoid this problem, some materialist theorists, such as Marvin Harris in anthropology, acknowledge free will on the individual level and then reject it on the cultural level, without resolving the inconsistency; see *Cannibals and Kings,* by M. Harris, 1991, New York, NY: Vintage. My point is this—if free will is an illusion, then all of Western jurisprudence (a cultural phenomenon) going back at least 3,700 years to the Code of Hammurabi, is based on illusion.

A sound, philosophical defense of free will is in Robert Kane's (1996) book, *The Significance of Free Will*, Oxford, England: Oxford University Press.

4. By the term *strong will* I mean that internal quality that sustains a person in persevering toward an end point and is directly linked to the good will (and a good will, or *eunoia*, as used by Aristotle, is goodness for the sake of others). A strong will without good will can lead to immoral acts, such as the bank robber persevering in planning and executing that deed. A strong will is not the same as perseverance, the latter being the behavioral demonstration of the inner quality of a strong will.

5. See *The Four Loves*, by C. S. Lewis, 1960, New York, NY: Harcourt, Brace, & World. I can almost hear Kant say something like this: Love is an end point of morality (what we are striving for), whereas a good will is what we need fundamentally at the beginning to make any moral response possible. I would argue, instead, that love is both a fundamental issue (existing at first in us as a capacity and as an actuality developing slowly in small ways) and as an end point. It is our essence (our fundamental building block of morality, along with rationality and a free, good, and strong will), and its perfection is our goal (as we grow stronger in it with practice and reflection).

6. I am not suggesting that a person can love (in the sense of agape) too much. I am saying that one can get out of balance, distort the essence of agape, and then push too hard and burn out. It is not agape itself that leads to burnout but its distortion.

7. See *Helping Clients Forgive,* by R. D. Enright and R. C. Fitzgibbons, 2000, Washington, DC: American Psychological Association.

8. See Enright and Fitzgibbons (2000). Christian theologians would argue that love and forgiveness are also dependent on divine grace. A free, good, and strong will is insufficient

to produce goodness in the form of either love or forgiveness. Because this is a book on psychology, not theology, I acknowledge these points. Even the monotheistic believer would probably agree that one has to cooperate with this grace. The points in this book thus concern your part in all of this. A theologian might say that this book is about your cooperation in producing love and forgiveness in the face of hurtful injustice from others.

9. See *Athenian Constitution, Eudemian Ethics, Virtues and Vices*, Eudemian Ethics (1.121 4b and 1.21 7b), by Aristotle (H. Rachman, Trans.), 1935, Cambridge, MA: Loeb.

CHAPTER 2. IF YOU ARE TRAUMATIZED

1. See "Forgiveness as a Psychotherapeutic Goal With Elderly Females," by J. H. Hebl and R. D. Enright, 1993, *Psychotherapy: Theory, Research, Practice, Training, 30,* pp. 658–667.

2. See "Effects of Forgiveness Therapy on Anger, Mood, and Vulnerability to Substance Use Among Inpatient Substance-Dependent Clients," by W. F. Lin, D. Mack, R. D. Enright, D. Krahn, and T. Baskin, 2004. *Journal of Consulting and Clinical Psychology, 72,* pp. 1114–1121.

3. See "The Effects of a Forgiveness Intervention on Patients With Coronary Artery Disease," by M. A. Waltman, D. C. Russell, C. T. Coyle, R. D. Enright, A. C. Holter, and C. Swoboda, 2009, *Psychology and Health, 24,* pp. 11–27.

4. See "Waging Peace Through Forgiveness in Belfast, Northern Ireland II: Educational Programs for Mental Health Improvement of Children," by R. D. Enright, J. A. Knutson Enright, A. C. Holter, T. Baskin, and C. Knutson, 2007, *Journal of Research in Education, 17*(Fall), pp. 63–78. A study of Primary 3 (first-grade) children also is described in this journal article. The three studies within Milwaukee's central city

are in "The Forgiving Child: The Impact of Forgiveness Education on Excessive Anger for Elementary-Aged Children in Milwaukee's Central City," by A. C. Holter, C. Magnuson, C. Knutson, J. A. Knutson Enright, and R. D. Enright, 2008, *Journal of Research in Education, 18,* pp. 82–93. These studies concern first-, third-, and fifth-grade children.

5. *The Velveteen Rabbit,* by M. Williams, 1922, New York, NY: Doubleday; *Rising Above the Storm Clouds,* by R. D. Enright, 2004, Washington, DC: Magination Press.

CHAPTER 3. HOW TELLING AND LISTENING TO STORIES CAN HELP

1. See "Forgiveness Education With Parentally Love-Deprived College Students," by R. Al-Mabuk, R. D. Enright, and P. Cardis, 1995, *Journal of Moral Education, 24,* pp. 427–444.
2. This issue of the distinction between forgiveness and reconciliation is addressed in Chapter 7.

CHAPTER 5. THE WORK PHASE OF FORGIVENESS

1. See "Forgiveness as an Intervention Goal With Incest Survivors," by S. R. Freedman and R. D. Enright, 1996, *Journal of Consulting and Clinical Psychology, 64,* pp. 983–992.

CHAPTER 6. THE DISCOVERY PHASE OF FORGIVENESS

1. See *Man's Search for Meaning: An Introduction to Logotherapy,* by V. Frankl, 1969, New York, NY: Washington Square Press.
2. See "Forgiveness as an Intervention Goal With Incest Survivors," by S. R. Freedman and R. D. Enright, 1996, *Journal of Consulting and Clinical Psychology, 64,* pp. 983–992.

3. I am indebted to Professor Eleanore Stump for this idea on agape love. See her lecture, "The Anselmian Tradition on Love and Forgiveness" (http://www.anselmphilosophy.com/mod/forum/discuss.php?d=13).

4. This view of Mozart's music was stated by the late conductor Bruno Walter.

CHAPTER 7. WHAT DOES IT MEAN TO FORGIVE?

1. These distinctions are made by C. S. Lewis (1960) in his book *The Four Loves* (New York, NY: Harcourt, Brace, & World), and by G. Outka (1977) in his book *Agape: An Ethical Analysis* (New Haven, CT: Yale University Press).

2. I have chosen Aristotle here and elsewhere as the ultimate authority on questions of moral virtue because his discussion of virtue is deeper and broader than that of any other philosopher. His insights into the meaning of virtue have never been surpassed in the history of philosophy. For those who differ, I have these questions: Which modern philosopher has seen the weaknesses in Aristotle's approach (to moral virtue in particular) and has corrected them? How is the new system by any philosopher a superior conceptualization of the meaning of virtue? Do you see any weaknesses in this modern view that are significant?

CHAPTER 8. THE FORGIVENESS PLAN

1. We discuss issues of forgiving people and society within the context of racial and ethnic injustice in Chapter 15.

2. The Mind Garden website is set up in such a way that you will be able to identify a particular person by his or her relationship to you (mother, son, relative, boss, etc.). The site currently

is not set up for you to list actual names of the people you are forgiving. You may keep note of the names separately from the site if you wish.

CHAPTER 9. MEASURING YOUR FORGIVENESS

1. If you work through the scales on the Mind Garden website, make sure you are using the Personal Forgiveness Scale and not the Enright Forgiveness Inventory. The Personal Forgiveness Scale is for private use only. The scale is not used for research purposes because the number of items is too small. The Enright Forgiveness Inventory, a 60-item scale, is for professional clinical use and for research.

CHAPTER 10. YOUR FORGIVENESS PATHWAY

1. See "Forgiveness as an Intervention Goal With Incest Survivors," by S. R. Freedman and R. D. Enright, 1996, *Journal of Consulting and Clinical Psychology, 64*, pp. 983–992.
2. I am indebted for the distinction between things and persons to the law professor J. Budziszewski in his book *The Line Through the Heart* (2009, Wilmington, DE: Intercollegiate Studies Institute). He has also informed me regarding the discussion to follow on ethical personhood, although he does not use that term.
3. Agape love may have the consequence of preserving the life of self and others, but that is not the endpoint or what Aristotle would call the *final cause* of it.
4. The discussion on personhood here centers on the notion of personhood in the philosophy of ethics. You should know that from the perspective of the law, there also are the issues of legal personhood and constitutional personhood. A legal

person is protected by the laws of the state, which define what or who a person is. As another nuance on legal persons, a corporation, for example, can be treated as a person if that corporation broke the law and is now brought to court. Constitutional personhood refers to the United States constitution, which protects persons with regard to life, liberty, and the pursuit of happiness. Personhood from the ethical position taken here can be thought of as the common sense view of who a person is regardless of how a country's laws define a person.

5. This idea of appropriating heroes as a way to understand this forgiveness unit is from Amber Flesch; see *Healing Through the Heroic Gift of Forgiveness*, by A. Flesch and R. D. Enright, 2010, Madison, WI: International Forgiveness Institute.

6. See *Left to Die*, by I. Ilibagiza, 2007, New York, NY: Hay House.

7. I am indebted to Allen Bergin for this idea of being a conduit for good as we bear the pain of others' injustice through forgiveness; see "Three Contributions of a Spiritual Perspective to Counseling, Psychotherapy, and Behavioral Change," by A. E. Bergin, 1988, *Counseling and Values, 33*, pp. 21–31.

8. See Freedman and Enright (1996).

CHAPTER 11. HOW DID YOU DO IN FORGIVING?

1. Please recall that if you keep trying to forgive but do not quite succeed in forgiving the person as you revisit the exercises in Chapter 10, then it may be time to switch to another person who has hurt you even deeper. You might be "stuck" in your forgiveness with one person until you unburden yourself of anger toward someone else.

CHAPTER 13. FORGIVENESS BETWEEN PARTNERS AND WITHIN YOUR CURRENT FAMILY

1. I use the word *gift* rather than *a gift* to make an important point: You are not giving "a" gift or you are not being "a" gift in the sense that you are a thing, a what, that engages only in behaviors such as gift giving. The word *gift* without an article in front of it is meant to tell you that you are the embodiment of gift for your partner. It is not your behavior alone that makes you "gift." It is your very being, your personhood, that you are willingly bringing in love to your partner that makes you "gift." He or she, then, is gift to you.

CHAPTER 15. SCHOOL DAYS, WORK DAYS, AND OTHER DAYS

1. See *Generation Me*, by J. Twenge, 2007, New York, NY: Free Press; *The Narcissism Epidemic*, by J. Twenge and W. Campbell, 2009, New York, NY: Free Press.
2. See, for example, "Anger and Aggression Among Filipino Students," by J. P. Campano and T. Munakata, 2004, *Adolescence, 39,* pp. 757–764; "Waging Peace Through Forgiveness in Belfast, Northern Ireland II: Educational Programs for Mental Health Improvement of Children," by R. D. Enright, J. A. Knutson Enright, A. C. Holter, T. Baskin, and C. Knutson, 2007, *Journal of Research in Education, 17*(Fall), pp. 63–78; *Anger,* by R. Thurman, 2006, New York, NY: Oxford University Press.
3. As you know, when you practice forgiveness, you practice it alongside the other virtues. Thus, if there is a serious problem in need of correction for your child in school, then you should not only forgive but also take steps to ensure justice for your child. As you forgive, this may help you seek an even better justice than might have been the case if you had sought it while deeply angry.

CHAPTER 16. SURVEYING THE LANDSCAPE FROM THE MOUNTAIN PEAK

1. This point, that moving in a positive direction is indicative of emotional improvement, is discussed in *Helping Clients Forgive*, by R. D. Enright and R. P. Fitzgibbons, 2000, Washington, DC: American Psychological Association.

2. The material to follow in this section is inspired by Aristotle's discussion of the moral character in Book 2, Chapter 3 of *The Nichomachean Ethics* (H. Rachman, Trans.), 1926, Cambridge, MA: Harvard University Press.

3. Please refer back to Chapter 10 if you need a refresher on the term *person*.

CHAPTER 17. QUESTIONS AS YOU GIVE FORGIVENESS TO OTHERS

1. See *Helping Clients Forgive* (pp. 310–311), by R. D. Enright and R. P. Fitzgibbons, 2000, Washington, DC: American Psychological Association.

2. See Enright and Fitzgibbons (2000), Chapter 15.

3. See Enright and Fitzgibbons (2000), Chapter 15.

CHAPTER 18. GIVING FORGIVENESS AWAY TO OUR CHILDREN AND IN OUR COMMUNITIES

1. *How the Irish Saved Civilization*, by T. Cahill, 1995, New York, NY: Anchor Books.

CHAPTER 19. YOUR FORGIVENESS LEGACY

1. See *Pensées and Other Writings*, by B. Pascal (H. Levi, Trans.), 2008, Oxford, England: Oxford University Press.

INDEX

ABOUT THE AUTHOR

Robert D. Enright, PhD, is a licensed psychologist and a professor of educational psychology at the University of Wisconsin–Madison. He has been a leader in the scientific study of forgiveness and its effects since 1985. *Time* magazine referred to him as "the forgiveness trailblazer." He is the author of more than 100 publications, including five books. He and his colleagues have developed and tested a pathway to forgiveness that has helped incest survivors, and people in drug rehabilitation, in hospice, in shelters for abused women, and in cardiac units of hospitals, among others. His recent work has been in schools within conflict regions, such as Belfast, Northern Ireland, assisting teachers to deliver forgiveness programs to students.